A History of Asking

A History of Asking

Steven Connor

()
OPEN HUMANITIES PRESS

London 2023

Cover Illustration: 'Portrait of an Old Man Begging' by Michael Sweerts, Hochenbuchau Collection, on permanent loan to Liechtenstein, The Princely Collections, Vienna.

Print ISBN 978-78542-127-3
PDF ISBN 978-1-78542-128-0

OPEN HUMANITIES PRESS

Open Humanities Press is an international, scholar-led open access publishing collective whose mission is to make leading works of contemporary critical thought freely available worldwide. More at http://openhumanitiespress.org

Contents

Wir sind Pettler. Hoc est verum
(Note found in Martin Luther's pocket after his death.)

I

Pretty Please

The intention of this book is to enquire into the ways in which the action of asking is performed, across the full range of its modalities, that is, across the spectrum that runs from the less self-authorising kinds of asking like begging, pleading, praying, imploring, beseeching, entreating, suing, supplicating and soliciting, through to the more self-authorising modes of asking, like proposing, offering, inviting, requesting, appealing, applying, petitioning, claiming and demanding.

Asking, or asking for, almost anything, whether directions, help, love, money, even for the time, can be asking for trouble, so we must take a great deal of trouble with the way we ask in order to head it off. Because asking is largely an intraspecific action – one does not ask animals or mountains for things, except by romantic or religious projection – it always takes place within a landscape of relative advantage and disadvantage, and asymmetrical relations of power, which the act of asking has the capacity to confirm or disturb. 'I only asked', we may protest when a request goes wrong; but one rarely if ever 'only asks'. To ask is to request some object or service, but it is always also by the same token to seek permission for one's request, or secure it by enquiring into the acceptability of making it. That is to say, to ask is usually to ask a shadow question about one's act of asking; hence the familiarity of formulae such as 'May I ask?', or the use of modal forms like 'could I take this chair?'.

The governing assumption in politeness theory is that this kind of delicacy in quisitive actions arises from the fact that making a request may be a 'face-threatening action', that potentially threatens the freedom of action of one's interlocutor. Asking anything of anyone is requesting a gift or benefit that they do not have to give. This can seem like an attempted theft, as neatly described by Gudrun Held: 'In R[equest] situations ego takes on the role of the "illicit taker", the person demanding a gift. This is tantamount to an attack on alter's territory and thus to an unexpected disturbance and inconvenience' (Held 1999, 30-1). Since, according to Robin Lakoff, one of the three most important principles of politeness is 'Give Options' (Lakoff 1973, 298), one must avoid giving the impression that one assumes any right to what one requests, while securing nevertheless one's right to make the request. Sometimes this acceptability is secured by a kind of excuse or apology in advance for the act of asking: 'Can I enquire whether...'; 'Do you mind my asking if...?' This can take subtle forms: 'I wonder whether you would be willing to give up your seat?' sounds like it is asking a question, but is framed in such a way as to ask for some preliminary reassurance as to whether asking the person to give up their seat is likely to offend or to achieve its end.

Asking is difficult not just because asking may seem like an aggressive imposition. For asking is an intimate act, or an act which intimates intimacy, which can be uncomfortable even where it is not aggressive. To enquire even of somebody's well-being is to reach into their personal space, if only in requiring them to give some sort of account of themselves, which is at the same time an affirmation of their shared commitment to the protocols of social exchange. Asking any kind of question always sings, like the Mock Turtle, '*Will you, wo'n't you, will you, wo'n't you, wo'n't you join the dance?*' (Carroll 1998, 90). Requesting or enquiring are both forms of requirement: if any asking simultaneously asks about the acceptability of its asking, it also asks its subject to agree to give an answer, whatever the content of that answer might be.

Asking is therefore always attended by moral, emotional and political tension. Asking is difficult because of our awareness that being asked can be what we call an imposition, in that it imposes a demand; that any ask is potentially a big ask.

Demanding

Like most actions, asking has both a negative and a contrary. The negative of asking is simply not asking. Like any negative, this can take a multitude of forms; I might decide to leave you in undisturbed possession of your bag of crisps, or I might simply steal them from you. But the contrary of asking is demanding, asking in such a way as to reduce the duality just defined, of asking for an object, by asking if one may ask, to nothing. A demand assumes that it need not ask any permission for its request.

The focus of this book will be on those kinds and occasions of asking which seem especially unstable, in that entreaty and demand seem to interweave or alternate in them. I will designate these as petitory acts. When I use the word petition, or petitionary, I will usually mean the act of addressing a formal request, usually in some public manner, in an authorised fashion and to some recognised authority; this kind of formalised petition will be the subject of chapter 3. Petition is difficult and interesting because of the ways in which it compounds the unauthorised and the authorising, and the ways therefore in which it must seem to raise and settle in various ways the question of its own legitimacy. In doing so, formalised petition in fact points to an ambivalence that is at work across the whole range of what I will try to remember to call petitory acts, which, though less formalised, are never entirely without formalisation.

One may see this compounding of request and demand in the two words *claim* and *bid*. To claim is to assert one's right to something, usually through the assumption or assertion that it is one's due, or indeed that one must be regarded as already a sense owning it. Indeed, so self-authorising is the act of assertion involved in claiming that one may use the word *claim* of a purely assertive action, an occupation of territory, for example, which seems to be an action that claims the right to be regarded as equivalent to the speech act involved in saying 'I hereby claim this territory'. And yet claiming is from *clamare*, to cry out, or call upon, as in the opening words of the Vulgate version of Psalm 129: 'De profundis clamavi ad te domine', 'Out of the depths have I cried unto thee, O Lord' (King James, Psalm 130). To claim is to stake a claim, with a stake being what one uses to make something stick, so, for example, a stick, on which might be hung some object that is hazarded during the course of a game. To claim is to try to make good one's claim. To claim is therefore in fact to bid.

Bidding has an even more complex semantic profile than claiming. In Old English, *bædon* and *biddan* could mean to ask, entreat or pray. In his *New World of Words*, (1678), Edmund Phillips explains 'to *Bid a boon*', as 'to ask a Boon', while noting that *bid* is an 'old word'. This usage survives longer in German, where *bitte*, I beg you, is the ordinary word both for 'please', and 'thank you' (as in 'I beg you to accept my thanks'). A bead is so-called by transference from the act of *gebed*, prayer, which the telling of rosary beads would accompany; so *to bid a bead* is to say a prayer, and a *beadsman* could be a man of prayer, that is, one licensed, or bidden to beg. At the beginning of 'The Eve of St Agnes', John Keats writes of the ancient Beadsman, doing the work of bidding for salvation as he has been bidden, that 'among/Rough ashes sat he for his soul's reprieve,/And all night kept awake, for sinners' sake to grieve' (Keats 1970, 195). To bid can still today mean to ask for, or solicit, as in bidding at an auction, and, in the archaic 'bidding farewell', a praying or wishing. But it can also mean to order, enjoin or command, as in 'forbidding', the negative form of command. These two functions are at work in the act of bidding someone 'farewell', or its more ceremonial form, 'adieu', thereby committing one's interlocutor to God. Bidding someone farewell is more than simply wishing them good faring or fortune: it contains and conveys a force of urging or requirement, the verbalisation, as it were, of verbal forcing, that is never entirely absent from the human act of wishing, or, rather perhaps, the more-or-less magical act of articulating a wish, about which there will be more to say in this book. *Entreaty* also has a buried intimation of force. To entreat is to attempt to negotiate a treaty, as between warring parties, treating in this sense deriving from *tractare, trahere*, to handle, manage, draw, or drag. This combination of asking and traction is at work to some degree in all the petitory acts in which I will be interested.

Perhaps because of our long and vocal dependency as infants, wanting becomes closely associated with asking, and desiring with requesting and requiring. The word petition derives from *petere*, to seek, and demonstrates the switch from looking for to asking for. The reverse seems to have happened with the word *crave*, which had the sense in various Germanic languages of demanding, or asking of right, along with the legal sense of summoning to court, or prosecuting. When Langland writes in *Piers Plowman* in 1393 'And non so bold beggere to bydden and craue' (Langland 1886, 133), he is referring to the beggar's action of asking, not his condition of need or desire. Suitors for benefits during the sixteenth and seventeenth centuries would often 'crave' them in their letters of petition: though they may indeed have been in a condition of yearning for them, it is the petitory action to which the verb reflexively refers, not the state of desire. But gradually the authority of the action of craving reduced, even as its urgency increased, as it began to be used to mean to beg or earnestly entreat something, as a gift or benefit rather than as of right. Nowadays, the word *crave* has moved over completely to the side of feeling, typically of intense longing, often for drugs or addictive substances, rather than verbal action.

It has been suggested that there is a link between the word *crave* and the Germanic root *kraf*, the root of German *Kraft* and English *craft*, the primary meaning of which is force or strength. The history of the word *crave* certainly indicates the differential distribution of force. When a court craves, in its early sense of demands or requires, the word enacts its own performative force. When craving begins to mean entreating or imploring, it is as though the petitioner seeks to impart a force of pseudo-requirement through the very urgency of their asking rather than the authority of the request. In archaic uses like 'craving pardon', that urgency has shrivelled to mere courtliness. In the third, modern phase of the word's usage, in which craving tends to mean intense or uncontrollable desire, as in the craving for nicotine or alcohol, the force seems to be being self-exercised over the one who feels the need. There need now be no external action of craving, or articulation of need, even if the word may still embody the force of an unuttered demand, or a demand to press forward into speech.

Performatives

In 1970, Jerrold M. Sadock proposed the term 'whimperative' for a question that functions as a request, or an imperative, such as 'Can you pass the salt?' or 'Why don't you just shut up?' In the online *Double-Tongued Dictionary*, Grant Barrett insists that the term is a portmanteau word formed from 'imperative' and 'wh-' as 'a wildcard formative for the interrogatives *which, who, when, what,* etc.' (Barrett 2007). But the success of the word does seem due at least to the suggestion of whimpering in this kind of request, implying something of the deliberate and paradoxically aggressive self-lowering of the beggar. There may also be an unconscious recall of the long tradition of antagonism towards the distinctively whining or nasal intonation of the beggar's 'canting'. One might say that petitory actions occur when some kind of begging may be in operation. This is more than a matter of interest to students of pragmatics, or the study of linguistic use. In fact, human societies are built around a huge range of actions, structures and even institutions for the forming of petitory actions and responses to them.

Petitory acts belong to the category of performatives, the term introduced by J.L. Austin for those verbal utterances or expressions which perform an action, rather than, say, referring to an object or state of affairs. But they are a special kind of performative action, which should be characterised as a kind of retracted action, an action that performs the act of minimising or modulating action. In this, petitory acts are not one kind of speech act among others, but rather a special kind of exception to illocution, a speech-unact, or redaction of the act of acting in speech. They are a form of assertive yielding, a giving way (Connor 2019b) or, to use the term I have proposed for the large class of such withdrawing actions, abstitution (Connor 2019a). Samuel Beckett provides an example of such an action of inarticulate begging in the story told in his radio play *Embers*, in which a character simply entreats: 'Please! Please!' without further specification. In …*but the clouds*… the character styled M recounts 'I began to beg of her, to appear, to me. Such had long been my use and wont. No sound, a begging of the mind, to her, to appear, to me' (Beckett 1984, 420). Begging need not be faint or mute, of course: indeed, it is often highly insistent or declamatory and always constitutes some measure of insistence: but it must often combine demand with the performance of incapacity, or anagential action.

Petition is a paradoxical act. It is a form of supplication which simultaneously emphasises the powerlessness of the supplicator and asserts a demand. Petition dramatises the petitioner's sense of their right to a benefit that they have no right to expect. It partakes of the same complication as the act of suing, in which the suer is in a condition of weakness, dependence or disadvantage, and yet brings forward a formal request. Petition is an exception to the principle that beggars cannot be choosers, since petition involves the active choice of the beggar's place, or at least speaking from that place. In the University of Oxford, when you have completed the requirements for a DPhil and been recommended for the award of the degree by your examiners, you are granted 'leave to supplicate', that is to say, to ask formally for what you in effect already have, or could no longer legitimately be withheld from you.

I write these words on Maundy Thursday, 18th April 2019, the day before Good Friday, on which Maundy Money is given out by the sovereign. Maundy derives from the mandate or command of Christ, given in accompaniment with the ceremony of foot-washing at the Last Supper: 'A new commandment (*mandatum novum*) I give to you, that you love one another' (John 13:34). It therefore conjoins humility and stipulation in the way I am characterising here. To *maund* subsequently came to mean to beg. The association of begging with obscure or unintelligible utterance seems to have encouraged a shift in the later seventeenth century to the idea of *maundering* as muttering, grumbling or incoherent utterance, and therefore, perhaps via association with *wandering*, and even *meandering*, to the idea of moving or acting in an idle, rambling or purposeless way. Following the logic that shifts the focus of begging on to questions of utterance, maundering usually means a particular kind of rambling speech, i.e., not begging, but borrowing the beggar's vagrancy. Maundering therefore becomes the senseless talk of the old, witless, or intoxicated. Often it is transferred to the inane quasi-utterances of nature, as in the dialect pastiche of W.N. Herbert's 'Featherhood':

> God speaks in sic undeemis weys
> that maist o whit he seys
> gaes maunderin awa
> in pirrs an pirlies lyk
> a speugie soomin thru a hedge. (Herbert 1996, 19)

Maundering is drawn into the constellation of words associated in the Protestant imagination with the vacuous sonorities of Catholicism, as in John Stuart Blackie's praise of the Protestant martyr Walter Milne:

> From land to land he pilgrimed, not to kiss
> The bones of maundering monks, and patter prayers
> To swart-faced Maries prinked with trumperies,
> But with free power to preach the eternal law
> Of truth and love and righteousness to men! (Blackie 1876, 144)

Louis MacNeice restores the pecuniary associations of the word in his poem 'Christmas Shopping', imagining the 'assault on the purse' of shop-windows on Christmas Eve:

> The eleventh hour draining the gurgling pennies
> Down to the conduits
>
> Down to the sewers of money – rats and marshgas –
> Bubbling in maundering music under the pavement
>   (MacNeice 1979, 66)

W.H. Auden revives the word beautifully to evoke a state of lassitudinous disconnection in his archaic exercise 'A Bad Night': 'time drumbles,/A maunder of moments,/Wan, haphazard,/And unaccented' (Auden 1994, 843).

Much ink has been expended on the question of when or whether there can be such a thing as an unconditional gift, this matter being an important one for absolutists of gift theory like Jacques Derrida, who insist that there can be no gift where there is any suggestion that the gift might either be regarded as any kind of recompense, or might be given in the expectation of any return. For the many people who have haggled at this question, the very possibility of the gift, that is said to be an ethical question of primary importance, or even to ground ethical relations themselves, is to the fore. It is more than curious that philosophers, anthropologists, psychoanalysts, theologians, economists, cultural historians and others who have striven to imagine how the giving of gifts can be stripped of any prompt, circumstance or consequence, have tended not to consider the operations of what might be seen as the complement of a gift on the demand side of the transaction, the supplication of gift-supply in the petitory practices that are designed to precipitate grace and favour. Gifts are by definition supposed to be beyond the possibility of any kind of transaction. But the phrase 'beg pardon' seems to indicate that begging might operate in such a way. That is, one might be able to see it as the attempt to solicit a gift that will be free of obligations on either side. More even than that, in circumstances in which the giving of charity is valued and admired, and there are many societies in which this is the case, the beggar offers the donor the gift of being able and being seen to be giving a gift. Perhaps it is because we possess an illuminating and influential book by Marcel Mauss called *The Gift* (2002), but not a work of equivalent reach and intent called *The Bum, The Pitch* or *The Cadge*, that we have so failed to notice the centrality of the petitory relation in human society.

The beggar wants something for nothing, thus, strictly speaking, a non-exchange. But in fact whenever there is an act, or even the appearance of an act, of begging, there is an exchange, since the beggar offers the evidence of their indigence as the price to be paid for the gift. One can certainly refuse to give the gift, indeed, to be a gift, and so for the giving of the gift to be properly gratuitous, one must be able to refuse it. But one cannot refuse the exchange, because refusal is necessarily an answer to the question posed by the solicitation. The beggar begs because they have nothing, except the having-nothing on account of which and through which they beg, and so confirm that they deserve the gift, even as their deserving converts the gift into a perverse kind of payment for their manifesto. The beggar must beg in order to demonstrate their condition as beggar, even as both parties must be aware and wary of this condition. Begging is a demonstration that one has been reduced to the condition of a beggar, even as it is possible in principle for anyone to offer such a demonstration. Begging depends on the fiction that nobody will voluntarily degrade themselves to the condition of the beggar (do you think I would do this unless I had to?), along with the uneasy recognition that in fact anybody can, and many, increasingly many as I will conclude, do.

The visibility of the beggar is often an act of indecent exposure, an aggressive display of helplessness. The beggar deploys and depends on the squeamishness of the one forced to behold their offensive being, squeamish meaning both prone to nauseated disgust and distant or disdainful. The beggar aims to induce recoil, and a donation which is payable for the right to that recoil. Begging monetises embarrassment. Begging is essentially corporeal and may be seen in fact as a kind of anti-prostitution. Where the prostitute offers bodily intimacy for payment, the beggar solicits payment for the removal of bodily intimacy, or as a fee for being permitted to look or move away from it. The social response to begging is a version of this aversion. Begging is transformed into a symptom or effect of various kinds, typically of social ills or problems, the assumption being that it is a necessary and unmediated response to indigence, unemployment or homelessness. The less funding for social welfare, the more begging there must, we are encouraged to assume, inevitably be. Historians have occasionally turned their attention to the history of beggars, sometimes encouraged by what is regularly represented as the scandal of people reduced by oppression and systematic inequality to indigence. But such histories are at once insufficiently focussed and insufficiently expansive. Begging and beggars are often understood as part of a larger picture involving vagrancy and the dynamics of social dissent and marginality. Such histories tend to have little to say about the styles, experiences and practices of begging in its own terms, and take for granted that we know perfectly well what begging is, and need to understand why it comes about rather than what it is and does. But begging is not accidentally a visible outrage, since its discomfiting of the eye and outrageous assault on and through visibility, are essential to its nature and practice. Chapter 3 explores the ways in which the theatricality of begging both stages and dissimulates the commerce of mercies, in many senses, it enacts.

We often prefer why-questions to what-questions, that is, questions about the causes of things, and how they might be abated or brought to an end, rather than questions about the kind of things they are. This is not because questions of causation are necessarily easier to answer, and indeed it may well be that the opposite is the case, so that it is precisely the difficulties in determining why things happen and how, as a consequence of that, they may be encouraged or mitigated, that makes them seem worth asking. What-questions, by contrast, questions about what things are, or, as we casually but tellingly tend to say, 'are like', may seem much less demanding, and allow less for transformative intervention. Why-questions seem at least by implication active and consequential, which demand and promise action, leading, as they seem to, to questions of how things might be changed, whereas what-questions can seem resigned to passive description.

Begging furnishes a telling example of this preference, in the strong tendency I have already noted to bounce quickly from accounts of begging to attempts to account for it, usually as the expression of some other problem altogether. I try in this book to reflect on the nature rather than the causes of begging, to treat begging less as a problem than as a phenomenon, and indeed to take the fact that begging tends to be regarded as a problem, and the kind of problem it is taken to be, as a persisting part of the phenomenon that it is. When one of the features of begging is its marketisation of intolerability and disgust, making it hard to fix and keep one's gaze steadily on a beggar and the act he or she performs, efforts to account for begging and explain what will be needed to remove it can seem to participate in this eye-averting response.

It seems strange to me that there should be no ready-to-hand noun for the practice of begging, leaving us dependent on the gerund form. 'Beggary' implies the necessity or likelihood of being forced to beg, but is subtly distinguished from it: you can be theoretically in a condition of beggary even though you are in fact too proud to resort to begging. 'Mendication' and 'mendicity' both exist, for example in the Mendicity Societies that grew up in England and Ireland in the early nineteenth century, with the aim of suppressing the more visible effects of street begging (Tighe 1965; Roberts 1991; McCabe 2018, 146-84). But both of these terms seem too formal and too tied to a specific and largely superseded religious or political history to be seriously available.

General Petition

Seeing begging as part of the history of outsiders or marginal social groups massively misses the massive centrality of begging to human affairs. In the medieval world, begging formed part of a culture of petition that operated at all levels of society. It may seem easy to accept Barry Windeatt's suggestion that the medieval culture of petition is far removed from the arrangements for seeking and delivering redress in modern societies:

> From the hindsight of modern society, where most of the contingencies and grievances that concern medieval petitioners would find resolution and redress through the regular apparatus and agencies of a modern state, the extant corpus of petitions serves to emphasise starkly the difference and distance of an earlier world where so much might depend so crucially on success or otherwise in petitioning someone with more power and resource. (Windeatt 2012, 192)

In fact, however, we should be aware that the move has not been from 'a culture where recourse to petition is part of how society functions' (Windeatt 2012, 207) to a culture of abstractly administered redress and adjustment, but rather from a formally petitionary to a more diffusely petitory culture. For it seems likely to be true of all cultures, if certainly, and for that reason, true in different senses, that 'recourse to petition is part of how society functions'. Supplication may give way to more abstract and emotionally flatter processes of application, but petition can be guaranteed never to be marginal in any human society. A culture of application rather than supplication, such as operates for the most part in more abstractly mediated and administered societies, does not remove the action of petition, it just changes its tone, modality and conditions of visibility. In such societies, for example, petitions will tend to have a much higher quotient of expectation to entreaty.

The process known as *application* begins as the simple bringing to bear or bringing into contact of one thing with another, as in the application of an ointment, or remedy, or, more abstractly, the application of a rule or principle. All the uses of the word by Shakespeare seem to involve this meaning of bringing to bear. The word seems to have become associated by sound with the act of appealing, or an approach for information or assistance. In the first citation given by the *OED*, Hugh Hilarie's satirical poem *The Resurreccion of the Masse*, the sacrament itself speaks, offering solace and uplift to all Catholic souls: 'to me therfore let all men applye/If to come to glory they do intend' (Hilarie 1554, sig. A7ʳ). However, the next recorded use in this sense is not until more than a century later, and it may be that the principal meaning is to approach, or come towards, rather than to ask something. It appears to have been in the seventeenth century that the word began to be used to refer to the kind of action that might formerly have been referred to as supplication, but with some of its drama drained away, into a formal or official kind of process. What has become the usual meaning, of putting oneself forward for a position or employment, does not come into use until the middle of the eighteenth century, though the reflexive usage, to 'apply oneself to', is found in the advice given in Spenser's 'Mother Hubbard's Tale' to one hoping for a priest's benefice: 'to some Noble man your selfe applye,/Or other great one in the worldes eye' (Spenser 1591, sig. N2ᵛ). This usage may perhaps be regarded as a softening complication of the force that might otherwise seem to be too directly applied. Indeed, the growing formalisation of processes of application (which indeed is ever more frequently conducted through written instruments known as 'application forms'), involves the diffusion of the dangerous kind of demand implicit in the I-thou, or face-to-face relation of an appeal of one individual to another. The application form objectifies the work of attenuating the sense that the one applied to may feel themselves to be worked on.

But the act of applying – applying for a loan, a place in university, or, most commonly, for employment – will remain and, where application and selection processes are means of fair distribution of limited resources, will retain many of the features of supplication, including most particularly, the necessity of actions of demand or solicitation. Human societies are bound together, it has sometimes been suggested, by different kinds of debt. There is at least as strong a claim to be made for the binding force of petition, the web of requirements caught up in the not-so-simple actions of asking and allowing.

An expanded view quickly discloses how huge the range of petitory practices is. All human beings are cognitively formed in the course of an enormously extended period of essentially helpless infancy, in which the only method of obtaining nutrition, care and the attention that is essential to survival is through practices of begging, practices that we should not be at all surprised to find, as we will in chapter 2, represented widely among very many social animals. For at least the first decade of life, the most cognitively formative of a human being's entire life – and, in the extended infancy characteristic of developed societies, which may extend into a second or third decade – the physical, cognitive and emotional lives of young humans are characterised by systematic relations of dependency, of which the psychosocial glue is the act of petition. Thereafter, the practice of systematic begging is a feature in different ways of most human societies, traditional and modern.

Petition is powerfully at work in the act of prayer, practised as a matter of religious duty, regularly and unselfconsciously, by millions of humans past and present, as though with no self-consciousness at all about the outlandish nature of what they are doing. Praying is far from a marginal or eccentric occupation. It seems certain that at any one time more human beings worldwide will be engaged in petition of or devotional action towards an absent but all-providing being than in acts of procreation.

Most societies have secularised systems of formal petition, addressed in approved ways to recognised authorities, meaning that petition also encompasses acts of legal appeal, supplication and what is still called suing. Much of the play of sexual seeking, tender and granting is driven through variations of suit, supplication and favour. A common view of the patriarchal division that has characterised almost every society we know of through human history is that it reduces the female half of society that is denied the opportunity for productive work to the condition of sexual mendicant, though the sexual mendicity we know as courtship, so widely spread across species, involves complex and highly-mediated exchanges based on asking and answering. The advertising industry has its roots in the supplicatory display of sexual opportunities, in which begging for custom represents itself as a display of charity. Insofar as they are the stylisation of imaginary yearnings and satings, art and literature are driven by petitory energies and investments. Before the rise of market relations in relation to art, all artists have subsisted in relations of patronage that depend upon begging, and artists remain the most skilful and inventive exponents of the arts of mendicant advertisement, in order to maintain the demand for their pseudo-supply of unsolicited goods.

Much of the time of those in senior positions in many professions, and in particular the educational and academic professions, will be taken up with the distribution of resources, in the form of grants and employment opportunities, through the administration of different sorts of application process, in which the fact of competition does little to conceal its essentially please-may-I-have petitory nature. As the similarity of the words, both of them derivatives of *petere*, might suggest, petition and competition are in company rather than in opposition. One should not have to resort, one might think, to petition to be given a fair share and for the most part what is meant by a fair share is precisely that for which one should not have to ask. But what one seeks or supplicates for in an application, whether for an award, position, privilege, or some other special advantage, is nearly always an unfair share. What is called open competition is the bureaucratic instrumentalisation of the act of begging.

Acts of petition imply and require the possibility of favour. Favouring implies a leaning away from equality, as when one is said to favour an arm or leg in performing an action, or when compensating for an injury. A petitioner may well claim justice, and justice may depend upon petition, since petition will often be prompted by the sense of unjust treatment; and yet petition implies the impossibility of equal relations, since petition always constitutes a kind of special pleading, for benefits or favours that are exceptional, discretionary or out of the ordinary. One hopes that one's petition will have a favourable outcome. Judgements that find in one person's favour restore balance by an act of unbalanced favouring. The more impersonal, complex and mediated the systems of petition, the more they will try to abstract away or even out the elements of luck, contingency or partiality, and operate 'without fear or favour', even as every petition will aim to reinstate more disequilibrium. One cannot ask a favour of the law, or ask the law to have favourites: yet a petition in or to the law is always addressed to one who may be favourably disposed to apply it. The word favour originally meant an attitude of liking, goodwill, kindness, regard or good opinion. From the fifteenth century onwards, the word was used to mean a special indulgence or privilege, or the lessening of some legal penalty that might otherwise be applied. By the end of the sixteenth century, it began to be used to refer to an object symbolising the favour of a lover or patron, and then as an action, a kindness or 'good turn'. Even today, when one asks for a favour, one is seeking some alteration in circumstances that moves away from equilibrium or necessity.

So petition always aims to elicit outcomes that are gracious or gratuitous, that is, more than are strictly required by the letter of the law. The only petitions that can work are those for which there is no guarantee of success. The formulaic pairing of favour with grace, in the phrase 'grace and favour', was originally applied to the Christian God and then transferred to the sovereign or their representatives, as especially in the provision of 'grace and favour' accommodation. In strongly urging a desired outcome that the fact of petition itself acknowledges is not necessarily due or to be expected, petition therefore involves in itself a tension that is similar to that tension between confession and petition involved in some acts of apology, as described by Andrew Escebedo:

> the confessive dimension implies that we believe we deserve and are ready to accept punishment, whereas the petitionary dimension implies that we wish to forestall punishment and obtain forgiveness. Confession gets us into trouble, and petition tries to get us out of it. An apology, in a sense, fights against itself. One cannot, it seems, be fully committed to self-condemnation at the same time one pursues pardon. (Escobedo 2017, 158)

To the examples of bureaucratised petition in modern societies must be added institutional begging. Many large public institutions, including very powerful and prestigious organisations and wealthy universities, depend on practices of what is hard-headedly known as 'fundraising', but consists of the professional soliciting of gifts, recalling the systems of extractive mendicancy of the religious institutions, themselves similarly already possessed of prodigious wealth, of the medieval world. The tendency for begging to solidify into transaction is at work firstly in the growth of formalised charitable activities, and then in the incorporation of charitable solicitation into the ordinary functioning of institutions or associations, such as schools, colleges, museums, hospitals, or political parties. There seems to be a shared sense that such activity must be a kind of agitation, both in the idea of 'raising' (an English equivalent to the Latinate 'levy'), and, more particularly in soliciting, which derives from Latin *sollus*, whole and *citus*, past participle of *ciere* to move. The link between raising and levying points to the long association between taxation, or the enforcement of giving, and the raising of funds through appeal. To raise funds is to try to induce a kind of voluntary tax. Appeal seems to become associated with appellation as naming (French *s'appeller*) through the idea that when subject to the driving action (*pellere*) of enforcement or inducement one is likely to be identified by name. To be subject to such pressure is to be nameable, just as to 'give one's name' is to stand surety for a debt.

In recent years, the suspicion that has traditionally attached to the honesty of the beggar has transferred to a suspicion of the probity of the giver. This leads to the necessary, if at times faintly absurd, existence of mechanisms of vigilance to ensure that contributions to universities, museums and the like come from reputable sources, or are given freely (*par don*), without the calculated expectation of return. The fact that powerful and sometimes conspicuously well-endowed institutions should appear to be so choosy as to those from whom they will agree to accept money is an indication of the need to try to regulate the forms of transaction taking place in the soliciting and giving of donations, lest the giver be seen to be getting more than their due, which should of course ideally be nothing, but never can be.

On the largest scale of all, human beings engage in prodigious acts of production that disguise the essential relation of parasitic dependency we have to the natural world. We not only keep vast numbers of animals in a domesticated condition that enables us to make economic use of them, we also 'keep' them, at a ruinous environmental cost, as pets, which is to say, in a petitory relation to us.

The Force of Petition

Petitioning is an instance of illocutionary force. But what is the specific form of petitory force? The force of petition is signalled in the Latin *petere* from which it derives, a verb which joins together two fields of semantic force. There is, first of all, to seek, demand, require or solicit, especially in applying or being a candidate for some office. Secondly, *petere* means to move towards or fall upon, both in a hostile sense, in attacking or assailing, and in affection, as when one moves toward or embraces another. *Impetus* embodies the same sense of advance, as also, some have maintained, does the word *perpetual*, endlessly seeking. That which is *propitious*, from *pro + petere*, is that which pushes positively towards. This dual origin alerts us to the advance or aggression involved in petition, which helps understand the feeling of force it tends to give.

A child is wheedling for an ice cream. 'Oh mum, plee-e-ase', she whines. And then, with greater urging, and even a note of angry menace, giving a sharply peremptory falling inflection in place of the rising inflection of appeal: 'Please!' What impels and imparts the passion of this petition? Perhaps to a large degree it is the omnipotence of thought found by Otto Rank and Hanns Sachs in petitionary prayer, the conviction that the articulation of a wish is identical with its fulfilment:

> The belief in the omnipotence of thought centers in the overvaluation of the power of speech, which is so deep rooted that it is considered sufficient to speak aloud the name of a person in order to influence him in the desired direction. This idea of the magical effect of speech is the foundation of prayer (Rank and Sachs 1916, 71)

Denied, the child assumes that what is required is simply increased urgency. This increased urgency generalises the demand, which begins to be, not so much the articulation of a desire as the defence of the belief in magical thinking itself, which requires the parent's performance of her support of the pleasure principle.

Why, on the parent's side, are the repeated demands so hard to resist, to the point of becoming physically painful? What is so commanding about the child's demand? Is it simply that the parent would naturally wish to gratify the child's wish? Perhaps, to some degree. But the emotional conflict is more intense than this. Perhaps the intention and effect of a petition is to infect the listener with the urgency of the petitioner's desire, as though appealing not for a particular object but on behalf of desiring itself. So 'give me what I want' turns into 'do not extinguish the force of desire which is currently identical with my whole existence. Have mercy on my need, for you too have felt the force of need, and you too have felt the blank void of having your omnipotent need defeated. How can you now put yourself in the pitiless place of the reality principle?' The adult subject to the appeal to keep hope in omnipotence of thoughts alive may have just enough of that hope flickering in themselves to share in the mourning for omnipotence and to feel the pain of participating in its deep and this time irreversible betrayal.

Rank and Sachs suggest that the child who has experienced rebuff of the omnipotence of thoughts does not give the doctrine up altogether (for who gives up anything altogether?) but transfers belief in its own omnipotence to belief in the omnipotence of God:

> On the one hand, the petitioner expects that the solemn voicing aloud of his wishes avails to cause the god to fulfill them, on the other hand, he has at the same time indirectly preserved the feeling of omnipotence which he has had to renounce by resignation to the godhead, with which he unconsciously identifies himself. (Rank and Sachs 1916, 71)

The growing desperation of the child's imprecations places the ever more remote parent in the position of the omnipotent deity they too once invoked in vain, and tempts them to make good the fantasy of a beneficent rather than sadistic divinity (a loving parent rather than a stonily remote god). Petition always offers something of what it solicits, 'par don', by way of a gift. That is, it offers to the one petitioned the possibility of showing their mercy and magnanimity, in the process reviving and preserving through impersonation their own imperilled belief in the omnipotence principle.

The child negotiates a conditional surrender of his omnipotence fantasy by displacing it into the figure of the all-powerful donor to whom he is given, or even gives himself, the right to pray. Petition results from the child's discovery, which, in that every social creature discovers its efficacy without needing to know it, need not be consciously recognised, that helplessness is a form of power in this transaction, which is made a transaction rather than simply an action by the very fact of this reversibility. The transaction consists of the process whereby the donor's gift, or their very power to give, has the power to turn helplessness into power. The struggle enacted in the petitory transaction is to substitute the ideal Donor of the petitioner's fantasy for the real donor.

Ultimately, the belief in this imaginary Donor will have itself to be given up, after the long and painful discovery that the omnipotence of the imaginary other cannot be relied upon to act as the relay through which the petitioner may grant themselves their own wish. This may be reinforced by the discovery by honest theological reflection that a God who could be relied upon to grant prayers could not only not be a just God, but could not in fact be a god at all. In this respect, prayer represents the gravest jeopardy it is possible for religious belief to encounter. The dissolving effect of prayer on the central principle of monotheism will be considered in chapter 5 below.

This recognition requires a strange second displacement of omnipotence. Having first been displaced from the ego's hallucination of power to the imaginary Donor, omnipotence is then displaced back into the act of wishing, but now kept at a distance from the force of the subject's narcissism, by having to pass through the forms of performative ritual. This means that the force of petition is transferred from its objection to the action of petition itself, to which both petitioner and petitioned are now ritually subject. Thus, the power of petition passes from the subject to its object, to petition itself. The sediment of force in the form and performance of the petition helps to maintain a potency which might otherwise be at risk from the withering of force into form. As petition takes ever more the form of a contract, it becomes increasingly the exemplary example of the contractual basis of social life itself, with its many obligations to recognise the force of obligation.

The fact that to be a human is to have been a child for a very long period during which such petitory dramas are played out almost constantly makes the act of petition naturally apt to recall or repeat these infant-adult relations. In this sense a large part of petitory force may lie in the reminiscence of these dramas, for which the word *re-petition* seems literally apposite, and which are characterised by the absolute helplessness of the child, moderated only by the vehemence, despairing or angrily assured as it may be, with which they can exhibit or proclaim their own helplessness. Every act of begging is a voluntary reduction to the condition of a child, in order in part to claim the powerful prerogative that only helplessness can confer.

But petitory force extends well beyond infant-adult relations. The force wielded by the one who petitions comes also from the offer the petition makes of a certain intimacy of relation, in which the one receiving the benefit they request will be, as we say, obliged to the giver. In this sense the power of the petition consists in part in the offer of power or advantage it seems to hold out, in the offer made by the petitioner of their future state of obligation to the petitioned. Pleading of this kind is always a kind of plea-bargain, in which the petitioner offers their obligation as exchange for the favour. Petitioning may often therefore assert a kind of bondage, or social ligature, in advance (the willed bondage of a loyal subject, or hard-working tradesman, say) of the obligation that is sought in the granting of the petition. This offering of a future condition of obligation seems to offer a force of obligation of its own, activating the force of the obligatory that seems to inhere in all such offers. For social creatures, it is a reminder of the general obligation we are all under to be prepared to recognise and respect ties of obligation. The petitioner demonstrates that they will be obliged to be obliged to the giver, attempting thereby to evoke an answering obligation on the part of the petitioned to accede to this obligation.

Pleading and petitioning take some of the most dramatically corporeal forms and may both enjoin and exploit an intensely corporeal rhetoric. Parent birds respond automatically to the display of the pink throats of their young, and petitioners may similarly seek to provide similarly irresistible pressure through their displays of respect, abjection, desperation, dignified restraint, etc. But petition has also been formalised, in written and other forms. Indeed, a very large part of the documentary record of public and political life, and the relations between private subjects and public institutions, is constituted by the records of petitions. In order for this to happen, petition needs to have a form as well as exerting a force. The complex relation between form and force is an essential part of all speech acts. Speech acts must do things, but there must always also be ways of doing those things; speech acts are forceful in that they are actions, but formal in that they must be actions that can be acted out, making every action recognisable as a kind of reenactment of an approved form.

Petitory relations have a distinctive relation to this complex because such relations always appear to break, or at least break from, the law, understood as a purely formal, wholly self-consistent set of rules, to be applied indifferently in all conceivable circumstances. The one who appeals hopes for some leavening or laying aside of law, that quality of mercy that cannot be constrained, but may, with luck or at a pinch, be granted. This makes mercy, clemency or leniency not things that may be counted on, but some excess, or some curtailing that is strictly unnecessary, because they loosen the strictness of necessity itself. As Jeffrie Murphy has justly observed, tempering the law is tampering with it (Murphy 1988, 167). Indeed the word tamper very likely derives from the word temper, in an evaluative shift that seems to parallel that in the word *meddle*, which means to blend, mingle or associate with until the seventeenth century, but comes increasingly thereafter, perhaps influenced by *muddle*, to mean to interfere with.

And yet the right of petition to appeal against the law becomes an intrinsic part of the law from very early times. This means that petitory force becomes focussed through prescribed legal forms, which both conduct and contain the force of petition. One of the most important effects of this interchange is that petition, which tends at first to be a way of taking account of individual circumstances that the generalities of law cannot deal with justly, itself becomes generalised, and petition enters the order of number, and begins to be shaped and driven by it. These changes will be the subject of the chapter on the political history of petitions.

Petition and Seduction

Petition is both an essential part of seduction and deploys seduction in most of its operations. The petitioner must draw the one petitioned into a dual identification. First of all, they must be induced to identify their desire with that of the petitioner; and secondly, they must have induced in them the desire to enter the powerfully longed-for and approved role of the granter of wishes, succumbing to what, in Brecht's *The Caucasian Chalk Circle*, is called the terrible temptation to do good (Brecht 1974, 160). The seductive aspect of petition consists in the offer of gratification it makes. Hence, perhaps the expression 'pretty please', a bit of babytalk sometimes elaborated in American usage by 'with sugar on top', or 'with six cherries on top', which attempts to mime for the hearer the idea that work has been done to craft the petition into a pleasing object for their consumption and benefit, meaning that the plea for a gift has become itself a gift. Perhaps, in fact, the object signified by these imaginary infantile-eat-me objects (the double-t of 'pretty' helps it double up with 'little') is intended momentarily to be identified with the petitioner himself, offering themselves up in person in their pleading as a pleasingly dainty sweetmeat.

Like *nice*, *pretty* has undergone both a lowering and restriction of sense from the seventeenth century when it could still mean fine or commendable, or, of a person, and especially in Scottish usage, doughty and courageous, as well as more generally admirable or accomplished, as in Pepys's praise of Dr Timothy Clarke, a founding member of the Royal Society and physician to Charles II, 'who I find to be a pretty man and very knowing' (Pepys 1995, 134). Like the words *nice* and *cute* again, both of which have softened from their early meanings of precise and acute, *pretty* could have the sense in earlier usages of tricky or cunning. *Pretty* derives from OE *praet*, a prank or trick, and Joseph Wright records *prettikin* as a Shetland and Orkney word for a feat, trick or gambol (Wright 1905, 614). Pretty continues to be used to mean elegant, or neatly-contrived, rather than just nice-looking, for example in *pretty as a picture*. Of course the teasing self-lowering involved in the childish patterning is just such an instance of a trick in action, the trick of tricking itself out as something pretty.

This would work pretty well even without the word *pretty* functioning as an implied diminutive of 'prithee', or 'I pray thee', reducing them both to little more than a bit of lilting prettiness, on the principle that, as the proverb has it 'little things are pretty' (Ray 1678, 169). Nevertheless, there is a kind of folk-assumption that *pretty* is a prettification of *prithee*, an attempt to make the act of pleading pleasing with a touch of innocent, because rather amateur decoration. The *OED* records no instance of *pretty please* before 1888 and compares it to German *bitte schön*, though without suggesting any reference to *prithee*. Kay Boyle uses the phrase *prithee please* in her 1932 novel *Year Before Last* (Boyle 1932, 94), but this is very likely the spelling out of a conjecture. It is nevertheless a conjecture that may be in unconscious operation, as an implied backformation for the phrase *pretty please*. The Gilbert and Sullivan song 'Prithee Pretty Maiden' from *Patience* (Gilbert and Sullivan 1976, 172-3) may suggest their latent association.

Anne Wichmann has pointed to the intonational complement involved in giving intensity to what is ordinarily a polite formula, observing that 'the unusual assignment of a high pitch accent on the word *please* often creates a sense of greater urgency, turning a neutral, courteous request into an emphatic request, plea or appeal' (Wichmann 2005, 244). The crafting of the phrase *pretty please* will often be accompanied by the distinctive rising pitch of the imitated child's wheedle, rather than the 'high dive' intonation from high to low pitch characteristic of an urgent appeal or vehement instruction. All of this is the work of rather trivial, or tension-diffusing play, designed to sweeten the work of petition.

Life begins and ends in beggary, the infant and the pensioner both assigned to the life of the dependant. Even the one who thinks they have accrued enough capital on which to live out their final days depends upon petitory relations to be able to make good that independence. And even between these two extremes of infancy and superannuation, we are caught in complex webs of dependence that are secured by something more or less than contractual relations. Increasing connectivity means ever denser codependency, in which the absolute distinction between the autonomously productive subject and the unproductive or parasitic dependant becomes ever more abstract and imaginary. For, as petitory relations become ever more formalised, so the distinction between social contracts and symbolic transactions is eroded. Petitory rituals and relations activate and consolidate these dependencies.

Nowhere is this more the case than in what is nowadays called 'networking'. The appearance of this word as a verb occurs almost simultaneously with technical uses which describe the construction of networks of relations, typically in communications. The idea of social networking is introduced in the work of psychologists Ross Speck and Carole Attneave, who use it to refer to the process of reviving or constructing family or kinship relations they call 'retribalization' to provide therapeutic support in the case of mental illness (Speck and Attneave 1973). This depends on the idea that kinship relations provide an alternative to more abstract, and potentially alienating kinds of social relation, like that of customer or employee. But the rapid spread of the term social networking to other kinds of contact, especially for the purposes of commercial or professional advantage, makes for a tight convergence with what might previously have been thought of as 'patronage'.

Patronage is in fact the symmetrical counterpart to petition. Networking flattens and micrologises the vertical relations of patronage, meaning that the power and the responsibility of the patron are distributed and made intermittent. In a network, every individual is called upon to act at different times both as petitioner and patron. Academic life in particular oscillates continually between contractual and patronal relations, and nowhere more so than in the power given to the archaic institution of the 'reference' or letter of recommendation. The more seniority one has, the more of one's time is spent confecting these extraordinary ceremonial documents. The writing of references is an expectation rather than a requirement, which is one of the things that makes its demands so imperious. One does not request a reference so much as appeal for it, in the sense that one calls on the referee to meet the conditions of their name – an anonymous reference is useless, because a reference is the proof of the willingness of one's referee to give the reference freely and without requirement – *par don*, rather than, as is always in fact the case, on demand. This makes the action of asking someone to write on one's behalf a tense affair. One is asking, as the beggar asks, with no sense that what is requested is one's due: but it is this very condition that exerts the petitory force. As so often, charity and menace combine in such a request. The one petitioned is offered the gift of having given a gift, with the enlargement of status that it involves; but they are also implicitly threatened with the disgrace of being seen to refuse.

The forms of Serresian 'natural contract' (1995) which are beginning to accord legal standing to trees, rivers and insects are widening these forms of dependency. Objects in the natural world, like trees, streams and mountains, come to have standing, in the legal sense, when they can sue for damages, or for protection of their rights to continued existence, which is to say, when somebody may be legally empowered to stand in for them (Stone 2010). So to be a legal subject is not to be self-governing but to have the right, and means of appeal. As so often, to be a subject is to be subject, and to be able to have been subjected to some wrong, against which petitory protest may be made. Natural objects are made not just subject to law but subjects of law by having extended to them the right of petition.

Begging and Discourse

Begging is a symbolic action and therefore requires some kind of symbolic system and form of discourse in which to operate. But there is reason to consider begging as more than just one interaction among others that occur in discourse. Any discourse requires as a minimum the capacity to make a signal to which a response is possible, the capacity, that is, to enter into discursive exchange, through the acts of replying (that is, etymologically, retying) and rejoinder that keep discourse joined together. Michel Serres proposes that all communication may be translated into the invitation-exhortation 'keep me warm' (Serres 1982, 76). Following the communicational energetics assumed by Serres, this would make every utterance, no matter what its manifest content, up to and including a dismissive imperative like 'avaunt thee!', or 'piss off!', a request for a response, 'keep me warm' translating directly into 'answer me'. What makes a language, otherwise an inert map of relations and correspondences, into a discourse is this activating activity, of askings and answerings, requests and requitings, proposals, renderings, demurrals and returns. It seems perfectly unsurprising that this process should be spoken of through the economic metaphor of exchange. What holds discourse together through these uncertain transitions is the fact of transaction, and the temporal hooking or implicature it effects, of one action that asks for another or, at the very least, asks what the answering action of speech will turn out to be.

Begging is both the confirmation of this tensile weave of petition and permission, and its violent jeopardy. This is because begging ruptures the reciprocity of discourse along with the distance which sustains it and which it allows for. Begging enunciates a demand that seems not to allow for the symmetry of any kind of exchange or transaction. The hostility which is never absent from begging is directed at the discourse it infects with its lethal absoluteness even as it parasites it. Begging affects to remove any trace of expectation or presumption from the act of requesting, but is, as a result, the imposture of request in its ruling out of reciprocity. Begging therefore does its work by demanding the dissolution of the very system of symbolic exchanges it deploys and on which it depends. Given the dependence of children, who do not have the resources of discourse available to them, on this means of short-circuiting discourse, it is not surprising that it should have this kind of force, or that interlocutors should be susceptible to it. The tension of begging comes from the fact of this parasiting of discourse, as it seems at once to affirm and to unloose the bonds formed in discourse and on which discourse must depend.

Begging, so often deployed as the evidence of a violation, or the attempt to avert it, is itself a violation, the ravishment of discourse, in just the same way as sexual rape is a violation of the contract enacted, in theory at least (but a theory that is powerfully regulative), in the relations of sexual love. The inversive force of begging derives from the petitioner's imposture, in the literal sense of the taking of a position, of a condition of helplessness and what may justly be called 'irresponsibility', that is, not being answerable to any prior requirement, but primary and self-motivated, which attempts to force the response it wishes to appear to be forced to petition, through seeming, precisely, unanswerable. Of course, discourse of all kinds depends on, and may perhaps be nothing other than, the deployment of many kinds of force and counter-force, but begging, in its paradoxical requisitioning of the force of commanding through the choice of abrogating choice, seems to be unique in its powers both to activate the essentially responsive structure of discourse and to pirate it. This may have something to do with the uncanny force that acts of begging and the figure of the beggar can seem to exercise.

In post-traditional, individualist societies, beggary is regarded with horror, or is supposed to be (if it really were such a horror, we would all do much less of it than it is this book's intent to show we do). To be reduced to the action of begging, or the condition known as beggary, which hovers at an intriguing distance from the actual resort to begging, is more than to be poor. It is to be outside the social world, even, insofar as being human is identified with the capacity to labour, to lose one's humanity, and so to become a kind of animal, or the semi-domesticated animal known as a child. Though beggars are entirely dependent on the existence of organised society, beggary desocialises, and the solitary condition thought to be appropriate to that of beggars brings suspicion on any kind of society of beggars, along with the strange dread that beggars will automatically cluster together into marauding mendicant assemblies. Beggary is an evicted, outdoor condition – one begs 'in the street', or 'from door to door'.

Few representations of begging go further in removing humanness from the beggar than the final verse of the Irish song, 'Johnny, I Hardly Knew You', often described as a folk song and assumed to date from the late eighteenth century, or the Napoleonic Wars, but in fact written in 1867 by music-hall singer Joseph B. Geoghegan:

> Ye's haven't an arm, ye's haven't a leg, ahoo!
> You're a noseless, eyeless, chickenless egg,
> Ye"ll have to be put in a bowl to beg –
> Och! Johnny, I hardy knew ye. (Geoghegan 1867, 5)

The penultimate line is sometimes smoothed out to 'put with a bowl to beg', but the original 'put in a bowl to beg' completes the savage grotesqueness of the preceding line, and may refer to the bowl in which amputee veterans would in fact be placed to beg. Not to be able even to be able to hold out a bowl for alms, but to be yourself an item deposited in such a bowl, reduces the being of the beggar to its condition of biological minimum. The image may recall the Irish story of Billy in the Bowl, the 'Stoneybatter Strangler', a legless mendicant who propelled himself through Dublin's streets in a wheeled bowl, yet managed impressively nevertheless to commit a series of murders on his almsgivers for their purses. Johnny and Billy may have converged in the various pot-bound and enurned characters who appear (only partially of course) in Samuel Beckett's *The Unnamable*, *Endgame* and *Play*.

The one who begs is helpless, not only without any source of help, but unable to help themselves, and so lacking in the self-relation that is held to be the condition of the adult human. Their condition is one of pure dependency. Oddly, this is not just a characteristic of the beggar, but also something of a requirement, and in fact a difficult one to fulfil. The beggar who gives any sign of having made a choice to beg is regarded as deceitful and parasitic. The difficulties of making good this condition of choicelessness are an important part of the discursive paradox of begging.

The most important thing about beggary is that it is a communicative action as well as a condition. This makes for a peculiar and defining tension between beggary and destitution. My *Giving Way* (2019) explored the many different modes of abstitution, of standing aside, or holding back, in human communication and behaviour. Here, I press further, to try to build acquaintance with the more ambivalent condition in which destitution, or extreme deprivation, nevertheless speaks on its own behalf. A poem, Archibald MacLeish tells us, 'should not mean but be' (MacLeish 1985, 107), audaciously overruling his own edict in the process. The scandal of the beggar lies in their disinclination simply to be, and their inclination to articulate their meaning, in the form of demand, thus proclaiming the claim that their being makes. Its scandal and perturbation of discourse is that of a destitution that, requisitioning for its purposes a discourse of destitution, must therefore be more or other than the pure or absolute destitution of which it discourses. The one who begs cannot in fact be destitute of everything, since they retain a capacity for discourse, albeit one that must itself approach the condition of a kind of destitute state. Such destitute discourse stands for, and stands forth as, that which has no standing. So the destitution of discourse itself is always at stake in the discourses of the destitute. The relation between the beggar's destitution and their communication of it is aptly encapsulated in King Lear's exasperated exclamation, as his daughters seek to bargain him down to absolute indigence, that 'our basest beggars/Are in the poorest thing superfluous' (Shakespeare 2011, 650). He means that there is always something of which a beggar has a greater store than they strictly need; but his words also allow the suggestion that beggary itself, the condition of needing and being able to beg, is itself one of those resources. In its capacity for begging, poverty may itself be the superfluity or something more than nothing that prevents absolute poverty.

It seems straightforwardly the case that people ask for things they want and ask for them as ways of obtaining them. But this is far from exhausting the range of uses and requirements that asking has. For if it seemed possible that asking for things provided other kinds of reward than their obtaining, the way might be open to an understanding of the primary value and reward of the act of petition. The first thing to be noted is that petition gives one the animation of grievance. The petitioner has the advantage of their disadvantage. The one who asks is armed with the necessity of their need. The one who is able to ask – and all humans who can speak can ask, for we are indeed *Homo rogans* – is supplied with a reservoir of possible needs.

Asking is, we have said, a primary action and orientation of discourse. Asking always introduces stress and the possibility of infraction into a relationship, but the family of words centring on the action of suing suggests that it also constitutes relationship, the relationship of one thing that follows another. To sue is to follow, from Latin *sequor*, which could mean to pursue in a hostile fashion as well as to follow subserviently, thus matching the active-passive duality of *petere*, as well as, more neutrally simply to succeed or ensue. Suing and suitage are what happen *ensuite*, as a matter of course. When I accede to a query or request with the words 'of course', I witness the way in which such actions indeed constitute the due course of things among humans, the primary meaning of *due* being the duty of that which is owed, the relations of *debt*, *devoir* or *debitus* that at once complicate and constitute social time.

Strong Weakness

In Samuel Beckett's story 'Ding Dong', the character of Belacqua Shuah is said by his friend, the unnamed narrator, to have had 'a strong weakness for oxymoron' (Beckett 2010a, 32). Beckett might perhaps be said to have made a speciality throughout his work of this particular form of oxymoron. But the principle of the strength of weakness is at once the distinctive discovery that made almost all of Beckett's work possible, and the discovery that if it is a speciality, it is one that is general across our entire species. One cannot beg except in weakness. One not only begs because one is weak, one must necessarily make oneself weak in the action. But why would one make oneself weak? This is a far-reaching question, with many more operations and applications than can be taken notice of in this book. But the short answer is often that becoming weak is a means of gaining strength. How?

We assume that strength and weakness are opposites, and also form a zero-sum game, like hot and cold or height and depth. The more strength I have, the less weak I must necessarily be; the weaker I grow, the less strength I must have. In an entirely abstract world there would be only those who want, the things they want, and the impediments to their attainment of those wants, which might obviously include other people who also want them. In the case of hunting prey, the wanted and the impediment may be identified, since that animal one wants to eat wants to continue its uneaten existence. But the evolution of social forms and the complicated reroutings of wanting and attaining through structures of communication mean that other wanters may also be able to assist the attainment of wants, as well as impeding that attainment.

This structure represents a further abstraction of the already highly abstracted functions set out in Vladimir Propp's *Morphology of the Folktale* (1968), which distinguishes in narrative various configurations of agents, aims, enemies, inciters and assisters. An essential diagram of wanting – and every narrative is driven by the need for the satisfaction of some kind of need, if only the need for story itself – need consist only of agents, aims and opponents. Games have the same structure, complicated only by their reflexivity: the apparent aim of a game is never the manifest aim but is subsidiary to the meta-aim of wanting to play with aims and aiming: I don't really want to knock a ball into a hole with a stick, I want to see how good I could be at doing it, that is, to play at doing it.

Petition arises from the recognition that opponents may be transformed into proponents, or, as we ought to be able to say, *copponents*, through being recruited to my aims, or by becoming a component of them. A tripartite structure of agents, aims and opponents thereby becomes a quadratic relation, of agents, aims, opponents and components and or, since it depends upon the indeterminate transformability of opponent into component, a quasi-quadratic relation. Systems of communication are not necessary to the emergence of such structures, but they certainly assist and accelerate them. Systems of communication mediate the process of turning impediments to my aims into mediations of them.

Grammatical structures seem to embody something like this variation. Many declension systems divide nouns into subject-cases and different forms of object cases. In Latin, there is the accusative case, for direct objects, or the effects of a cause, from which the word 'accusative' derives (to accuse is to bring someone *ad causam*, to the case, cause or trial). Then there are the indirect cases of the genitive, for objects that belong to other objects, the dative, for objects that are given to other objects or subjects, and the ablative, to name what is taken from, or by means of, other objects or subjects. Strikingly, the essential relations between these cases of 'to-ness' and 'from-ness' are circumstances of giving and taking. The ablative case is so named from the past participial stem of *auferre*, to carry away. The act of begging aims at effecting a relation that is successively ablative with respect to the one solicited to give, and dative with respect to the direction of their giving. So it may be thought that petition is not only inflected through grammar; grammar, or at least this form of it, is the schematisation of petitory relations. Communication is necessary to the to-and-fro of petitory relations; but the need for petitory relations itself drives the formation of communication systems that mediate this reciprocation – reciprocation deriving from *reci-* backwards + *procare*, to ask or demand, in particular to ask in marriage.

The reciprocating engine of many grammatical systems allows for the conversion of weakness into strength, by providing an economy of borrowing, in which the weak can become strong by drawing on, or drawing off some portion of the strength of others. They cannot do this by compelling the strong, since they are too weak. They can only do it by means of their weakness, a weakness that infiltrates strength and dulcifies the obdurate.

The power of the powerful is always potential rather than actual, an assumption or promise or menace in the future perfect tense of what will have been able to be done. This means that power is always symbolic, which also accounts retroactively for much of the power accorded to symbolism. Power is not that which is exercised but that which is threatened, proclaimed and accorded. All force is show of force, even and especially that kind of exercise of force that aims to prove its reality goes beyond mere show. The strength of the strong and the weakness of the weak are both indeterminate, because they are matters not of simple fact but of probability – both in the sense of what may be more or less likely and what may prove to be the case. This indeterminacy gives power to the signs of power and weakness. Demonstration of potential is the very power of power. One enacts power in action in small doses in order that the future demonstrations can be used to show that there is no need for the power to be demonstrated in action. But if being able to be exercised in intimation rather than action is the strength of power, then it is also its weakness, for having to be displayed makes power no longer autonomous but dependent on demonstration and recognition. The show of force also shows that force may be all show.

But, where the strength of the strong is assumed to be identifiable as a kind of autonomy, even if it will almost always in fact depend on forms of alliance or the expectation of supplementation, the strength of the weak must always be of a heteronomous or second-order kind. For it depends on allusion and implication and derives what force it seems to have from its expectation of the ethnic-moral force that may be evoked on its behalf. It is a sort of ethical currency, both symbolising and also in part realising the credit that every society, considered in the light of a system of mutual insurance, must at least in principle be willing to extend to those in need or at risk. Among humans, there will always be at least one group who will need this kind of protection, namely children, given the extraordinary length of time that children remain dependent on other humans. No society that did not deploy some kind of power to defend the interests of its vulnerable young could thrive, or even survive. Such force is the promise held open by any social coalition that offers protections to its less powerful members. To take the most obvious example, the theoretical monopoly of violence enjoyed by the state is intended to offer protection, and therefore potentially realisable power, to potential victims of violence. The penalties for violence or abuse practised against defenceless members of a society by the powerful are particularly exacting, or, where they are not, such abuse will be viewed a moral scandal. The weak, or those taken to be weak, or taking on the position of weakness, have access to the inhibiting power exercised over power which is unavailable to the strong except by dissimulation.

More often than not, however, the second-order force deployed by weakness is moral-political rather than a matter for the police. This is to say that it offers a challenge to the psycho-social standing of the powerful rather than any kind of direct physical threat. The power of the weak may appear more symbolic than actual compared to the power of the strong, but loss of symbolic power is in reality far more debilitating to the strong than loss of physical power. In fact the dependence of the strong on symbolism is the source of all the strength of weakness. As we will see later, the political action known as the demonstration has a large repertoire of methods for forcing the authorities into the ultimately debilitating use of unnecessary force.

Up to a point, display functions as an embodiment of power. Power tends to try to achieve a monopoly of communicative methods and messages. But as communication becomes common currency, it becomes correspondingly more difficult to exercise power through it, and over it. This view of things would allow the prediction that the move from relatively restricted communication to relatively generalised communication would produce ever more occasions for the insurgence and ramification of the strength of weakness, achieved through reversal of valence. Developments in recent years seem to bear this out. In part, this is a matter of simple strength in numbers, but it is much more essentially a matter of the density of communications, in which the strong are not so much wiped out by the weak as shouted down. This is why the weak can turn the strength of the strong against them, as noted by Henry Kissinger following the American withdrawal from Vietnam: 'we lost sight of one of the cardinal maxims of guerrilla war: the guerrilla wins if he does not lose. The conventional army loses if it does not win' (Kissinger 2000, 314).

One of the most telling examples of this aggression through symbolism is the taking of offence, or what almost always amounts to the same thing, the articulation of this offence. I cannot remember a time when people were so likely to take offence, or, rather, what comes to the same thing, when we were more edgily aware of the risk of giving it. Contracts, corporate guidelines and codes of conduct of all kinds warn against words or actions that are 'liable to cause offence'. Artists and writers, and those who transmit their work, like producers, publishers and broadcasters, must maintain a constant state of vigilance with regard to the possibility of causing offence.

The striking thing about the word 'offence' is that it is so symmetrically shared out between offenders and their victims. If I offend someone, then in an obvious sense, the offence is mine, as the offending party. But, under those circumstances, the offended party is also entitled to speak of their offence at what I have said, thought or done. So now, in a strange way, the 'offence' is theirs too. And this offence, in the sense of a sense of having been offended, is far from being a passive or even reactive state of feeling. Indeed, in speaking of taking offence, our language recognises that offence is not a passive state of being offended, but rather an active seizing of an advantage. When you take offence, you get a golden chance to go on the offensive. There is also a curious somersault of time involved in the taking of offence. In contrast to a kiss or a right cross, which must be given before they can be received, taking offence is a primary and inaugural act: you can try, but you cannot be said to have succeeded in giving offence unless it has first been taken.

To offend someone is to hurt their feelings. This is a revealing phrase. Why not just hurt them? It makes no sense to say that you have hurt someone's feelings, because hurt already is a feeling. You can hurt a person, by giving them a feeling of hurt, but how on earth do you go about giving their feelings a feeling of hurt?

Now I know all too well what it is like to offend someone, which is to say I am pretty familiar with the ways in which people are likely to act and speak in such a circumstance. But I find it almost impossible to attach any content to the feeling of being offended. It is not that I am too soggily tolerant to be offended by anything, and I hope it is not that I am too affectively inert to be able to sympathise with such feelings. It is that I honestly do not know what being offended is meant to feel like, in the way that I am sure I know what it feels like to be angry, humiliated, jealous, envious, tearful or fearful. What is more, and no offence, but I do not think other people know what this feels like either. Hence the bizarre, but giveaway phrase 'I feel personally offended'. For one never in fact does feel personally offended, because offence is always a vicarious feeling, which is felt, or claimed on behalf of some other putatively injured party. Being offended is therefore not something you feel, but something you do, in laying claim to it, in lieu of feeling it. It is an aggressive appeal, right over at the demand end of petition, a claim to entitlement and, very likely, reparation, if only the symbolic reparation of an apology, that self-weakening which is the only way for the strong to escape the enfeeblingly shameful consequences of their strength.

So why do people insist that they feel offended? It is surely because, if you recognise that taking offence is an active demand you might have to take responsibility for it. Whereas, if you can pull off the trick of persuading yourself and others that you are the helpless victim of an offence that has been gratuitously done to you, then you will seem to have no choice in what you say and do in response. To have no choice, to be able deliciously to conceal from ourselves the choices we cannot but make by robing them as destinies, is our deepest and saddest craving.

The action of petition, the subject of this book, is just one form of the strength of weakness. But it has a right to be thought of as possessing particular potency, and even of forming an essential part of the grammar of symbolic power. Petition is an essential form of the convertibility of weakness to strength, because it is its discursive actualisation, the taking up of simulacral arms in the more or less militant assertion of the strength that is reserved to weakness. More than this, it is the actualisation of the potential for the transvaluation of power that is probably the essential function of discourse. Perhaps the essential function of discourse is therefore not to say 'keep me warm', but 'keep calm'.

The push and potency of petition rest in the frail audacity of its arising. Really, it takes courage to beg: most people are not up to it. For this reason, petition is always also protestation, a testimony to and angry protest against the assumed and ostended necessity of its own daring. There is therefore a kind of aggression in petition, which makes the petitioned the target for its bitter reproach; for they are the one taken for that moment to be the cause as well as the occasion of the petitioner's self-prostration: if not for the opportunity your wealth offers, I would not be forced into this humiliation, for which alone I deserve recompense. The beggar asserts, without needing to assert it, for their action itself insists on it, that they have no choice but to beg, for our regulating assumption is that no human would beg by choice, or would choose the humiliation of choicelessness that begging seems to prove. Through their begging, they then convey that condition of helplessness to the one petitioned, who is in turn constrained, if only for the brief period of the encounter, to execute a role they cannot themselves freely assume or easily decline.

It is right to look to infant-adult relations in seeking to understand begging and petition, because childhood represents the most extended period of helplessness in human life. But at the same time, childhood is the period in which human beings discover the power of their weakness. Indeed, the discovery of the power of their weakness is an important stage in the overcoming of that weakness. There is no simple once and for all and irreversible move into adult, independent life. It is not just that old age inevitably involves a return to something like the condition of the child, as we become dependent on other humans and healthcare systems. All the way through, and at every level, every human society is a web, constantly being respun, of dependence and independence, along with the dynamic patterns of reciprocity, and relative or quasi-autonomy assured through alliance, that bind them together. At the apex of a traditional society is the leader or sovereign whose power can never rest in their own personal strength, but must always derive from some external principle, whether it is the supposition of some kind of divine right, or the shared assumption of the continued consent of the ruled to her rule. Her, because I here insist that all absolute power is female, in the sense of secondary, or derived, so that sovereigns must consent to be feminised. In patriarchal societies, nothing embodies this ambivalence better than female monarchs, especially when they assume the posture that Elizabeth I does in her Tilbury Speech of 1588, first recorded in a letter from Leonel Sharp to the Duke of Buckingham in 1623, which turns the fearful exposure to danger that had been a characteristic of her reign into her strength:

> My loving people, we have been perswaded by some, that are careful of our safety, to take heed how we commit our self to armed multitudes for fear of treachery: but I assure you, I do not desire to live to distrust my faithful, and loving people. Let Tyrants fear, I have alwayes so behaved my self, that under God I have placed my chiefest strength, and safeguard in the loyal hearts and good will of my subiects. And therefore I am come amongst you as you see, at this time, not for my recreation, and disport, but being resolved in the midst, and heat of the battaile to live, or die amongst you all. (Anon 1654, 260)

Proclaiming famously 'I know I have the bodie, but of a weak and feeble woman, but I have the heart and Stomach of a King, and of a King of *England* too' ((Anon 1654, 260), Elizabeth becomes the 'armed *Pallas*' (Anon 1654, 259) of popular mythology. Elizabeth's speech shows how essentially heteronomous, derived from and dependent on external circumstances, apparently absolute power can be.

In social creatures, these relations of interdependence are always dynamic, which is to say, not just changeable, but subject to pressures and negotiations. The emphasis on independent selfhood, and the famed captaincy of one's soul, in contemporary societies produces an obsession with the assertion of what is known as 'agency', not least in the universities and the pop-psychopolitics the discourse derived from them underpins, which is so absurdly, if also sometimes deliberately inattentive to the force of weakness in human society. We may risk the articulation of the following principle: the more complex and diversified the social forces that arise to channel and inhibit the ingenious aggressiveness of creatures like primates, the greater the force of weakness will thereby become, and the more diverse its forms will be.

Roger Gomm drew attention to one particular form of this in 1975, in an account of the social uses made of the experience of spirit possession among the Digo people of Southern Kenya. Gomm draws on the suggestion of I.M. Lewis that spirit possession is 'an oblique aggressive strategy' (Lewis 1971, 32), built on the expectation in many societies that elaborate and expensive steps must be available and taken where necessary to dispel demons. A society that offers elaborate forms of welfare and support for conditions of affliction or disadvantage (it is easy to see the analogies in developed welfare states, but there are no societies that offer no such compensations) will always give encouragement to these forms of oblique aggression, among humans who have any memory at all of being observant children, whether or not they were well cared-for (and children had better be observant, if they have any hopes of staying alive long enough to stop being children). Gomm associates spirit possession with a large class of social phenomena 'in which someone can be represented as bargaining for something, not on the basis of what he or she has to offer in return, but on the basis of what he lacks, is about to lose, suffers from or is deficient in' (Gomm 1975, 536). The beggar is only one among a number of social roles or types which may give rise to such negotiations, including invalids, the poor, victims of discrimination and 'the suicide on the parapet', but Gomm proposes that they may all be characterised by the term 'mendicity', since all involve 'asymmetrical transaction', and begging is the form of transaction that most obviously negotiates on the basis of weakness (Gomm 1975, 536). Such transactions are attended with certain conditions: the person conducting the transaction must be thought not to be responsible for their condition and therefore their actions; and their condition of helplessness must bring special kinds of privilege or status (including, we must suppose, a kind of immunity from the accusation that they might possibly be exploiting their condition), along with a genuine cost in lowered dignity and esteem, and the risk of suspicion that they may be fraudulent, along with certifying measures to protect against this (Gomm 1975, 536-7). All of these conditions require strong and intricate reciprocal expectations, which will be highly specific to different societies and social set-ups, but universally present as the condition of reciprocity in general.

Concern is sometimes expressed about what is sometimes known as 'aggressive begging'. But perhaps there is aggression in all begging, even of the most apparently passive kind. For the beggar always offers a moral affront to the one from whom charity is sought, in the very fact of their appeal, insofar as it represents a demand. An appeal differs from a demand in that it does not include any sense of entitlement, and therefore seems to leave the one to whom appeal is made free to refuse. But the beggar's appeal includes a kind of demonstration of absolute need that in fact amounts to a demand that the potential giver recognise their moral duty to help restore the human dignity of the one who has been forced to relinquish it. Insofar as dignity is everyone's due, then help to restore their dignity is indeed the due of the beggar. The appeal leaves one free to refuse, but the fact of making the appeal, which always includes the implication that the one making it has no choice but to make it, is an absolute demand. It is this demand which represents an incursion on the freedom of the one solicited. This is not at all to say that it is an unjust assault, but it is what in the literature of politeness is known as a 'face-threatening-action'.

The complex dynamics of begging often include a visible mitigation of this affront, often through transposition of audible into visual terms. One of the commonest forms is mute appeal, in which the beggar may substitute a posture or gesture for spoken words. Seeming to subtract significance, this action in fact adds it, acting out the suggestion that the beggar is not only without every kind of material resource, they are also deprived of the very medium of entreaty. In extreme forms, this can involve the hiding of the face, through lowering of the forehead to the ground, as though in the posture known as 'kowtowing', which entered English in the early nineteenth century, but with the open hand held out. A less extreme form of this apparent threat-mitigation is the substitution of a written sign for the spoken appeal, typically in a form that itself demonstrates the indigence of the beggar, like biro scrawled on a piece of cardboard. This allows also for the conveying of more information, and the adoption of a more informative mode in place of the act of imploring. In Shakespeare's *Measure for Measure*, Lucio, urging Isabella to beg for her brother's life from Angelo, articulates the power of corporeal pathos: 'when maidens sue,/Men give like gods; but when they weep and kneel,/All their petitions are as freely theirs/As they themselves would owe them' (Shakespeare 2011, 807): that is, as a corporeal intensification of the act of formal suit, the actions of weeping and kneeling ensure that what is sought in the maidens' petition will be theirs as surely as if they already owned it.

My book *Giving Way* concerned itself with the diversified powers of negative virtue in social life– the ways in which social beings maximise benefits and diffuse the threat to social existence posed by aggressive assertion through the variously self-inhibiting modes of abstitution. Here, I will often pay attention to instances of what must often be considered an inversion, or parasiting, second-order variation on this. Where politeness is the assertion of a willed weakness, petition assumes the position of weakness in order to deploy it as unexpected strength, for the gain of a particular individual or group. Assuming and assumption, from Latin *ad*, towards + *sumere*, to take, is one of the most complex social functions and ideas we know. It can mean supposing or 'taking for granted' (a pressing enough expression when it comes to considerations of petition), but it can also mean appropriating, usurping, or taking on, as when one assumes control or assumes a position of power. The relation between supposing and imposing means that assuming also implies deception, the taking of a role, as when 'takes on' an assumed identity, in order to 'take in' others.

Beggary and petition play variations on all these forms of assumption, in taking as, taking on, and taking in. The conversion of weak into strong reaches its high point in the idea, which is particularly prominent in Catholicism, but apparent also in other religious and mythological systems, of the Assumption, referring to the taking up of Mary the Mother of Jesus into heavenly glory. Where Christ ascends, Mary is passively-positively assumed, consumed, or assimilated into godhead, or more strictly, godhood. Assumption is particularly appropriate for the figure also known as Θεοτόκος, the bearer of God. Surprisingly, this theological use of 'assume' is not in English a derivation from other uses, but the earliest reference of the word, as found in the closing line of the poem 'The Libel of English Policy', in a 1436 manuscript in the Bodleian Library (MS Laud 704), which prays 'He us assume, and brynge us to the blisse' (Wright 2012, 2.204). The ambivalence of dependency and appropriation in the idea of assuming has a telling relation to the ambivalent economics of petition. Petition takes for granted the claim and even charisma that, for highly-socialised creatures with a strong memory of the experience of infantile helplessness and therefore a high degree of awareness of the implication of the other in the 'I', will always be immanent in the condition of privation, disadvantage, suffering or destitution. The strength of petition, of the one who bargains with the very fact that they have nothing to bargain with, is the strength of this weakness.

Nietzsche notoriously blamed Christianity, with its puling addiction for suffering and sacrifice, for the milksop resentment of the truly strong that he saw everywhere in European civilisation. But he would have been hard put to it to find unambiguous approval of the value of pure strength in many times at all. Heroic subjects, whether male or female, are heroic because of that to which they are subjected, and it is their subjection that permits their overcoming. Tragic and comic heroes alike become strong through their aggrandising exposure to their own weakness. We tend to be told, and pretend to agree when we are, that we want to be and to emulate strength, but the evidence of history is strongly against this. Rather, we crave the strength that comes from weakness, from craving, meaning begging, or asking earnestly.

This book follows Roger Gomm in seeing the 'mendicant situation' (Gomm 1975, 540) as at the heart of a slowly swirling helix of seemingly anomalous reciprocities that propagates energetically through human societies, and is characterised by complex and dynamic forms of commerce between weakness and strength. The particular set of relations established in the act of petition is the focus of the book, the aim of which is to show the intricate continuities between different kinds of petition and requisition. But the possibly unsuspected breadth of reference and significance of the act of petition exists because it is part of this even larger phenomenon of mendicity in Gomm's sense. The more examples of the convertibility of power into weakness and vice versa one takes under one's view, the less like a local variation on stable background conditions it comes to seem, and the more like a central principle of the functions of discourse and mediation in human society, which is to say, a defining principle of human society as such. But perhaps even this view of the special powers available to the powerless, or the power of signs to reverse these relations, is too parochial. The next chapter will ask how far the mendicant situation extends into nonhuman animals.

2

The Begging Animal

Allow not nature more than nature needs,
Man's life is cheap as beast's. (Shakespeare 2011, 650)

Begging and petition are matters of credit, in the discursive and economic senses of that word. One begs for some allowance or benefit to be given, on the basis of the credibility of the account given of one's circumstances, and the claim that it may be allowed to constitute. Though financial credit depends upon social credibility, the original sense of Latin *credere*, to believe, was in fact commercial, meaning to extend a loan, with the more general senses of trusting or believing being bred from it. Giving and begging are therefore closely tied to questions of believing, and, since believing is always in part a question, disbelieving. *Believe* is close to words meaning to love, desire (Latin *libido*) and hope (Old English *lufen*). This means that, as we will regularly have cause to recognise in this book, mendicity always consorts with mendacity.

Cultural theorists, especially those informed by Lacanian psychoanalysis, used regularly to evoke a 'symbolic order', or sometimes, more portentously, 'Symbolic Order', into which infant humans entered through the development of speech, and then, later, and much more powerfully, and so also insecurely, the acquisition of the skills of writing. It was assumed that this mythical passage marked the process of what Giorgio Agamben calls anthropogenesis, 'the caesura and articulation between human and animal', the emergence of the human out of the condition known as the animal, an emergence of and into 'the *meta* that completes and preserves the overcoming of animal *physis* in the direction of human history' (Agamben 2004, 79). With the symbolic order comes power, but also duplicity (and the power of duplicity): secrecy, deceit and man's first disobedience.

More and more, however, the event of this entry into the field of the symbolic has been pushed back in time and generalised across species. The field known as zoosemiotics, inaugurated by Thomas A. Sebeok (1963, 1968), finds signage and signalling almost everywhere among animals, and, increasingly, well beyond them.

Closely related to the privilege accorded to symbolic language is another privilege which humans have given themselves, or at least allowed only very select groups of animals to share with them, namely the capacity and appetite for play. Play operates in the subjunctive space of the as-if, and involves play with the signs and appearances of actions. Play opens up in the world a pocketed sphere which is suspensively both in and out of the world. Here again, the capacity for play, once accorded only to primates and mammals, has been progressively generalised, to include ever more organisms.

There is one particular activity that seems to bring together semiosis and play in the relations between the young and adults of a species: the signalling and interpretation of need involved in begging, or solicitation behaviour, usually for food, but also for other benefits. This is not at all to suggest that begging is nothing but play, or indeed is ever simply 'playful', as climbing, chasing and rough-and-tumble games among the young of many species are. Quite the contrary, in fact, for the actions of begging are among the most urgent and serious that a young animal will ever engage in. We may say that all animals which beg begin by begging for their lives, which is what imparts to begging behaviours of different kinds their particular tonality, in the urgency of their urging. Such begging is too important to be entrusted to conscious systems of choice or preference. But to point to an association between begging and play is also to suggest that begging, as the exhibition and interpretation of need, involves complex kinds of probabilistic behaviour, in which the coordination of actual and projected states of affairs is paramount. In creatures assumed to be able consciously to take account of such factors, one might assume the operations of psychological actions like conjecture and calculation. This is one of the features that would no doubt confirm for many that the Lacanian symbolic order is exclusive to humans, in which symbolising and subjecthood are so co-constitutive. One does not need of course to assume anything of this psychological kind among, say, meerkats, leeches or songbirds, but it seems plain that the coordinated actions of hunting, feeding and communicated signals themselves form a system that allows for different possibilities to be kept in play. The two meanings of 'in play' – that is, 'pretended' or 'not serious' on the one hand and 'under negotiation' on the other – are therefore closely associated. We must assume that among animals it is the communication system as a whole that does the conjecturing and calculation, 'reasoning the need', in King Lear's sense (Shakespeare 2011, 650). This kind of play, and playing out, means that the *meta-* is in the *physis* from the very beginning. So, among living things, to go no further than this, the order of things seems always already to be, or be able to be, or be on the way to becoming, a symbolic order. When things are both themselves and the signs or tokens of being themselves, what they are includes the capacity of both being and not being what they are.

Begging behaviour is seen in many if not most forms of social animals. It is most familiar in nesting birds and many mammals, such as dogs, cats, bats (Kuczaj et. al. 2001, 166-7) and dolphins (Connor and Smolker 1985, 399), but is also operative in insects such as bees, where begging is an important distributor of food gathered by foraging bees on their return to the hive

(Núñez 1970, 531), beetles (Andrews and Smiseth 2013), ants (Creemers at. al. 2003; Kaotein 2005) and termites (Kawatsu 2013), as well as amphibians like frogs (Dugas et. al. 2017). 'Social animals' is hardly a very exclusive category, for there are very few organisms that have no contact with each other following reproduction. There is also substantial evidence that one of the effects of domestication or captivity is the development of begging behaviours in relations with humans, suggesting that there is a very widely-spread propensity to it, or at least a capacity to discover its benefits very quickly, in the animal world. The begging paradigm has even been extended to plants; though there is obviously no equivalent to the visible and vocal interactions between parent plants and their progeny after parturition, the production of particular hormones by embryos allows for relations of solicitation at an earlier stage, as articulated by Da-Yong Zhang and Xin-Hua Jiang: 'In plants, the progeny solicit resources by presenting "begging" signals; developing plant embryos signal by producing hormones' (Zhang and Jiang 2000, 124)

At the heart of efforts among biologists to understand begging behaviour is the question of what is rather strangely called 'honest begging', but is probably best understood as 'reliable', or just 'immediate' begging. Begging proves to prompt questions at the junction of economics and ethics. One must wonder whether the question of honesty would have arisen in quite the same way if 'begging' had not been adopted as the standard term for this behaviour, when other terms, such as 'food solicitation' or 'food requisition' are in fact available and sometimes used. We will see that questions of honesty are never far away when it comes to human begging.

Taking a nest of young chicks as the model for the conditions under which solicitation occurs, the essential issue for the parent bird, bringing back food to the nest to feed their infants, is one of resource allocation. The simplest model would assume that chicks solicit food because they are hungry, and that the hungriest chicks will solicit most energetically, prompting the parent bird to feed the chicks in proportion to their need, thereby producing a reduction in the intensity of the solicitation. There are several difficulties with this model. The first is that chicks seem to be designed to solicit food as energetically as they can, whenever it is available, and whether or not they are hungry. In the evolutionary long term, we must assume the chicks who beg and are fed most assiduously and successfully would begin to be selected for, producing a runaway situation in which the insatiable demands of chicks would gradually outstrip the capacity of parents to supply them. In 1991, H.C.A. Godfray outlined what seemed to be a more dynamically stable model, which balances the advantages that may accrue from solicitation with the costs of that solicitation. Solicitation behaviour offers potential benefit, but is likely to bring with it potential costs: first of all, it is itself very energetic, meaning that the cost in energy may be greater than the nutritional gain it brings. Secondly, it may possibly alert predators to the presence of young. In 1975, Amotz Zahavi suggested an explanation for the many mating signals and displays that seem to involve conspicuous excess, and therefore to constitute a handicap (for example in the peacock's tail, or the costly act of singing in male birds). Zahavi argued that, since only genuinely fit mates can afford to squander resources in this way, such voluntary self-exposure through excess may come to function as an insurance of reliability (Zahavi 1975), Godfray argued similarly that begging costs acted as regulators to the system, reducing the intensity of solicitation in a nestling with reduced need: 'Although some signals may be physiologically constrained to be unfalsifiable, most have the potential to give false information. For the latter type of biological signals to be evolutionarily stable, they must be costly for the signaller to produce' (Godfray 1991, 328). This balance of costs and needs is assumed to produce accurate information that allows the parent bird to respond optimally in their allocation of food. Put more simply, it seems that honest signalling of need depends upon signalling itself exacting a cost (Grafen 1990).

In 1991, John Maynard Smith devised an influential mathematical model for the various pressures and constraints involved in signalling and meeting need. He based his analysis on the story told by Fulke Greville of Sir Philip Sidney during the siege of Zutphen in 1591. Sidney, who had been wounded with a musket shot to his thigh, was offered some water, but, seeing another wounded soldier looking longingly at the bottle, passed it across to him with the words 'Thy necessity is yet greater than mine' (Greville 1907, 130). Maynard Smith tabulated the various outcomes arising from this action, involving the donor, the beneficiary, the value of the resource, the cost associated with giving the signal and the chances of survival (as it happens, Sidney died, of his wounds, or his treatment, a couple of weeks later, and of the outcome for the thirsty soldier we know nothing). Although 'the Philip Sidney game' is very simplified, it seemed to verify that 'honest signals must be costly if there is a conflict of interest between signaller and receiver' (Maynard Smith 1991, 1035), and provided a theoretical framework for considering much more complex scenarios.

Subsequent work has added new dimensions of need, cost and benefit to this model. It seems, for example, that individuals in a brood who will tend to have a close genetic relationship with each other also have a collective interest in regulating absolute levels of begging behaviour, since they will all benefit from not advertising the presence of a noisy nest to a predator. This is indicated by the fact that brood parasites, such as cuckoos, do not seem to be affected by the same group-constraint, and so will cry more loudly and frequently than their genetically unrelated nestmates (Redondo and Zuñiga 2002). Begging, a behaviour that is in the first place concentrated in animals with high levels of intraspecific relation and dependence, especially between the young and the mature members of the species, is increasingly being understood nowadays by reference to the communication networks that sustain them and to which they themselves give rise, with a communication network being defined as being formed 'whenever several individuals communicate within transmission range of each other's signals' (Horn and Leonard 2005, 170). The communication network may include the production of hormones that will themselves act as signals to induce the production of begging signals (Smiseth et. al, 2011). Takata et. al. have reported the production in female burying beetles (*Nicrophorus quadripunctatus*) of a pheromonic signal designed to signal their readiness to provide food and therefore to stimulate begging behaviour in their larvae, this behaviour consisting of waving the legs toward the parents' mouthparts. They surmise that this signalling exchange, the pheromone inducing in the young the act of induction by begging, acts to prevent redundant and potentially costly begging in the young when there is no food available (Takata et. al. 2019, 1257).

Hormones may mediate relations between care-giving adults as well as between siblings and their caregivers. José C. Noguera et. al. found evidence that female yellow-legged gulls selectively induced more energetic begging in chicks when they produced higher levels of yolk testosterone in their eggs. Since male gulls responded to this energetic begging more than female gulls, this provides evidence of what has been called the Manipulating Androgen Hypothesis (Noguera et. al. 2013). Brood reduction is common in sea-birds, for example the Dalmatian pelican (*Pelecanus crispus*), in which multiple eggs will be laid but only one chick selected for rearing to adulthood, on the basis of the intensity of its begging, which 'can apparently be amplified by androgen-dependent hypertrophy of a muscle necessary for hatching and begging' (Schuppe et. al. 2019, 27), leading a recent review to propose that 'AR [androgen receptor] differences present in pelicans and their relatives is more likely to increase transcription of genes that express begging-related traits' (Schuppe et. al. 2019, 28). Quite as much as mating and aggression, with both of which it has important overlaps, begging is formative of communication networks, not least because it communicates between bodily states and communicative actions.

The question of begging in animals has stimulated a great deal of experiment and investigation over the last three decades, and these investigations have thrown up very uneven results, some seeming to confirm the game-theoretical model, others introducing complexity into it (the question of whether those who study begging behaviour are part of or independent of the game will have to be deferred to another occasion). One of the difficulties that has arisen is the idea that begging is to be seen as a signal of need, which has tended to be identified with the signalling of hunger. But it is perfectly possible for a young animal to be in pretty good nutritional shape and yet to be ravenously hungry because its stomach is temporarily empty. Human babies furnish convenient examples of this behaviour, as do intelligent and well-nourished adults who may nevertheless sincerely declare 'Let's eat: I'm starving'. Conversely, it is possible for an offspring to be completely sated after feeding, and yet still to be malnourished. So it has come to seem unwise in many circumstances to take signal of hunger as a reliable proxy for signal of need, or a signal, as it were, of a signal of need. As Douglas W. Mock crisply observes, 'Desire is not a synonym for need' (Mock 2016, 181). Somewhat unexpectedly, this chimes with Jacques Lacan's observations on the displacing effect of language on the articulation of a need through a demand:

> desire is situated in dependence on demand – which, by being articulated in signifiers, leaves a metonymic remainder that runs under it, an element that is not indeterminate, which is a condition both absolute and unapprehensible, an element necessarily lacking, unsatisfied, impossible, misconstrued (*méconnu*), an element that is called desire. (Lacan 2018, 154)

Even more perplexing is the fact that the hypothesis of honest need signalling in the hungry seems to contradict a principle that seems elsewhere to be commonly enforced in animal behaviour, especially in mating behaviour, namely that animals tend to advertise their fitness rather than their weakness; if one asks why this should be, the most intelligent and far-reaching answer may well be, because they can. Indeed, the original articulation by Amotz Zahavi that signalling might impose a handicap, the overcoming of which then becomes part of the signal, since only the fittest animals can afford such excess, of plumage, say, or energy-sapping complexity of song, would predict the opposite of what has taken to be the case, namely that the fittest animals would tend to be the ones that could afford to beg most energetically. In fact, Zahavi has gone on to make the handicap of excess a general principle of signalling, with the claim '*all* signals have a cost – they impose a handicap – … this is what guarantees that they are reliable' (Zahavi and Zahavi 1997, 58). Douglas W. Mock crisply summarises the idea that begging might be a 'signal of quality' rather than a 'signal of need': 'Echoing the advertisement roots of sexual signals, that hypothesis requires no inversion of message and no voluntary abstention. Instead, it proposes that strong offspring are essentially bragging' (Mock 2016, 181). In an earlier paper, Mock had suggested in passing that the almost total neglect of this possibility among investigators of begging might have something to do with the sedimentation of the word 'begging' itself, which 'connoted impressions of pleading rather than boasting' (Mock 2011, 913), as opposed to words like 'solicitation', 'stimulation' or 'demand'. Rather than enabling the parent bird to allocate resources differentially to weaker offspring, signal of quality may help in the strategy of brood reduction, which may be optimal under conditions in which food supplies are uncertain, a prospect that must obviously impart an extra spurt of urgency to the energetic imposture of need. This was the conclusion of a large study of variable feeding strategies across 143 species of bird:

> Overall, a clear pattern emerges: the probability of successfully raising all offspring from a nest determines the system of

communication between parents and their offspring across
species. In predictable and/or unusually good environments,
offspring in worse condition are more likely to beg, and parents
are more likely to feed individuals begging at a higher rate. These
results are predicted by signal of need models, where parents
expect to rear a complete brood. In contrast, in unpredictable
and/or poor environments, offspring in better condition have
more intense structural signals, and parents are more likely to
feed chicks that are larger or have more intense structural signals.
(Caro et. al. 2016, 5)

In fact, even the assumption that begging is a risky or costly form of
behaviour has not been unequivocally verified. For one thing, it is not as
simple and straightforward as might be supposed to measure such costs;
and where such measurements have been made, it has been possible to
conclude that 'current data on energy expenditure during begging indicate
that in the species studied to date it is a small and arguably trivial proportion
of the energy budget', and indeed that 'begging appears to be an extremely
energetically efficient way for nestlings to communicate with their parents,
at least in terms of the energy expended during begging itself' (Chappell and
Bachman 2002, 158, 159).

All of these factors suggest that solicitation is not merely to be
'contextualised', by insertion into the communicative networks that seem
to enable and diffract it: rather, solicitation gives rise to the very diffractive
processes which form communicative networks. Solicitation is not merely a
signal that discloses a pre-existing set of circumstances – the level of need or
fitness in a chick, say, or the 'honesty' with which it is signalled. In a sense, it is
the signal that actualises the circumstances that give it its meaning and effect.
The analogy with a game is a good one, because a game refers both to a fixed
and finite set of rules and conditions, and also to the uncountable number of
games to which a game may give rise. So 'a good game', as one might say after
a particularly exciting or absorbing encounter between two teams, is a game
that plays out the possibilities inherent in something that seems essentially
like a 'good game', by which is meant, in circular fashion, a game capable of
giving rise to 'good games'.

It is not the ambition of this book to develop a unified theory of the way
in which begging functions across different organisms in nature. But what the
investigation of begging behaviours suggests is that begging precipitates an
intense swirl of communicative action, an action that may extend well beyond
what may appear to be the immediate partners in a solicitational transaction.

The most important feature of begging is the dynamic link it forges
between economy and signification. It is by no means unique in this respect
of course, but, considered in its largest sense, as part of a spectrum that
includes all kinds of bidding, betting and solicitation, it can be regarded as

the principal means in which economies 'take time', that is reach forward into new and unpredictable conditions, and achieve – or, of course, fail to achieve – their own condition through the unfolding of time.

It should not be surprising that the questions around which considerations of begging in biology revolve are those of the accuracy and reliability of begging signals and the honesty of begging behaviour. Wholly reasonably, biologists are interested in how such behaviours may have arisen and what their continuing rationale might be. Even where it may be a matter of deceptive signals, as in the case of brood parasitism, there must be an assumption that the behaviour must in some sense *work*, that is contribute to the evolutionary fitness of the organism in question, for the simple reason that, if it did not, it is very unlikely that there would still be any such organisms going about their business in this way. One can of course object that it is always in fact too early to make absolute judgements about the evolutionary fitness of any organism, since that fitness will have to include its fit with environmental conditions that might well change. The fact that many, and perhaps most organisms do not make the grade can be taken as evidence both that the idea of fitness fits the circumstances and that it does not. But it is surely wholly reasonable for biology to take as its theme the reason for, and reasonableness of, solicitation behaviour in animals, so far as that goes.

Studies of animal begging are showing signs of moving away from the apparently conclusive game-theoretical models of the Philip Sidney type. Nevertheless, the point of these remarks is not to articulate any objection to the ways in which begging in animals has been considered by biologists, but rather to suggest that they are not the only ways conceivable. One might, for example, wonder if the conditions in which such behaviour arises may resemble the conditions within which other kinds of petitory and solicitation action arise, along with the questions to which they may give rise. And giving rise to questions will itself be at the heart of the question. This approach would focus, not on the role of signalling in creating systems of resource distribution, and resolving parent-offspring conflicts of interest, but, inversely, on what economies of begging and solicitation might be able to intimate about the nature of signalling itself. The question might then be able to become, not How does begging signal need? but How does need inflect signalling? and How does signalling inflect the nature of what is thought of as 'need'?

A strictly Newtonian view of the physical world might see it as consisting solely of actions and reactions. Translated into a communicational register, actions can be thought of as autonomous assertions, or theses, literal takings of position, of which the most elementary might be the graffiti-like predication 'I am here', sometimes with adjectival modifications, such as 'I am strong' or 'take note of how big I am'. This assertion of states of affairs is the way in which many forms of signalling and symbolism have been understood by biologists and zoosemioticians. But communicative acts are not necessarily all best understood as statements. As linguists and literary-cultural analysts have

realised since the work of J.L. Austin, many utterances are better thought of
as performative rather than constative, or as attempted transmissions of force
rather than neutral statements of fact.

Performative actions certainly seem meant, or are at least apt, to
produce reactions, many of them much more obviously than the making
of statements. But there is a large class of performatives that seem designed
specifically to operate in an unpredictable field of reactions, and to take
account of that unpredictability. Indeed, given that all performances appear
to be performances for others, we might wonder whether all performatives
must operate in such an unpredictable field, even if they aim to increase
predictability on the side of the performer. Prominent among these are
actions that might be thought of as interrogative rather than assertive, that is,
utterances that ask a question rather than making a statement. Perhaps these
are best thought of as transactions rather than actions, trans-actions because
their action goes across to that of which the question is asked, aiming to
produce not just an effect in the world, but an answering reaction in a receiver
of the signal. It seems strange that biological actions of signalling that seem
so strikingly to correspond to actions of inquiry, inquisition, or requisition
in linguistic behaviour should so regularly have been treated as statements,
with the most important question to be asked of them therefore taken to be
whether or not they are true, or, as the moral correlate of truth, honest. If one
is to take crying in a baby as a signal, it would seem much more rational to
translate it into terms like 'Please feed me' (plus or minus 'or else', or 'without
delay') rather than 'Bulletin on current nutritional condition in process'.

Actions that are to be regarded as interrogative are obviously different
from linguistic interrogatives, the purpose of which is usually to procure
information or some other linguistic response, while a solicitating action
seems designed to produce a response in the form of an action. Nevertheless,
one may regard such actions as part of a communicational system, in that
the solicitation is in the form of a sign or signal that in some way substitutes
for an action that would deliver the desired action directly – snatching food
straight from the parent's bill, for example. In the case of food solicitation,
the substitution is metonymic, in the opened beak that is both the sign of
and prelude to feeding. The action is symbolic in that it at once proposes
and stands aside from the action it proposes, in what I call an abstitution
(Connor 2019a).

If a solicitation of this kind is successful in its aim, it has the effect of
doubling the action that forms its response, making it simultaneously an
action of feeding, that might have been performed spontaneously and
autonomously in any case, and an action of responding to the solicitation.
This makes the feeding response both a primary action and the sign of that
action: it does, and says, yes. The solicitation need not imply anything like
a hope or expectation of such a response in the one issuing the signal, since
it is the sheer fact of the temporal scansion of such actions that forms them

into a communicative structure, precisely by giving it the structure of a communicated and granted demand, or question and answer. One may say of such actions what has been said of gestures of pointing in infant humans, that they are 'proto-interrogative' (Rodríguez 2002). Where a child may seek to elicit information through such a proto-interrogative – 'Yes, that's a bus, it's taking the children to school' – it may also, and just as importantly, suggest and secure a degree of attentiveness in the parent (Begum and Southgate 2012). In non-linguistic animals, whatever that means precisely, a proto-interrogative may nevertheless also cement the intra-specific solidarity that communicational signals bring. The forming of such signalling solidarities may be as much what signals are 'for' as for the conveyance of information about nutritional states.

Already, we have turned the baby's crying into a vocal act that is more like a demand than a polite enquiry, in that mixture of the imperative and the interrogative that we will find is a feature of many of the forms of petition to be considered in this book. But this requires us, and permits us too, to ask a question that our familiarity with actions of questioning may normally inhibit us from asking. What is a question? The easy answer to this might be, a question is an utterance that expects or demands an answer. As long as one remains within the domain of language, in which questions and answers are regularly and reliably linked in this way, a circular answer of this kind may do much of the work we want from it. But if we ask this question of an action of signalling like infant solicitation in animals, this kind of answer is not so readily available.

Obviously, nestlings and newborn infants do not knowingly or purposively emit any kind of signals, interrogative, or otherwise. What makes the action of cheeping, bleating or bawling a signal is the coincident fact of the likelihood of it giving rise to a response in the receiver of the signal. It is the fact, or possibility, of this response that turns the action into the kind of transaction that a signal is. The most important feature of a transaction is its suspended and therefore suspensive action. The transaction opens on to the not-yet of the action that may answer and complete it. It cannot be a transaction without this negative possibility of turning out not to have succeeded in being one. Time is held back in the tension of what is anticipated yet unfulfilled, and it is this tension which brings into being the discontinuously continuous time lived out by, and in, living creatures. The tension, of need, desire or concern, a tension that is focussed precisely on the desire of the creature to continue in being (tension and continuity being variations on the same word) stretches time out into a continuum. But this continuum is continuously broken into by the reaching beyond the present instant of which every present instant consists for a living creature impelled, without needing to be able to formulate this for itself, by its own need for persistence.

It is the sign or signal which makes this tension possible. In a world without any kind of signals, nothing would announce or anticipate or answer or originate from anything else, so there could be no links or relations, whether of continuity or discontinuity. In such an unimaginable circumstance, there could also be no entities for which there could be such relations. A signal is an action that calls on or calls for an answering action, even though this relation of calling can only exist as a consequence of the answering action having already occurred. A signal is an expectation of, even the requisition of, a recurrence. Of course, the expectation is a state of affairs rather than any kind of state of mind, so it is more like a propensity in things than a representation of how things may turn out.

The differences between these perspectives is that between a completed and an uncompleted understanding of time. Begging may resolve into conditions of certainty or equilibrium, but these conditions only emerge in the long run, while the practices of petition and solicitation can only take place in the short run, in which outcomes are uncertain.

The very word *solicit* may give us some hints here. Its earliest meaning is not to request, but to disturb, stimulate, harass or provoke. It combines Latin *sollus*, whole, entire and *citus*, shaken or aroused, past participle of *ciere*, to shake or move (thus 'excited' or 'incited'). To cite contains this same idea of disturbance or displacement, with the added idea of calling or summoning to appear, and the same idea of agitation is contained in the word *resuscitate*. So soliciting is to be understood as disturbing the peace, discomposing what is settled or entire; 'solicitous' still means giving oneself trouble or subjecting oneself to difficulty. When the person known as a 'solicitor' concerns themselves with the criminal offence that has come to be known as 'soliciting' (originally an action performed by libidinous males, but then, from the early eighteenth century onwards, increasingly associated with female prostitution), the taking and making of trouble converge.

Solicitation therefore indicates the very two dimensions, of the complete and incomplete, just now distinguished, in the difference between the extrapolated calculus and the open occasions of solicitation. The very word solicitation is a model of the two possibilities that are always at once in and out of equilibrium in the passage of time, the continuity of one moment with the next, and the discontinuity introduced at every moment. Solicitation is an allegory of time, a way of working on time that is also a model of time's workings. Solicitation propels time, because it is the question that time asks of itself, in its irregularly baulked and permitted quest for a return to itself. The answer for which it asks is either that things will persist as they were, or that they will change. It is solicitation that is the prompt or provocation that sets in motion the game of forking possibilities, asking for what will or will not be given, which either will or will not mean a movement forward and away from a given starting point without the prospect of return to it.

If solicitation is a kind of interrogative, in its opening on to a temporality that it cannot be sure of controlling, it is obviously a different kind of interrogative than a simple request for information, or a speculative question like the one just asked, 'what is a question?' A solicitation does not leave its response open, but rather urges a particular response. This is the difference between a nestling's gaping beak and the leaves of a plant turned towards the sunlight. In the first case, there is the force of a demand as well as an opening to a possibility. This force will be a feature of most of the petitory actions summoned for discussion in this book. It will make it uncertain quite how to we are to distinguish the interrogative from the imperative function in petition. So it will always be difficult to see a petition as a question intensified into an imperative, or as the modulation or 'abstitution' of an imperative into a question, so, not 'give me' but 'please may I have?' In fact, there will always be a kind of question, or *demande* in that ordinary French usage, in every imperative, since an imperative will never be sure of its fulfilment, just as there will always be a kind of imperative force in every question, in its very demand for an answer.

In their concern with questions of honesty or reliability, biological investigations of begging behaviours tend to construe them as what may be understood as signs rather than signals. A sign tends to be used to refer to an object rather than initiating an action. Sometimes, the word signal places emphasis on the material action of forming or performing a sign, as opposed to merely showing or displaying signs involuntarily – thus one may 'show no signs of life', but 'signal' one's existence by breathing or pulse. So when one 'makes a sign', as opposed to giving or showing signs, one is usually regarded as signalling. Signs tend to indicate signifieds that are currently in existence, with which they have only a relationship of signification. A signal tends to be a sign viewed as being intentionally formed: a signal is not just a sign, but a signalling, and sometimes too a signature, the making of a sign that signals the fact of its own making, and the maker of the sign that it makes into that maker. For this reason, a signal is more temporal than a sign, and has an orientation to some possible or future condition, that it will likely have some role in bringing about. So signals tend both to be intentionally made, and to signal some intention: signals, in short, are tensive. Signals tend to be regarded as initiating or altering states of affairs, and so themselves tend to have a dynamic or variable form. Traffic signs give static information ('24 hours from Tulsa'); traffic signals both indicate the necessity of moving or stopping and themselves modulate the flow of traffic. A signal is a signing which is a doing, or a sign of something to be done. Where signs are indicative, signals are predicative or imperative: signals are signs with designs. They are the kind of performative known as perlocutionary, in that they not only do things, but urge, enable or require things to be done: not 'I declare you man and wife', therefore, but 'You may now kiss the bride'. Pallor is a sign of fear or fatigue: a starting pistol signals, and simultaneously effects, the start of a race.

It is for this reason that hormones, neurotransmitters and other forms of 'chemical messenger' are known as chemical signals, in that they both impart information and themselves initiate change. They are instructions, differences capable of making a difference, to adapt Gregory Bateson's formulation (Bateson 2000, 459). C.S. Peirce argued that all signs depend upon interpretants, in that they must be signs for entities for whom they have significance, and can only be signs for such entities: 'a definition does not reveal the Object of a Sign, its Denotation, but only analyzes its Signification, and *that* is a question not of the Sign's relation to its Object but of its relation to its Interpretant' (Peirce 1977, 118). Signals can be regarded as having a particular orientation to interpretants, since their relation to their interpretant seems much more important than their relation to any existing state of affairs. A traffic light which turns green may be regarded as an indication that the road ahead should be clear, but this is really an accessory purpose, for it will only be clear if all traffic users obey the signal. This might make it sensible to call a traffic light an inductive indication, or *inducation*. If signals are a sign of anything, it is their own condition of being a signal for some signalled-to entity.

This is particularly the case with solicitation signalling. As a signal, solicitation actually makes a double demand. There is first of all the demand for that which is its object – food, comfort, information, sexual release. But, coupled with this, is a demand issued to the one capable of meeting the demand. Even though signals can only ever be a signal for entities for whom they act as a signal, this abstract condition of dativity, or being a signal-*for*, is also a feature of signals in themselves. Indeed, as we will see when we come to consider the act of prayer, which may be thought of as a purely intrasymbolic petitioning or soliciting, it can be a demand for there to be one capable of receiving and meeting the demand. This makes it a signalled demand for a response to the signal, which, as a response, must then itself be able to be regarded as a signal. The signal therefore simultaneously solicits both an object and an answering or countersigning signal. This means the soliciting solicits another and the time in which they will (might) appear. Solicitation is the quisitory imperative that makes time by its reaching into it.

Seen in this way, the modalities of demand and urging so insistently present in living creatures can be seen as more than a method for sustaining an economy or calculus in action. Rather than a way of reasoning out need according to variously reliable and adjusted sources of information, demanding is the reason supplied by the existence of need itself, and the need to give expression to it. This need to express need is what charges every signal with endeavour and impulse, the principle of striving known from the Stoics onwards as *conatus*, in the process forming, and itself being formed by time. In linguistic creatures like humans, the soliciting imperative – the *imperogative*, as it might perhaps be styled, as a variation on Jerrold M. Sadock's *whimperative* introduced in chapter 1 – is a question impelled by an imperative function. In a non-linguistic, or proto-linguistic creature, it is the imperative that forces its way into the condition of the sign through the signal.

It is this process of forcing which keeps need in play in signalling. Biologists investigating begging behaviour are overwhelmingly interested in that behaviour in juveniles, as aimed at caregivers. But in creatures in which social interaction continues beyond weaning begging behaviour often persists, sometimes adapted for other purposes. Some female birds seem to advertise their fertility with vocalisations modelled on juvenile calling (Ellis et. al. 2009). In European robins, males may evolve to use these signals as signs of mating opportunities (Tobias and Seddon 2002). Such adaptations are particularly apparent in domesticated animals, which tend to display neoteny, the retention of, or reversion to infant behaviours. Begging behaviour in cats and dogs may be combined with submission displays which can themselves be adaptations of begging behaviour: the dog who greets you by excitedly licking at the side of your mouth is reverting to the begging behaviour used by puppies to solicit food from adults. Cats, who mew as kittens but do so rarely as adults in the wild, develop a large mewing repertoire when they are domesticated, as well as simulating the sensations of being licked by their mother by seeking out human stroking and recapitulating the scratching or 'kneading' behaviour that kittens use to stimulate the flow of milk in the mother (Morris 2002, 16; Bradshaw 2014, 193). Animals who become used to human contact, such as seaside donkeys and bottle-nosed dolphins (Hazelkorn et. al. 2016), may also develop begging behaviours. A correspondent to the Philadelphia journal *The Friend* in 1893 described the behaviour of a mendicant elephant, who had been trained to beg for money, and was even known to escape and beg on his own account, by collecting coins and depositing them on the table of a fruit merchant, who would allow him to eat sugar-cane at will (Knox 1893).

It is tempting to see these as secondary or derivative behaviours, divorced from the circumstances in which they form part of the assembly of actions that determine a creature's survival. But as soon as something has become a signal, it has the capacity to be reappropriated and recontextualised in this way, in the process I have characterised as being put into play. It has not been the purpose of this chapter to offer a rival understanding of begging or solicitation behaviours in animals. But it does aim to disclose some of the complexities attaching to those behaviours, which seem to be much more open to contingency, adaptation and reappropriation than might at first be thought. As transactions, solicitation behaviours perform a general act of solicitation that is at work in every signal, inducing a difference into the world.

The interplay between signal of need and signal of quality is in fact an indication of how signalling may itself enter into the economy it is supposed to be signalling. In so-called 'honest signalling', the signal of need may also come to signal the need for signal, as need is displaced into the need to signal. Similarly, the signal of quality may also come to signify the quality of the signal. There is no more convincing display of excess vitality than one in which all the energy is expended on the act of display itself. Perhaps, rather than attempting to decide between begging, as signal of need, and boasting, as signal of quality, we might attempt to characterise a kind of signalled urging – the urge that leads the organism to signal, and the urging to a kind of reciprocal action that the signal effects – that could include both. And we might find such a signalic urging in what we call bidding, understood as making a play; for in fact, as we have seen, bidding already compounds the senses of offering, attempting, entreating and demanding.

This view of animal begging as a kind of bidding or putting in play is at odds with what has been, since the work of Karl Groos (1898), the dominant view of play, namely that it is a kind of practice or rehearsal of skills that will be required in adult life. It is indeed hard to see what begging in infants could possibly be practice for. But, as Gordon M. Burghardt astutely observes, the 'delayed benefit' assumption 'is so basic to virtually every definition of play that demonstrating a current utility to behaviour labelled play is tantamount to proving that it is *not* play' (Burghardt 1998, 6). The kind of play involved in begging is a gamble on a broader front than the development of motor skills. Play of the kind involved in entering the order of signals is a meta-play, or play with the possibility of play, a play with the possibility of a utilitarian outcome *at some time or other*. Once you enter the order of signalling, you just never know, and the order of signalling is precisely this not knowing.

The suggestion to which this chapter has conducted itself is that begging is taken up in a complex, unpredictable and formative way with the process whereby it is signalled. The consequence of this is not only that begging is necessarily dependent on signalling, but also that signalling in general is driven by the range of urgings and biddings characteristic of begging behaviour. Such an argument has similarities with the ways in which the psychoanalysis of Jacques Lacan sees human desire as infiltrated and inflected by the linguistic structures in which it must find expression, meaning that demand does not issue from desire, as we tend straightforwardly to think, but vice versa. Needless to say, it does not follow from this that we should see animals as having the same complex relation to symbolic life as human beings, mediated as that latter is by what we call consciousness, or alternatively that animals might be possessed of anything like an 'unconscious', in the sense considered by Maud Ellmann (Ellmann 2014, 331-2). Nor is it to suggest that human beings are to be regarded as simply subject to the same mechanical or instinctive kinds of drive that operate in animal behaviour. But there may nevertheless be continuities in the way in which demand is signalled and the demands of signalling itself across human and non-human animals.

There are not two domains to be reckoned with, the human and the animal, with the human defined exclusively by its possession of, and subjection to, the symbolic order. There are instead perhaps three domains, each intersecting with and exercising a pressure on the two others: the animal, the human, and what may be called the domain of the demand, signalised, and signalising. Animals are not comparable to humans in having knowing access to language, but rather in the very fact of their automatism, which is usually taken to mark them off from self-aware humans. Having an unconscious and not being conscious converge in the force exerted and transmitted through bidding, begging and urging. In being subjected to, rather the subjects of their own demand, as displaced through the imperatives of the signal, animal begging-bidding in fact anticipates the automatism of the *bêtise*, the beastly, babbling, chattering stupidity that performs the function of psychoanalytic disclosure for Jacques Lacan. As Peter Buse writes, concluding his defence of Lacan against claims that he maintains an absolute Cartesian separation of the animal from the human:

> *La bêtise*, so instrumental in the clinic and in Lacan's teaching, is there from the start, but intensifies in the later seminars. The animal, meanwhile, fixed in its coding in the early seminars, so as to be passed over by Lacan, becomes in the later seminars a reason to pause. The dog and the parakeet are not known in advance, but rather puzzles or puns. Their desire is as much a riddle as the desire of the human animal. (Buse 2017, 142)

A riddle is in fact close to German *Rätsel*, a sifting, sorting, reading or reasoning. It is not just a question in need of answering, but also the means whereby it plays itself out, a means for reasoning need, and the need of that means. Equipped with this mesh of intersections, between signal, need and quality, suggested by various kinds of animal behaviour, and our behaviour in relation to it, the next chapter will consider the questions of appearance and apparence in the begging act that makes man's life 'cheap as beast's'.

3
Theatres of Begging

Begging is not only a widespread phenomenon, both in nature and in human society; it is also a stubbornly recurrent problem, a big issue. It is worth asking why the act of begging and the figure of the beggar attract so much hostility and excite so much suspicion – as well, perhaps, as being the source of such suspicious excitement. There is something, or perhaps many things, about the act of begging that seems to disturb. This chapter will explore the possibility that we (for the nonce nonbeggars) find the sight of beggars disturbing (and in various ways arousing) in large part because of the affront that begging offers to visibility. But this affront to the eye is the very thing that fixes and draws it. Something about the act of solicitation seems to excite and incite, and especially it seems the sight of the act of solicitation. Begging is a scandal – from Greek σκάνδαλον, a trap or snare – for the eye, for it forces us to see, and even to want to see, that which our seeing shows us should be kept withdrawn from our greedy view. Inseparable from the dynamics of exposure, exhibition, obscenity, ostension and manifestation, begging is a highly visible, even, I am going to have to insist, an essentially scenographic affair.

Beggary, or as it might even be termed, the condition of beggarhood, may be thought of as a summarising name for a range of different styles of disaffiliated life. The beggar is the role assumed by one who secedes from a social role, and the act of begging is an act which emblematically affiliates one to this condition of nonaffiliation. It is this oxymoron, of the one who makes a profession of having no profession, that seems to create the eye-offending scandal of the beggar. The beggar is not only disaffiliated, they show their disaffiliation, and that demonstration is part of the disaffiliation.

To be reduced to the condition of a beggar may be a source of dread to those engaged in productive life in a recognised social role; but it is also a kind of temptation, to a careless life of animal irresponsibility – and more than metaphorically animal, given that so many domesticated animals exist in a permanently petitory relation to human society.

Against this, one must recognise the institutional nature of begging. Begging cannot be performed spontaneously, or without preparation. The ambivalence of begging is that it is at once a desertion from, and a defiant affront to accepted styles of social relations, and yet also itself an intense but alternately styled condition of life, which in fact depends upon its social visibility for its existence. Indeed, the affront represented by public begging may consist in its very display of the horror of the unstyled life, a horror that is nevertheless itself styled.

Beggary is close, in act as well as word, to buggery. Vagrancy, often assumed to be synonymous with begging, is often associated with the suspicion of unnatural acts. People known as *hijra*, or 'eunuchs' were the target of oppressive legislation in nineteenth-century India. Alok Gupta notes the convergence of laws against vagrancy and sexual immorality, arguing that 'vagrancy and sodomy provisions stemmed from the same motive: to place not just behaviours, but classes of people, under surveillance and control' (Gupta 2008). This theme of control recurs in the writings of social theorists about beggars, though beggars usually provide the signs of that which has escaped control. To be a vagrant is to be extravagant, from *vagari*, to wander, like Horatio's 'extravagant and erring spirit' in Shakespeare's *Hamlet* (Shakespeare 2011, 294)

Tableaux

The iconography of begging, as exemplified in paintings and photographs, and then reechoed in the characteristic postures of beggars, is conservative and consistent. It is important both for the act of begging and for the depiction of that act that the viewer should be able to see straight away what it is that they are seeing. So it is characteristic of such emblematic scenes and sights that in seeing them one also sees one's seeing of them. Beggars typically squat or kneel, withdrawing themselves thereby from any action aside from that of being exhibited. Sometimes recumbency is combined with a characteristic hunching, visible in Rembrandt's self-portrait *Beggar Seated on a Bank*, suggesting a defensive withdrawal from the very visibility their posture draws in. Part of the drama of the beggar's posture is the interplay between the mouth, which may be depicted, as in Rembrandt's etching, mutely open, to signify the scarcely-articulate call for alms, and the open hand, or, its scooped and scooping substitute, the cup, bowl, or hat. The drama involves a displacement of the view from the soliciting open mouth to the body which turns out, often surreptitiously, to echo the gaping appeal of the face. The beggar offers a nesting of concavities, spaces of emptiness which beckon the eye. In the case of the Rembrandt etching, it seems clear that we are meant to read the image, not as a depiction of a beggar, but as a self-portrait of the artist *as* a beggar, rendering the act of incitement in the image also a citation, of the many images of beggars that Rembrandt would expect his viewers to recall. As Stephanie Dickey suggests, the etching is a response to the artist's vexing condition of dependency (Dickey 2013), which at once protests against and grudgingly accedes to it; it attempts to solicit business in the very advertisement it offers of the artist's skill in capturing human suffering, or the recognised signs of 'suffering'.

Rilke's 1908 poem 'Die Bettler' ('The Beggars') offers an aggressively grotesque fantasy of the concealed aggression in the display of beggary, all centred in the painful visibility of oral-corporeal concavity.

> Du wußtest nicht, was den Haufen
> ausmacht. Ein Fremder fand
> Bettler darin. Sie verkaufen
> das Hohle aus ihrer Hand.
>
> You didn't know what the heap
> was made of. A stranger found it
> full of beggars. They are offering for sale
> the hollow of their hands. (Rilke 1930, 3.169; my translation)

Hands turn into mouths, being eaten rather than eating:

> Sie zeigen dem Hergereisten
> ihren Mund voll Mist,
> und er darf (er kann es sich leisten)
> sehn, wie ihr Aussatz frißt.
> They show the newcomer
> their mouths full of muck
> and he can see (he can run to it)
> the canker gorging on them (Rilke 1930, 3.169; my translation)

Michael Sweerts's *Portrait of an Old Man Begging* provides another example of the deflected interplay between the mouth and a mutely mimic receptacle. The old man in the portrait looks away to the side and slightly upward, suggesting that he is seated humbly and, as unaggressively as possible, only obliquely meeting the gaze of a passer-by. His eyes are wide and his lips slightly parted, as though in an inarticulate murmur. The bottom of the picture-frame is almost entirely occupied by the hat which he is holding out, the hand demurely concealed behind it but for the thumb that secures it like a latch over the brim. The little highlighted glint of the thumbnail rhymes and communicates with the scintillation suggested by the tiny dab of white in the man's rolling right eye, and so looks toward without looking at the empty space of the hat, with its interior bowl tilted encouragingly towards the potential donor. The thumb securing the hat reappears in many paintings, as a sign of its gathering function: examples include Jan Adriansz van Staveren's *A Beggar* (c. 1650-69), Jozef Huttary's *An Old Beggar* (1887), Rafael Romero Barros's *Mendigo* (c. 1865-70), Edward Ritter's *Der letzte Groschen* (1848) and Lewis Dewis's *Old Beggar* (1916).

The hat appears again in Jozef Laurent Dyckmans' popular sentimental painting *The Blind Beggar*. Here, a beggar is sitting in the porch of a church, with a pretty, contemplative girl next to him. His face is raised and the eyes closed as though to bathe in the golden light that falls like a benediction upon it. The radiance falling upon the blind beggar's upturned face forms a wildly ridiculous contrast to the illumination cast on the feet of the crucifix visible in the interior of the church. The hat is held discreetly low, as though it has been taken off only in humble acknowledgement of the blessing being shed from above, though the gaze of the beggar's putative daughter directs the gaze of the viewer into its empty interior and the thumb clasped over the brim ensures that nothing dropped in it will tumble out. A rosary held over the hat hints at the satisfying, sanctifying transaction into which the donor will enter with their offering, prayer in exchange for charity. The delicate hand of the beggar's daughter is laid across her father's hand, doubling the cross of the rosary that rests on the brim of the hat. Its half-open gesture at once seems to say 'behold' and is held ready for any gift that may come. Everything in the picture seems to challenge the viewer not to read and acknowledge the staging it effects: the woman in the church, lifting her hands in rapture to the dimly-lit Christ, the woman who exits the church clutching a prayerbook, her eyes directed out at the viewer, doubling the fiercely unrelenting gaze of the girl right at the centre of the picture. All insist on the irresistible legibility of the scene they participate in staging and the imperative to give that comes from the impossibility of sharing the beggar's knowing unseeingness.

In Jean-François Millet's *Charity* (1859), the beggar is reduced to a mere sliver, as he can be made out through the angle of the open door, with the central expanse of the painting showing the mother giving her daughter some bread. But enough is visible for the viewer to be able to recognise the bare head of the beggar, at once exposed and bowed and his hat, held down low as the sign both of abasement and appeal.

Often, there is no receptacle for offerings, but simply the curled or cupped hand of the beggar. El Greco's *St Martin and the Beggar* (1597-9) shows the saint on horseback about to cut off half of his cloak for the beggar who grips it expectantly in his left hand, while his right hand hangs with the index finger extended, with the mime of an appeal still lingering in it. In Adolphe William Bouguereau's *Indigent Family* (1865), a mother squats, with three children curled around her, staring straight out at the viewer, turned by her gaze into a potential giver, but enjoining nevertheless the characteristic deflection from her eyes to the half-open hand, the slightly loosened fingers half-withdrawing the visibility of their own appeal.

In such examples, the body of the beggar is a miniature opera, which is at once larger than life, and yet also discreetly attenuated. Like the photographs of the hysterical patients in the nineteenth-century Salpêtrière discussed by Georges Didi-Huberman (1982), the painting seems to render a person who is himself trying to remind his viewer of the posture of a genre painting.

Begging often constitutes a kind of outdoor theatre. It is unsurprising that early modern theatre should have been as preoccupied as it was with the lives of rogues, beggars and vagabonds, given the theatricality of the lives led by such persons. The closing of the Wells Road entrance to Finsbury Park underground station in July 2016 made thousands of passengers arriving at bus-stops walk 200 yards under Stroud Green Bridge to the other station entrance. This coincided with the arrival of a number of rough sleepers, who set up their stations along the route. Begging near stations and other such busy interchanges is of course extremely common, and railway bridges provide a particular combination of shelter from the elements and social exposure, as suggested in Bud Flanagan's 1932 song 'Underneath the Arches', prompted by the sight of men sleeping under Derby's Friargate Railway Bridge during the depression year of 1927. The song became popular ten years later during World War II, when the experience of outdoor collective sleeping became common in air raid shelters and underground stations. The space under Stroud Green Bridge is unusually long, for the bridge supports some seven separate railway lines coming into and out of Finsbury Park, and therefore offers the opportunity for a sort of enforced passeggiatta of begging display. It was not unusual to see people sleeping on the streets in the daylight – this is partly because it is so much more secure for the sleepers than at night. But the distinctive feature of the Stroud Green Bridge was the growth of a kind of daytime dormitory theatre, made up of mattresses, duvets, pillows, bin liners and cardboard. Islington Council regularly distributed leaflets to passers-by claiming that most of those who set up their pitches under the bridge had in fact been offered accommodation elsewhere, but had returned to the bridge to take advantage of the footfall for begging, in order to purchase the drugs on offer from dealers in nearby Fonthill Road and other neighbouring streets. Many hostels and refuges refuse to tolerate drugs on their premises, making it more likely that addicts would be forced to resort to the streets.

The bed is a potent addition to the dramaturgy of indigence precisely because it emphasises idleness, or possibly Lazarus-like infirmity. In contrast to those who come and go through urban spaces in pursuit of what they think of as their livings, the most characteristic pose of the beggar is that of repose. The stasis of the beggar, whether in the sedentary position or in the exaggerated form of daylight recumbency, asserts their exclusion from, or refusal of, employment, identified with purposive mobility.

Gradually, during 2017 and 2018, the improvised beds became more elaborate, becoming wittily-devised stage sets suggestive sometimes of amateur nativity plays, sometimes of home-sweet-home hearths. Bedside rugs appeared, sometimes extending far enough out in front of the grubby mattresses that passers-by were forced to step over them. One resident was able to set up a kind of awning with two supports at the head and foot of the bed, making a kind of enclosed cubicle. Shoes were sometimes left out or tucked cutely under the end of the mattress, and there were battered paperbacks suggestive of bedtime reading. The principle of the display here was not the ostension of suffering and want, which is traditional among beggars, but the creation of a kind of wrecked cosiness, and the enactment of an unavailing effort at withdrawal from the humiliation of public exposure. Rather than invading common space, these displays forced on passers-by the painful sense that they were violating the pathetic and fragile privacy of the sleepers by tramping through their boudoirs as they had somewhere to get to and walked calmly on. One or two of the arrangements featured a cloth or blanket draped over the sleeper, as though to shelter their intimacy from the pain of public exhibition, though the aim and effect was of course to exhibit this very circumstance. The most elaborate set-up I remember seeing involved a box-like framework, curtained off by rags or dirty counterpanes, like a gimcrack four-poster bed, which could accommodate two sleepers. One of the principles of the outdoor diorama was that it should seem to represent a piteous last island of personal dignity and fragile retreat for its occupant; in fact, though, the beds seemed to be used in shifts by different sleepers, and were more likely to be occupied during the hours of daylight, and therefore footfall, than at night, when there was no audience, so much slimmer pickings for the sleeping display. Very few if any sleepers were in fact to be seen at night, and there were reports of shopping trolleys being used to transport the bedding scenery into position in the morning.

The traditional way of thinking about begging is either to see its subjects as powerless, or as malign tricksters. But the two reactions do not in fact exclude each other. To say that one performs one's predicament as a beggar for charity is not at all to say that one is not genuinely in need; it is merely to say that one's need includes the necessity of performing that need.

Swindling in the Head

For these reasons, it is hard to get or keep the act of begging sharply and steadily in focus. Beggars are defined by the acts of earnest petitioning in which they engage and yet the representations of beggars often seem to omit or elide the specificity of that defining action. Nowhere is this more true than in sixteenth- and seventeenth-century literature, in which the topic of begging and the figure of the beggar are extremely prominent. This is the period in which the figure of the beggar becomes particularly common in the rising art of the theatre. And yet, even as beggars become staple figures in seventeenth- and eighteenth-century drama, the act of begging is rarely itself displayed on the stage. So ingrained is imposture in the idea of begging, it might seem, to be a beggar is in fact to be assumed to be something else, a cover for one of the many roles that began to proliferate in the imagination of the underworld. The most successful and well-known drama of criminal life, John Gay's *The Beggar's Opera* (1728) has a cast of characters that does not include a single beggar, among its company of highwaymen, hucksters, pickpockets, prostitutes, fences, bent jailers and chancers. The only personage named as a beggar in *The Beggar's Opera*, and it is in fact the only name he has, is not strictly in the play at all, for he is a representation of the author of the piece himself, who opens and closes the play as 'The Beggar' with the words 'If Poverty be a Title to Poetry, I am sure No-body can dispute mine. I own myself of the Company of Beggars; and I make one at their Weekly Festivals at St. *Giles's*' (Gay 2013, 3). So there are either no beggars in the play at all or the entire company can be taken as beggars in their dramatic work of petitory pretence. Since to be a beggar is to be, or be taken to be, a swindler in and of appearance, it can scarcely be expected that they would often appear in the *propriae personae* they disclaim. Swindle is from early modern Dutch *swindel*, vertigo or giddiness, and German *schwindeln*, to daydream: in Laurence Andrewe's 1527 translation of Hieronymous von Brunschwig's *Vertuose Boke of Distyllacyon*, lettuce juice is said to be 'good agaynste the swyndelynge in the hede' (Brunschwig 1527, sig. Kiv[v]). It developed its deceptive sense in English only in the later eighteenth century.

Two themes in the literature of beggary perform together the work of displacement: dissimulation and vagrancy. The beggar is suspected of begging as a way of avoiding working, hence the prominence of sardonic phrases like 'sturdy beggar' or, 'valiant beggar' both in legislative documents and in the many guides to the tricks and counterfeits of beggars that appeared from the mid-sixteenth century onwards. And the fact that the beggar is, or pretends to be, unable to follow a trade or profession, makes for the assumption during the fifteenth and sixteenth centuries that they are physically removed from the places where they should be pursuing some determinate and legitimate occupation, pursuing an occupation and occupying a place being closely associated, as indicated by the survival still of the words 'place' and 'position' to signify a job. Even though trade and employment were beginning by the sixteenth century to be more mobile, with the rise of London in particular eroding the sense of local belonging, to be out of one's physical location was thought to be the same as being out of one's social station. This is both part of an emerging order of professional mobility and the source of dread. For vagrancy and begging, though closely related, are not identical. Indeed, vagrancy is less of a problem than the aggressive kind of residence asserted by beggars, in their different kinds of 'pitch'. Because the beggar is assumed to be a person in the wrong place, it is imperative that they be subject to further, remedial displacement, by being moved off or on. From the end of the sixteenth century, vagrants and beggars even began to be transported to colonies.

The analogies between vagrancy, begging and acting are spelled out emphatically by Paola Pugliatti:

> It would seem that at the core of the shorthand definition of 'vagrancy' as comprising all street activities that threatened to

produce disorder was the intention to marginalize and degrade in the eyes of the population, and eventually suppress, all the trades of those people whose subversive potential was seen both in their idleness and in their instability in location and role, that is, in their 'theatrical' quintessence. (Pugliatti 2003, 5)

A general 'fear of a changeability concerning place, role and identity' (Pugliatti 2003, 5) explains why 'professional begging may have been considered as a form of unlicensed acting' (Pugliatti 2003, 8).

The emphasis on the theatrical figure of the roguish beggar has encouraged a disciplinary dichotomy between poetic and social-historical readings of beggary, with proponents of the facts of the matter as far as poverty is concerned contending against fictionalisations of various kinds. For Patricia Fumerton, the rogue pamphleteers transformed 'the *fact* of a vagrant economy grounding on a shifting mass of itinerant labour into the *fiction* of role-playing rogues' (Fumerton 2004, 197). The fabular rogue thereby becomes a way of rendering the actual vagrant invisible, and it is the fictionalising pamphleteers rather than the beggar they take as their subject who becomes the dissemblers. But whatever fact of the matter there may be about beggary, the ways in which begging does and does not imply being 'a beggar' must be a part of it.

Beggars are often said to be 'bold' because they must learn to break through a web of social discretions and inhibitions that otherwise prevent people asking those more fortunate than they are for charity. Even, and especially, when they appear to display themselves and their sufferings passively, beggars must always also be exposing themselves purposively to view. And yet, in another sense, in the very work of representation which seems to put begging and beggary metaphorically on display, the act and consequently the actuality of begging seems somehow withdrawn from visibility. In fact, just because begging forces itself into the field of the visible, in a kind of tormenting solicitation of the gaze, an extortion through self-exposure, it is experienced as a consequence as something one must take steps to avoid seeing. The very construing of the beggar as figure, whether of aversive contempt or amusement, serves to screen off the recognition of begging as action: what the beggar is allows one not to have to dwell on what a beggar does, and what is done by and through the begging that they do. The building of the profile of the beggar, through legal documents, popular denunciations and dramatic representations, is itself a way of putting the beggar in his or her place, even if it is as a representation of shape-shifting instability:

the anxiety about unlicensed begging, exactly like that about unlicensed acting, stemmed not only from preoccupations about public order but also from the same, unspoken and maybe half-conscious intolerance towards all forms of illicit and devious impersonation; in short, that the *mendicitas* of beggars and the *mendacia* of players may have been the object of the same antitheatrical prejudice. (Pugliatti 2003, 10)

Lying and begging, mendacity and mendicity, do seem to be related by something more than accident, or by a mishap that has method in it. Both derive from Latin *mendum*, a fault or blemish (de Vaan 2008, 372), hence something to be mended. There may also be a link to *mens*, mind. De Vaan proposes that '[i]f the original meaning was 'sign, mark', one might tentatively derive the noun from PIE *mn- 'to think', as *mn-dr or as *mn-dhr to set the mind, be attentive.' (de Vaan 2008, 372). To lie may derive from mind, following the sequence to change one's mind, have second thoughts, invent, lie. So there appears to be suspicion of the beggar from the beginning. The fault of the beggar lies in his reduced condition, which must often have included a physical infirmity. But the faultiness of the body is often allied to the falseness of speech which claims or manufactures such a fault. Indeed, there is often the suspicion that the beggar's fault is in itself a falsehood, in the form of a simulated limp, or pretended blindness, or madness. In such simulations, the defect itself is defective. The mistrust of the simulating beggar is a protection against the more taxing conundrum, of the beggar who simulates their actual condition. In such cases, what beggars simulate is not just their condition, of need or suffering, but the condition of not being able to conceal their condition. Beggars pretend that they are unable to pretend. This is the essence of mendicant theatrics.

If any intelligible sense may be attached to the idea of 'collective anxiety', which is perhaps doubtful, it would be wise to mistrust the assumption that it will express itself in widely-shared and readily recognisable representations. It is much more likely that such representations will protect against an anxiety that remains unformalised and unspoken, difficulty of formalisation being an essential feature of anxiety. We can be confident that an anxiety to which expression is given as uninhibitedly as in the case of the representation of beggary is an anxiety thoroughly sedated.

The theatrics of beggary, whether in the representations of beggars in plays, or in the more figurative evocations of the beggar in his or her scene of operations, enact the essential duality of the scene, that allows simultaneously for exposure to and insulation from the spectacle. Making of the beggar a *dramatis persona* allows the scenic ambivalence of the begging encounter to be held at bay in the stabilising work of the scene itself. To revive Derrida's tart characterisation of the theme of castration in psychoanalysis, the figure of the beggar is a lacking of which there can be no lack, an omission that can never go missing from its place (Derrida 1997, 441).

One of the most distinctive features of 'beggary', that hardening into noun-form of the gerund 'begging', is how wide and slippery it is in its reference.

The characteristic of beggars is that they are, or are thought likely to be, many other things alongside, yet also aside from, being beggars – runaways, thieves, pimps, fornicators, gamblers, wastrels, confidence tricksters, rioters, atheists, even seditious traitors to the realm. The word *rogue*, meaning a rascal, does the work of summing up all these suspected characteristics, but it is less easy to understand why the word *beggar* should so often have the same range of associations, given the specificity of the action it names. In fact, the origin of the word rogue is itself somewhat obscure. There may be a connection with the Norman forename 'Roger', but an appearance of the word as a verbal noun in one of the earliest of the sixteenth-century rogue pamphlets, Robert Copland's *The Hye Way to the Spyttell Hous*, suggests some reference to the Latin *rogare*, to ask:

> But to our purpose / cometh not this way
> Of these Rogers? that dayly syng and pray
> With Aue regina / or De profundis
> Quem terra ponthus / and Stella maris
> At euery doore there they toot and frydge
> And say they come fro Oxford or Cambrydge
> And be poore scolers / and haue no maner thyng
> Nor also frendes, to kepe them at lernyng
> And so do lewtre only for crust and crum
> with staffe in hand / and fyst in bosum
> Passyng tyme so bothe day and yere. (Copland 1536, sig. B4ʳ)

A little later, Copland distinguishes 'another company/Of the same sect / that lyue more subtylly/And be in maner as mayster wardayns/To whome these Rogers obey as capytayns' (Copland 1536, sig. B4ᵛ). The connections between rogation and the learned beggar are reiterated in the description of this group:

> They say that they come fro the vnyuersyte
> And in the scoles haue taken degree
> Of preesthod / but frendes haue they none
> To gyue them ony exhybytion
> And how that they forth wold passe
> To theyr countree / and syng theyr fyrst masse
> And there pray for theyr benefactours
> And serue god all tymes and houres
> And so they lewtre in suche rogacyons
> Seuen or eyght yeres walkyng theyr stacyons

> And do but gull / and folow beggery
> Feynyng true doyng by ypocrysy (Copland 1536, sig. B4^r)

The link between rogue and beggar in this case may simply be through the play in the Latin *rogare*. But there may also be an allusion to the feast of Rogation, days of fasting that precede the feast of Ascension on Holy Thursday, with prayers for the success of the harvest. Rogation days were also known as 'gang days', days of walking, because they often involved processions, perambulations and ceremonies of the beating of parish bounds. This cluster of associations, of learning, Latin, vagrancy and deceit may suggest a particular association between wandering beggars and academic and ecclesiastical deceivers: Copland goes on to distinguish a number of 'fals brybours, deceytfull and fraudelent/That among people call themselfs Sapyent/These ryde about in many sondry wyse/And in straunge aray/do themself dysguyse' (Copland 1536, sig. B4^v). It is tempting to linger on the word 'exhibition' in the statement 'frendes haue they none/To gyue them ony exhybytion' (Copland 1536, sig. B4^r). The primary meaning of 'exhibit' in the early sixteenth century is to provide, furnish or administer, as when one endows a school or college: the word 'exhibition' is still used in this sense in Oxford and Cambridge to mean a scholarship. But the transfer of meaning from providing to bringing forth, presenting or displaying has already begun in the 1520s, for example in a decree of 20th February 1529 which records that 'our true and faithful subjects, artificers and handicraftsmen … exhibited unto us a lamentable bill of complaint' (Pickering 1763, 189). This coalition of meanings, incipient in the 1520s and completed by 1656, when Thomas Blount's *Glossographia* could define 'Exhibite as 'to set abroad, to present, to give, to shew it self' (Blount 1656, sig. Q2^v), allows us to see the beggars in the business of furnishing themselves in vision as a way to gain provision.

One can never be quite sure that the sinuous synecdoche of 'the beggar' really belongs to the social world or the world of rhetoric. Since the condition of beggary was identified with vagrancy in general, the definition of begging was therefore itself a highly mobile and even vagrant one. And yet, for this very reason, begging is frequently lost sight of, or kept offstage by the engrossing figure of 'the beggar'.

Perhaps the most important feature of the figure of the beggar, and the means whereby its reference can slide across into so many other things, is the suspicion of trickery it involves. Much of the rogue literature that begins with the figure of the beggar moves quickly across into pseudo-warnings about the modes of trickery and deception that are used to dupe the unwary. The principal synonyms for cheating or deceiving, gulling, cuckolding (as 'cuckooing') and coney-catching, all have reference to ideas of eating, consumption and being 'taken in', ideas that may implicate the primary action of begging for food, in human and non-human animals.

By the sixteenth century, the word *beggary* had already expanded well beyond the meaning of beggarliness, in the sense of poverty, or a condition of destitution requiring one to beg. Beggary stood for the condition of destitution in general. A sermon of 1597 urged that his audience should cast out from their lives 'the Ionas of adultery, the Ionas of fornication, vpon whom beggery waiteth many a time' (Abbott 1600, 148). When the Captain in Shakespeare's *Henry IV Part 2* concludes his denunciation of Suffolk for the ruin he has brought upon the kingdom with the words 'reproach and beggary/Is crept into the palace of our King' (Shakespeare 2011, 519), he is really evoking a condition of moral wretchedness rather than indigence. Kent's intemperate and assiduously all-inclusive insulting of Oswald builds up similarly to a climax in the imputation of beggary:

> Oswald. What dost thou know me for?
> Kent. A knave, a rascal, an eater of broken meats: a base, proud,
>   shallow, beggarly, three-suited-hundred-pound, filthy, worsted-
>   stocking knave; a lily-livered, action-taking knave; a whoreson,
>   glass-gazing, super-serviceable, finical rogue; one trunk-inheriting
>   slave, one that wouldst be a bawd in way of good service and art
>   nothing but the composition of a knave, beggar, coward, pander,
>   and the son and heir of a mongrel bitch; one whom I will beat into
>   clamorous whining if thou deniest the least syllable of thy addition.
>   (Shakespeare 2011, 645)

Beggary is conspicuously to the fore in *King Lear*, through Lear's own mad vagrancy across the heath, but the play itself seems to offer an object lesson in the distinction between begging and beggary. For Lear, the descent into beggary does not cause him to have to beg; rather it is the humiliation of finding himself having to beg that precipitates him into his more general and diffuse condition of beggarly humiliation.

Licence

There were two features of the idea of beggary that seem to be vehicles of this fluctuation between the representable and the unrepresentable: the licensing of begging, and the fantasy of beggar society. Begging, as the sharp and visible end of vagabondage in general, had prompted attempts at legal provision from the Ordinance of Labourers of 1349-50, which responded to the depletion of the labour force following the Black Death of 1348. The emphasis of laws like the Statute of Cambridge of 1388 was on control of the movements of beggars, who were held to be the responsibility of the authorities in their home parishes, and punished harshly for straying from them. The Vagabonds and Beggars Act of 1494 (11 Henry VII c. 2) decreed that 'Every beggar suitable to work shall resort to the Hundred where he last dwelled, is best known, or was born and there remain'. The dissolution of the monasteries from 1538 onwards took with them the networks of almsgiving provided by monastic institutions, producing the need for more systematic provision for the poor, accompanied necessarily by efforts at regulation.

An important part of this attempt at regulation was the practice of licensing beggars. There were in fact different kinds of licence, issued by different authorities in differing circumstances. Students and soldiers were expected to carry a letter or testimonial accounting for their movements. Particular districts, finding themselves unable to cope with high numbers of the poor, would issue licences that allowed begging outside that district. There were also 'briefs', official letters stating that the holder had suffered a particular misfortune, such as a fire or injury and was permitted on that account to beg. Most peculiar of all were licences issued to vagrants convicted of begging outside their own localities, which allowed them to beg to sustain themselves on their journeys back to where they came from, presumably to ensure that they made it to their home parishes. Thomas Harman affirms in 1567 that

> they wyl cary a cirtificate or pasport about them from som Iusticer of the peace, with his hand and seale vnto the same, howe hee hath byne whipped and punished for a vacabonde according to the lawes of this realme, and that he muste returne to. T. where he was borne or last dwelt, by a certayne daye lymited in the same, whiche shalbe a good longe daye. (Harman 1567, sig. C1ᵛ)

As A.L. Beier observes, 'The distinction between true and false beggars almost guaranteed that there would be frauds, as did the licensing provisions in the poor law' (Beier 1985, 112). The misuse of licences to beg among convicted vagrants who could extend their journeys back home indefinitely was almost bound to occur. The pressure to regularise begging even extended to potential donors, who were enjoined to restrain their spontaneous urges to charitable giving, and sometimes even fined for giving shelter to beggars and vagrants. As Evan Gurney observes, 'It seems odd that the penalties for interpretive error were so rigorous, given the persistent admission among Elizabethans, one implicitly corroborated in law, that correctly reading the poor was an incredibly difficult task' (Gurney 2016, 555).

Sometimes, the very forms of bodily stigmatisation designed to transfix and control the beggar, like branding or the boring of the ear, could act as a kind of legitimating sign. The effort to reduce beggars could not help but produce them. The effort to distinguish real from counterfeit beggars themselves provided more opportunities for the multiplication of counterfeit signs.

The licence mediated the relationship between action and figure, begging and the beggar. The essential feature of the act of begging is that it arises from a condition of need which sets aside all other considerations, breaking through social restraints and conventions. It assumes and asserts an essential form of social relatedness beneath or before every other kind of social relation. The act of issuing a licence legitimises that action of spontaneous appeal even as it makes it impossible for it any more to be spontaneous. Only licensed beggars are allowed to beg; but this means that licensed beggars are no longer in fact begging, in that primary sense, for the piercingly intimate, aggressive-erotic I-thou encounter is mediated by an authority that turns the action of begging into a request for an allowance, and makes the action of giving alms the paying of a kind of unofficial, semi-voluntary tax. Only unlicensed beggars, who are therefore not countenanced as 'beggars' at all, are in fact able (because forced) to *beg*, as opposed to performing the licensed action of begging. The beggars who licensed themselves, through the purchase or manufacture of forged documents, therefore simultaneously enabled and disabled their capacity to beg.

In addition to the counterfeiting of licences, there were many attempts at bodily and performative self-authentication. The most perversely versatile form of counterfeit self-licensing was that of the Abraham or Abram Man, possibly named after a ward in Bedlam, the hospital of St. Mary of Bethlehem, founded in 1247 in St Botolph's in London. The Abraham man provided the proof of his pedigree as a Bedlam inmate through the very distractedness of his display, and, of course, display of his distractedness, in comportment and speech. John Awdelay wrote that the Abraham Man 'is he that walketh bare armed and bare legged, and fayneth him selfe madde, and carieth a packe of Wooll, or a stycke with Bakon on it, or such like toy: and nameth himself Poore Tom' (Awdelay 1603, sig. A2ʳ). Such beggars went to some lengths to license themselves through forms of self-stigmatisation. Writing in the second part of the seventeenth century, John Aubrey recorded that

> Till the breaking out of the civill warres, Tom ô Bedlam's did travell about the countrey. They had been poore distracted men that had been putt into Bedlam where recovering to some sobernesse they were licentiated to goe a begging: *e.g.* they had on their left arm an armilla of tinn, printed in some workes, about four inches long; they could not gett it off. They wore about their necks a great horn of an oxe in a string or bawdrie, which, when they came to an house for almes, they did wind: and they did putt the drink given them into this horn, whereto they did putt a stopple. Since the warres I doe not remember to have seen any one of them. (Aubrey 1847, 93)

Thomas Dekker gives rather more detail about the process of forming these marks:

> Some of these *Abrams* haue the Letters *E.* and *R.* vpon their armes: some haue Crosses, and some other marke, all of them carrying a blew colour: some weare an iron ring, &c. which markes are printed vpon their flesh, by tying their arme hard with two strings thrée or feure inches asunder, and then with a sharpe Awle pricking or raizing the skinne, to such a figure or print as they best fancy, they rub that place with burnt paper, pisse and Gunpowder, which being hard rubd in, and suffered to dry, stickes in the flesh a long time after, when these markes faile, they renew them at pleasure. If you examine them how these Letters or Figures are printed vpon their armes, they will tell you it is the Marke of Bedlam, but the truth is, they are made as I haue reported. (Dekker 1616, sig. M2^v)

It appears that there were many more licensed ex-inmates of Bedlam than can ever have been entertained within its walls, since there were hardly more than 30 such in the early seventeenth century (Beier 1985, 115). It is not even clear that any kind of licence to beg was in fact issued by Bedlam, so that the licence carried, or believed to be carried, by Abraham Men, is perhaps to be regarded as fictitious rather than forged.

If you know yourself to be mad, and know yourself to be known as mad, you cannot really be: whereas, if you can give a convincing appearance of having no understanding of your lack of understanding, you may be warranted, as having leave to be taken as having authentically taken leave of your senses, and so be permitted to make a living from it. The method acting of the methodically mad was one of the strongest and strangest responses to the pressure for licensing of the licentious act of begging. The linking of madness, folly and beggary in Shakespeare's *King Lear* is secured by the reference to the 'all-licensed fool', the one licensed to be able to take liberties, and the conspicuously unlicensed feigned madness of Edgar/Poor Tom. It is an intimation of the way in which beggary commutes between rationality and irrationality.

Abraham Men got their living from their performance of madness. But there is a sense in which by the sixteenth century madness had already started to become in some more primary sense performative. This was not just because of the frequent appearance of madmen, and references to Bedlam hospital, on the Tudor, Jacobean and Stuart stage, but also because by the later sixteenth century Bedlam had become established as a place of popular exhibition and entertainment (Carroll 1996, 100). The performative nature of madness is not exactly or invariably that it involved imposture of the kind engaged in by the Abraham-man, or *King Lear's* Edgar in his impersonation of a Poor Tom, but it certainly involved exhibition: to be mad was not just to be out of your senses, but to make a spectacle of yourself.

Mendicant Uncanny

The three-way association between playacting, madness and begging is perhaps also to be linked with another feature of begging in this period. In the medieval world, the most familiar and approved kind of traveller might have been religious, and to be a mendicant provided an oxymoronic yet stabilising example of a profession that entailed vagrancy. Borrowing and building on A.L. Beier's description of the 'desanctification of the poor' with the Renaissance humanists' praise of worldly striving over the Franciscan ideals of the late medieval period (Beier 1985, 4), Mark Koch has described what he calls the 'desanctification of the beggar' both in the theology of Wycliff, Luther and others and in the rogue pamphlets of the fifteenth century, arguing that 'If capitalist logic was to prevail, the sanctity associated with poverty, beggary and alms-giving had to give way to a work ethic and a rational, secular system of charity' (Koch 1992, 93). Though the last words Martin Luther ever wrote, on a piece of paper found in his pocket after his death, were '*Wir sind Pettler. Hoc est verum*', 'We are beggars; that is true' (Metaxas 2018, 432), his hostility to begging, and identification of begging with the corruptions of the Catholic Church, is strongly marked through his writing. In a preface he contributed to his edition of the *Liber Vagatorum* (1528), Luther wrote that:

> whereas people will not give and help honest paupers and needy neighbours, as ordained by God, they give, by the persuasion of the devil, and contrary to God's judgment, ten times as much to Vagabonds and desperate rogues,—in like manner as we have hitherto done to monasteries, cloisters, churches, chapels, and mendicant friars, forsaking all the time the truly poor. (Luther 1860, 4)

Paola Pugliatti argues that, not just in England, but across Europe

> the hostility towards the masses of unemployed determined a stigma of disrepute, that is, it helped to establish the equation between misery and deviance, which supplanted and wholly transformed the primitive Christian *ethos* of poverty into suspicion and even contempt of the poor and the praise of almsgiving into an act to be condemned in that it encouraged idleness and parasitism. (Pugliatti 2003, 22)

The desanctification of mendicancy seems also to have left, not just a certain power to fascinate, but also a residue of mystical or even occult feeling attached to the figure of the beggar. Thomas Harman describes mock-mad Tudor beggars as follows:

These Abraham men bee those that fayne them selues to haue bene mad, and haue bene kept eyther in Bedleant, or in some other prison a good tyme, and not one amongst twenty that euer came in pryson for any suche cause: yet wyll they saye howe pitiously & most extreamely they haue ben beaten & dealte withal. Some of these be mery & verye pleasante, they wyl daunce & syng, some others be as colde and reasonable to talke wyth all. These begge money, eyther when they come at Farmours howses they wyll demaunde Baken, eyther cheese, or wooll, or any thinge that is worth money. And if they espy smal company within they will with fierce countenaunce demaunde somewhat. Where for feare the maydes wyll geue theym largely to be ridde of theym. (Harman 1567, 19)

Thomas Dekker repeats some elements of this account in his *Belman of London* of 1608:

Of all the mad Rascalls (that are of this wing) the *Abraham-man* is the most fantasticke; The fellow (quoth this olde Lady of the Lake vnto mee) that sat halfe naked (at Table to day) from the Girdle vpward, is the best *Abraham-man* that euer came to my house, and the notablest villaine: he sweares hee hath beene in Bedlam, and will talke frantickly of purpose: you see pinnes stuck in sundrie places of his naked flesh, especially in his armes, which paine he gladly puts himselfe too (being indeed no torment at all, his skin is either so deade with some foule disease, or so hardned with weather: only to make you beléeue he is out of his wits,) he calls himselfe by the name of Poore Tom, and coming neere any body cries out *Poore Tom* is a colde. Of these *Abraham-men*, some bee excéeding merrie, and doe nothing but sing Songs, fashioned out of their owne braines, some will dance, others will doe nothing but either laugh or weepe, others are Dogged, and so sullen both in looke and speech that spying but a smal company in a house, they boldly and bluntly enter, compelling the seruants through feare to giue them what they demaund, which is commonly bacon, or something that will yeeld ready money. (Dekker 1608, sigs. D3^r-D3^v)

Dekker's characterisation is almost contemporary with *King Lear*, which was first published in a quarto of 1608. Edgar's evocation of the figure he will simulate as 'Poor Tom' includes the detail of the mortified flesh, and the mixture of menace and absurdity found both in Awdelay and Dekker:

I will preserve myself, and am bethought
To take the basest and most poorest shape

That ever penury in contempt of man
Brought near to beast. My face I'll grime with filth,
Blanket my loins, elf all my hair in knots,
And with presented nakedness outface
The winds and persecutions of the sky.
The country gives me proof and precedent
Of Bedlam beggars, who, with roaring voices,
Strike in their numbed and mortified bare arms
Pins, wooden pricks, nails, sprigs of rosemary;
And with this horrible object, from low farms,
Poor pelting villages, sheep-cotes, and mills,
Somctime with lunatic bans, sometime with prayers,
Enforce their charity. Poor Turlygod, poor Tom,
That's something yet: Edgar I nothing am. (Shakespeare 2011, 647)

O per se O (1616), the second of Dekker's two sequels to *The Belman of London*,
gives more detail about the means used by this form of beggar to elicit
donations through superstitious terror:

These, walking vp and downe the Countrey, are more terribly
to women and Children, then the name of *Raw-head* and *Blody-
bones, Robbin Good-fellow,* or any other *Hobgobling Crackers* tyed to
a Dogges tayle, make not the poore Curre runne faster, then
these *Abram Ninnies* doe the silly Villages of the Countrey, so that
when they come to any doore a begging, nothing is denyed them.
(Dekker 1616, sig. M2ʳ)

The importunate demands of beggars may inspire unease simply on the
grounds that they may seem to threaten violence – Edgar proposes to 'enforce'
charity with a mixture of curses (bans, banes) and prayers. But the suggestion
of madness in beggary may also suggest something uncanny in beggars'
behaviour or powers. The songs that grew up around the figure of the 'poor
Tom' suggest that there is something fearsome in the thought of him, even as
they might seem to offer reassurance:

From the hagg and hungry Goblin
That into raggs would rend yee,
All the Spirits that stan
By the naked man
In the book of moons defend yee.
That of your five sound Senses
You never be forsaken,
Nor Travel from
Your selves with *Tom*
A broad to begg your Bacon.

Chor: *Nor never sing, any food any feeding,*
Money drink or clothing:
Come dame or mayd
Be not affrayd,
Poor Tom *will injure nothing.* (Anon, 1672, 17)

In Shakespeare's rendering of Edgar's imposture (if it is in fact simply or entirely imposture) of madness, there are strong suggestions of diabolical possession, his disordered talk being threaded through with allusions to the extravagantly fraudulent exorcisms condemned in detail in Samuel Harsnett's *Declaration of Egregious Popish Impostures* (1603). Edgar proposes to 'elf' his hair, by knotting it, a usage which Shakespeare seems to have originated. Germanic elves were dangerous and terrifying rather than pretty, flitting mischief-makers, and the elf-knot was a particularly fiendish magical charm, having the power both to disorder things and to lock them helplessly in place – knots were superstitiously avoided by pregnant women lest they magically prevented parturition (Connor 2009). As well as madness, beggars were said also to feign convulsive conditions, such as epilepsy, or falling sickness. According to Thomas Harman, exponents of this specialism

> neuer go without a peece of white sope about them, which if they see cause or present gaine, they wyl priuely conuey the same into their mouth, and so worke the same ther, that they wyll fome as it were a Boore, & marueilously for a time torment them selues, and thus deceiue they the common people, & gaine much. (Harman 1567, sig. D2ᵛ)

The modern word *crank*, meaning an eccentric, may represent a confluence of a word meaning crooked with the term 'counterfeit crank' in rogues' cant, borrowing Germanic *krank*, ill, this preserving the association between craziness and imposture.

The arrival at the beginning of the sixteenth century of groups known as 'Egyptians' or gypsies also assisted these associations between beggary and the occult: vagrants became subject to prosecution not only for begging but also for fortune-telling and acts of pretended sorcery. When Shakespeare's Fool first hears Edgar in the hovel, he warns Lear 'Come not in here, nuncle, here's a spirit' (Shakespeare 2011, 652). The link between gypsies, 'such, for the most part, that call themselves *Egyptians,* but are no other than stroaling Beggars, Vagrants or Wanderers' and 'pretend to devine Magick' and Abraham Men was still being made by John Shirley in 1688, in a volume of verses and entertainments, which defined the Abraham Man or 'Abraham Cove' as

> one that dresses himself ridiculously, and pretends at sundry times to be Mad, and in Fits, when indeed he do's it to draw people about him to procure the advantage of the rest, either in

telling Fortunes, or giving them the opportunity of picking the
Pockets of the Gazers. (Shirley 1688, 205-6)

The power of the Bedlam beggar is derived, not from his pitiable weakness,
but his unnerving insensibility to pain, and his power to 'outface/The winds
and persecutions of the sky' (Shakespeare 2011, 647). The proof of spirit
possession was often furnished by insensibility of this kind – and suspected
witches were probed with pins in order to test for *stigmata diaboli*, numb spots
(Fontaine 1611; Connor 2003, 127-8). Shakespeare was particularly attuned
to the uncanniness of insensibility (Connor 2020), and *King Lear* focusses in
particular on the uncanny mixture of endurance and wretchedness in the
figure of the beggar. Edgar imagines the Bedlam beggar reducing himself to
a 'horrible object' – alluding specifically to Latin *horrere*, to bristle or stand
upright – in order to extract money from villages which seem uncannily to
resemble him, for they are, in his words, 'poor, pelting'. Pelting may mean
paltry, mean or meagre; indeed, it is used by Thomas Harman to describe
beggars' cant itself, as 'vntowarde talke and pelting speache myngled &
without measure' (Harman 1567, sig. G4^v). But it is also echoed in Lear's
evocation, immediately before his encounter with Edgar in the person of Poor
Tom, of 'Poor naked wretches, wheresoe'er you are,/That bide the pelting
of this pitiless storm' (Shakespeare 2011, 652), where it implies the literal
stripping away of the skin, or pelt. The thought of the 'poor, bare, forked
animal' that Poor Tom impersonates (Shakespeare 2011, 653) is uncanny in
its mixture of terror of this reduction to the condition of a thing, and desire
for the omnipotence in being able to subsist in this ultimately condition of the
'thing itself' (Shakespeare 2011, 653). The Bedlam beggar seems to embody
this power of undead endurance.

Freud surmised that sensations of the uncanny arose from the return
or persistence of beliefs belonging to the magical or animistic stage of
human belief, characterised by 'the over-accentuation of psychical reality
in comparison with physical reality', or 'omnipotence of thoughts' (Freud
1953-74, 17.244). Though Freud does not quite succeed in articulating
the connection between the 'animism' of primitive human life and the
uncanniness of the inanimate come to life, we may surmise that the beggar
embodies a kind of omnipotence in his toleration of wretchedness. The
ambivalence of the apparently living dead, the capacity of the Bedlam beggar
to embody the persistence of life amid the ultimate indigence of the reduction
to embodiment itself, and to demand what is necessary to sustain this deathly
animation in life, acts out a kind of undimmed desire. Theatre, the capacity at
once to be and not to be, is the essential vehicle of this omnipotence fantasy.
Abraham Men in particular, whose most characteristic disguise was their
nakedness, embody the greatest ambivalence. Thomas Harman reports of the
dissembling 'cranks' that 'any of these do go without writings, and wyl go
halfe naked, and looke most pitiously. And if any clothes be geuen them, they

immediately sell the same, for weare it they will not, because they would bee the more pitied' (Harman 1567, sig. D2ᵛ). Eventually, Nicholas Jennings, the crank whom Harman pursued, is exposed as a fraud:

> they strypt hym starcke naked and as manye as sawe hym sayde they neuer sawe hansommer man wyth a yellow flexen hede and fayre sknned wythout any spotte or greffe then the good wyfe of the howse fet her mans olde clocke and cawsed the same to bee caste abowte hym beecawse the syght should not abashe her shamefast maydens nether lothe her squamyshe syght. (Harman 1567, sig. D4ʳ)

It is strange that the exposure should substitute one kind of nakedness for another, and that the 'fair' truth of the exposed crank's body should nevertheless threaten to 'lothe her squamyshe syght' (squeamish, nauseating, but with a tilt at 'squamous', scaly).

It may well be that the figure of the secularised beggar maintained some of the quasi-supernatural power previously invested in religious mendicants, with magical rituals of propitiation taking the place of the religious duty of almsgiving, or perhaps simply preserving the magical function of that almsgiving. Beggars were thought to have the power of cursing those who refused to give them alms, or buy their undesired goods; as late as the 1800s, beggars were reported to do good trade around the university in Paris at examination times, from students not wanting to risk the bad luck that might come from refusing to give. In more general terms, the aura of the uncanny that hung around beggars may have to do with the fundamental disturbance of the structure of discourse that begging can constitute, as considered in 'The Force of Petition' in chapter 1, shifted into the register of epistemic unease.

The desanctification of begging that took place after the Reformation broadened into a secularisation of petitory practice, in a process that continues into the present. The medieval mendicant offered a pedagogic-ceremonial ostension of unworldliness, and the systematised occasion for transactions, at once actual and symbolic, between the orders of the temporal and the spiritual. But the dissolution of the wandering friar's or pilgrim's mendicary charisma did not imply a decline in actions of petition, so much as a generalisation and diversification of them in an increasingly complex economy of destitutions and remedies as well as purchases and exchanges. In a world in which many more kinds of people, in many different kinds of circumstance, participated in forms of secularised petition, bidding and solicitation, the mendicary was not so much overtaken by the mercantile, as absorbed into, and operationalised by it. As petition became more worldly, more widespread and more everyday, to the point where it became as much of a transaction as buying and selling, hiring and firing, the links between the many different modes of petitioning – for remittances, positions, privileges, remissions, exceptions, advancements and opportunities of many different kinds – and their earlier forms became almost impossible to discern, beyond the wan echo in the word 'application' of the archaic act of 'supplication'.

But the secularisation of the beggar may itself have led to a new kind of fascination with a figure who seemed so ambivalently placed in emerging economic conditions, at once a residual anomaly and a central figure. As Mark Koch observes, the reduction of the religious mystique attached to the figure of the beggar gave way in the later seventeenth century to a vision of the fraternity of beggars as 'a thoroughly romanticized utopia' (Koch 1992, 101). 1992, Beggars and players may both sometimes have been an irritant, but we must try to stay awake about historical matters such as this, which means retaining the capacity to doubt whether they were any more a source of anything like dread or anxiety to sixteenth- and seventeenth-century readers than they are to contemporary critics and their readers. Rather than being the pitiable jetsam of the Gradgrinding 'capitalist logic' of theoretical romance, it seems much more likely that, then as now, representations of beggars, literary and legal, abounded in large part because they were enjoyable to tease oneself by thinking about. Academic historians and literary critics, who mostly read for pay, may find their appreciation eroded of the pleasure principle that impels people to part with good money for things to read. Given the increasing importance of the economics of entertainment, this is all, of course, as much, or as little, a part of the logic of capital, whatever that is, as the working week. And even if there were also sometimes concern or anxiety at the figure of the beggar, or a fear of the 'subversion' that the beggar might seem to represent, this is so far from being incompatible with the forming and farming of pleasure in that figuration as to be an essential feature of it.

Cant and Descant

Perhaps the most insistent feature of the theatrics of beggary is the secret language that beggars and rogues were supposed to speak, and that was spelled out in the dictionaries of cant speech that held sway from the middle of the sixteenth century. The usual, indeed the almost universal explanation of cant, along with other examples of secret languages or cryptolects, is that they are used for concealment. Thieves, tricksters and other rogues will use such languages, it is maintained, in order to hatch plots and communicate criminal intentions to each other unknown to their victims or to the authorities. In line with this, the explications and lexicons of beggars' and thieves' cant which became common from the late sixteenth century onwards proclaim their intention of laying bare what the canters would wish to keep dark, for the purposes of protecting honest citizens. Thomas Harman seems to be the first person to use the word 'canting' of the language spoken by a group of 'bolde beggers', proposing that 'as far as I can learne or vnderstand by the examination of a number of them, their languag, which they terme peddelars

Frenche or cantig began but w⁴in these .xxx. yeres lytle aboue' (Harman 1567, sig. A3ᵛ).

Other authors of rogue pamphlets followed Harman in providing a word list of cant terms. In the first volume of her *History of Cant and Slang Dictionaries*, Julie Coleman does not hesitate to affirm that 'Cant goes one step further than jargon. Its primary purpose is to deceive, to defraud, and to conceal. It is the language used by beggars and criminals to hide their dishonest and illegal activities from potential victims' (Coleman 2004, 4). Daniel Heller-Roazen agrees that the primary purpose of cant 'is to deceive, to defraud, and to conceal' and reaffirms that standard belief that '[i]t is the language used by beggars and criminals to hide their dishonest and illegal activities from potential victims' (Heller-Roazen 2013, 31).

There is no reason to doubt that private languages or specialised argots do arise among criminal or socially marginal groups, as well as among professional elites and trades (academic life providing many examples); public schools and the armed services also develop their own slang. But it is extremely hard to see what advantage could possibly have been derived from communicating in such a conspicuous and outlandish manner, which must have served only to draw attention to its users' alienness, or determination to mark themselves out as different, rather than allowing them to escape notice. This is all the more the case because cant does not ever seem to have come close to being a 'language' in its own right, even though this was often affirmed of it, but rather a set of lexical variations or substitutions effected on a grammar and syntax that remained obviously and substantially English. Daniel Heller-Roazen follows Marcel Cohen in seeing them as 'parasitic languages' (Heller-Roazen 2013, 37). So, far from allowing for the concealment of criminal intent, the use of cant must have acted as an unmistakable beacon of shady goings on. Of course, beggars and rogues may for this reason have avoided using cant in public. In such a case, though cant might have a right to be thought a secret language, or, following Heller-Roazen perhaps, a secret use of language (Heller-Roazen 2013, 37), it would not be of any use in keeping things secret.

It is common for writers on canting to record the vexation of rogues and beggars at the publicity given to their secret talk. Thomas Harman wrote 'me thinketh I see how these peevish perverse and pestilent people begin to fret, fume, swear and stare at this my book, their life being laid open and apparently painted out, that their confusion and end draweth on a pace' (Harman 1567, sig. A3ʳ). This complaint is frequently repeated, very likely for reasons of self-advertisement, in books that purport to be exposures of rogueish tricks and language. Samuel Rid's *Martin Mark-all*, a reply to Thomas Dekker's *Belman of London*, makes it clear how a protective secret speech has actually become a liability for its users:

> yet such is the malice of some enuious il-willer of ours, that hath
> we know not how, not onely discouered our maners and fashions,

but also this our language and spéech, whereby we are often times ouer-hard, and taken and sent to prisons and tortures, and onely by our owne confessions, which we haue vttered in this our language, and which haue truste vnto vs boldly, as if wee had beene safe bolted in a Castle or strong hold. (Rid 1610, sig. C1^r-C1^v)

As late as 1673, one of Richard Head's informants for his *Canting Academy* told him 'that the mode of canting altered very often, and that they were forced to change frequently those material words which chiefly discovered their mysterious practices and villainies, lest growing too common their own words should betray them' (Head 1673, 56-7). This is just what one might expect in a language that was genuinely used for concealment; yet the canting dictionaries produced in the century following Thomas Harman, including Richard Head's own, show very little of this protective evolution, as they shamelessly raid and churn each other's wordlists and definitions. As Julie Coleman remarks, 'Anyone who actually wanted to converse in a secret language would have been well advised to avoid anything included in these works' (Coleman 2004, 187).

Cant, a word that itself belongs to canting, has other associations, beyond the signifying of a secret code. To cant also meant to speak in a particular high-pitched, wheedling whine that was believed to be characteristic of beggars and the act of begging. Harman actually uses the word canting as a synecdoche for begging, rather than as a term for the language of beggars, quoting the 'upright beggar' who uses his authority to declare formally to another 'hence forth it shall be lawefull for the to cante, that is to aske or begge, for thy liuing in al places' (Harman 1567, sig. B4^r). Robert Copland's evocation of the rogatory rituals of university and ecclesiastical begging suggests that this particular accent may have been derived from, or associated with the singing of Latin, which itself, in words like *patter*, from *paternoster*, and formulations like *hocus-pocus*, commonly glossed as an eroded form of *hoc est corpus*, suggested the sneaky weaving of verbal spells. Canting here is not so much a language as a kind of accent, a word the derivation of which, from *ad canto*, suggests a speech tending towards song, as in chant or incantation. This musicality may draw in another usage of the word cant, to mean list, leaning or camber, as of a road. The cant of the beggar is the verbal enactment of an attitude or posture of speech, which cooperated with the characteristic physical postures of the beggar, like the outstretched palm, the hands clasped in entreaty, or the fist driven into the bosom evoked by Copland. Rather than a language, canting is a kind of angling or disposing of language, which conveys meanings but also pulls away from the making of meaning into the performance of meaning-making. In his *Infidel Poetics*, Daniel Tiffany aligns this mode of speech with the seductive or mesmeric powers of the spell, charm or riddle, suggesting that

> The beggars' chant operates according to what may be called
> the "the logic of the lure." Anomalous, itinerant, promiscuous,
> the beggar's chant, as well as the space it engenders, calls
> forth erotics of social anonymity.… [T]he beggar's chant –
> a vexing, foreign sound – is a prelude to captivation, aiming
> to lure the stranger off course, to cull the anonymous mark.
> (Tiffany 2009, 147)

The erotics of the anonymity which the chant allows is, for Tiffany, the sign of
the potent obscurity represented by the beggar's discourse, an obscurity that
puts mendicancy into contact with secret underworlds and countercultures
that depend on not being easily legible by official cultures. But the anonymity
of the chant is surely also designed to make the beggar and the disturbing
act of begging recognisable. It is of a piece with the obsequious 'sorry for
troubling you today' with which a beggar may begin their spiel as they
approach you, reassuring you that this is not the terrifyingly immediate
and piercing proximity that the act of petition must always threaten, but in
fact recognisable and determinable as a petitionary act without the need
for any words in fact to be uttered or understood. Like many acts of social
ritualisation, the singsong of the beggar's canting mediates this immediacy,
sweetening its force, making it an anaesthetic repetition of a well-established
social form rather than an act with sets aside all social structures. It is a speech
act which is designed to avert itself.

The allegedly 'dark tongues' (Heller-Roazen 2013), or secret languages
of beggars embody something distinctly different from what they have
been regularly construed as, namely ways of maintaining an underworld of
outsiders, deviants and criminals free from legal oversight and interference.
They are in fact just the opposite of a means of concealment, for they are
part of the theatrics of beggary, a theatrics in which the constant exposure
of pseudo-secrets is entirely of the essence, for it is their exposure that
constitutes them as secrets, their dispelling that secures the dispersal of their
spell. Far from muttering and whispering surreptitiously, rogues are imagined
as roisteringly, liquidly loquacious: as Thomas Harman writes, 'At these
foresayde pelting penish places and vnmannerly, metings O how the pottes
walke about, their talkig tounges talke at large. They howle and bowse one to
another, and for the tyme bousing belly there' (Harman 1567, sig. B3ʳ).

Although the provision of cant glossaries becomes a regular feature of
rogue literature, there are very few examples to be had of canting understood
in this rhythmic or prosodic sense. It is the feigned distraction of the bedlam
beggar that is most likely to stimulate examples of begging discourse in action.
Thomas Dekker's *O Per Se O* sets out to describe what he calls the 'seuerall
gesture' of the Abram Man: 'some make an horrid noyse, hollowly sounding:
some whoope, some hollow, some shew onely a kinde of wilde distracted
vgly looke, vttering a simple kinde of *Mawnding*, with these addition of words

(*Well and Wisely*)' (Dekker 1616, sig. M2ᵛ). Dekker emphasises the deliberate incoherence of these actions, all of which 'shew them to be as drunke as Beggers: for not to belye them, what are they but drunken Beggers? All that they begge being eyther *Loure* or *Bouse*, (money or drinke)' ((Dekker 1616, sig. M2ᵛ). Dekker does not seem to be able to decide, or perhaps does not really want to be able to decide, whether being proverbially 'drunk as beggars' means really being drunk, or the intoxication of the pretence that will allow them to be drunk.

Dekker then provides an extended specimen of the style of the beggar's 'maund', or style of petition (this is not usual in writing on beggars, but Dekker is, after all, a writer for the stage):

> He first beginnes *Good Vrship. Maister, or good Vrships Rulers of this place, bestow your reward on a poore man that hath lyen in Bedlam without Bishops-gate three yeeres, foure moneths, and nine dayes, And bestow one piece of your small siluer towards his fees, which he is indebted there, the summe of three pounds, thirteene shillings, seauen pence, halfe-penny,* (or to such effect,) *and hath not wherewith to pay the same, but by the good help of Vrshipfull and well disposed people, and God to reward them for it.* (Dekker 1616, sig. M3ʳ)

Here, the numbing distraction is formed by the chains of pseudo-particularity, which diffuse attention, even as they draw it in: - so not just 'Bedlam', but 'Bedlam without Bishops-gate', and not just 'bestow your reward', amplified into 'bestow one piece of your small siluer', but help towards paying off the sum of 'three pounds, thirteene shillings, seauen pence, half-penny', the whole thing more suggestive of an invoice than an entreaty.

> The second beginnes: *Now Dame, well and wisely: what will you giue poore Tom now? one pound of your sheepes feathers to make poore Tom a blanket: or one cutting of your Sow side, no bigger then my arme, or one piece of your Salt meate to make poore Tom a sharing horne: or one crosse of your small siluer towards the buying a paire of Shooes, (well and wisely:) Ah, God blesse my good Dame (well and wisely) giue poore Tom an old sheete to keepe him from the cold, or an old dublet, or Ierkin of my Maisters, God saue his life.* (Dekker 1616, sig. M3ʳ)

Here the refrain 'well and wisely' turns the appeal into a song, something citational that floats equidistantly between beggar and begged, this assisted by the third-person self-distancing of the beggar. The whole performance is sealed by what Dekker calls his epilogue, which further diffracts the attention and generalises the encounter by the evocation of various absent but rhetorically attendant authorities:

> Then will he daunce and sing, or vse some other Anticke, and
> ridiculous gesture, shutting vp his counterfeite Puppet-play, with
> this Epilogue or Conclusion, *Good Dame giue poore Tom one cup of the*
> *best drinke, (well and wisely,) God saue the King and his Counsell, and the*
> *Gouernour of this place, &c.* (Dekker 1616, sig. M3ʳ)

The literature of roguery does more than to encourage dramatists to
incorporate beggars and beggary into their work, more even than to suggest
the elective affinities between vagrants and players. It creates its own
dramaturgy of beggary, a performative cycle in which rogue literature is as
much a scripting as a documenting of beggary and indeed in which the writing
of beggary operates on and in the social drama it creates. This intertwining of
action and representation begins with the chapter in Thomas Harman's *Caveat*
dealing with Nicholas Jennings, the 'Counterfet Cranke' (Harman 1567, sig.
D2ᵛ). Harman not only tells us that he interrupts the printing of his book to
investigate Jennings, he actually requisitions a couple of servant boys from the
printer to help conduct the pursuit (Harman 1567, sig. D3v). Harman thereby
documents in his own book the process of procuring the printer's help in
procuring his own copy.

   The documentation of beggars' cant brings out more metatheatrical
intertwining between acting and scripting. Thomas Dekker opens his
Lanthorne and Candle-Light with an elaborate fantasia of a rogues' parliament,
in the form of a brawling, brabbling, chaotic convocation of devils in
hell. Curiously, Dekker sets out this parliament as a papery rather than
parliamentary scene, figuring it as forgery effected through the devilishly
corporeal apparatus of writing:

> The Inck where-with they write, is the blood of Coniurers: they
> haue no Paper, but all things are engrossed in Parchment, and
> that Parchment is made of Scriueners skinnes flead off, after they
> haue béene punished for Forgerie: their Standishes are the Seuls
> of Vsurers: their Pennes, the bones of vnconscionable Brokers,
> and hard-hearted Creditors, that haue made dice of other mens
> bones, or else of periured Excecutors and blind Ouer-séeers, that
> haue eaten vp Widdowes and Orphanes to the bare bones: and
> those Pennes are made of purpose without Nebs, because they
> may cast Incke but slowly, in mockery of those, who in their life
> time were slowe in yéelding drops of pitty. (Dekker 1616, sig. C1ᵛ)

The parliament is interrupted by 'an intelligencer sent by *Belzebub* of *Batharum*,
into some Countries of christendome, to lye there as a Spie' (Dekker 1616,
C3r) who brings letters giving news of the revelations made about roguish
life by 'the Belman', or town crier, that is, Dekker himself, in his previous text
The Belman of London. The spy's letter represents the counter-spy who is the

Belman as a '*Childe of Darkenesse*' (Dekker 1616, sig. C2ᵛ), walking the night and knocking at doors to warn against roguery. Confirming the performative convention articulated by Daniel Heller-Roazen that 'each increase in the scholar's knowledge brings about a corresponding decrease in the effectiveness of the hidden tongue' (Heller-Roazen 2013, 37), the Belman's revelations are said to threaten the entire society of rogues/devils. The Belman

> had of late not onely drawne a number of the Deuils owne kindred into question for their liues, but had also (onely by the help of the lanthorn & candle) lookt into the secrets of the best trades that are taught in hell, laying them open to the broad eye of the world, making them infamous, odious, and ridiculous: yea, and not satisfied with dooing this wrong to his diuelship, very spitefullie hath hée set them out in print, drawing their pictures so to the life, that now a horse-stealer shall not shew his head, but a hailter with the Hang-mans noose is ready to be fastned about it: (Dekker 1616, sig. C3ʳ)

Following the Belman's revelations, canting will no longer be a means of disguise, but a means of recognition, interrogation and unveiling: 'A Foyst, nor a Nip shall not walke into a Fayre or a Play-house, but euerie tracke will cry, looke to your purses: nor a poore common Rogue come to a mans doore, but he shall be examined if hée can *cant*' (Dekker 1616, sig. C3ʳ). So the inquisition in the interest of beggarly belonging practised by the Upright Rogue on the aspirant beggar becomes an inquisition designed to detect this belonging. The letter ends with a warning about the threat offered by the Belman to the rogue-devils, in which the impersonations of the Belman are playfully confused with those he unmasks:

> if such a fellow as a treble voic'd *Bel-man,* should be suffer to pry into the infernall Misteries, & into those blacke Acts which command the spirits of the Déepe, and hauing sucked what knowledge he can from them, to turn it all into poison, and to spit it in the very faces of the professors, with a malicious intent to make them appeare vgly, and so to grow hatefull and out of fauour with the world, if such a coniurer at midnight should dance in their circles, and not be driuen out of them, Hell in a few yéers would not be worth the dwelling in. (Dekker 1616, sig. C3ᵛ)

O per se O is the title of Dekker's pamphlet, but also the name he adopts as the spy or secret agent, the '*disordered person*' (Dekker 1616, sig. C2ᵛ) whose designation itself rhymes with 'per se o', giving intelligence of the rogues' world. The phrase is a mingling of Latin and English, meaning simply 'O, on its own, or through itself'. The word *ampersand* includes the little tag 'per se', since it is a contraction of the form in which children would recite the end of the alphabet 'X, Y, Z and, per se "and" ', to signify the symbol &. *Per se* therefore functions as a rogue particle of learned language, set adrift from full understanding, in the devilish condition of Babelian fragmentation evoked by Dekker at the beginning of *O per se O*. Its comic diabolism is echoed in the 1616 text of Marlowe's *Doctor Faustus*, in which it functions as a magical formula read by the clown Robin from a conjuring book: 'ROBIN [*Reading*] "A" per se "a"; "t", "h", "e", "the"; "o", *per se* "o"; "deny orgon, gorgon"' (Marlowe 1999, 410). A little later in Marlowe's play, Dick and Robin together attempt to defend themselves from an angry vintner by drawing a magic circle that may be identified with the 'O' of their magical incantation, as well, of course, as with the 'O' of the stage, the scene of hollow utterance:

> ROBIN Dick, make me a circle, and stand close at my back, and stir not for thy life. [*As Dick draws the circle*] Vintner, you shall have your cup anon. Say nothing, Dick. 'O' per se 'O', Demogorgon, Belcher and Mephistopheles. (Marlowe 1999, 428)

The O is part of a play with vacuity and devilishness that resounds across writing in England in the early seventeenth century. The devil is identified as the nothingness of simulation, since, according to orthodox Christian doctrine, the devil could do nothing but simulate power. But simulation has a power in itself, the very power of signification signified by signs like 'O' that are both empty signs and signs of emptiness. In the formula adopted in Samuel Harsnett's richly theatrical denunciation of the false theatre of exorcism in his *Declaration of Popish Impostures*, '*O, that oh is the devil*' (Harsnett 1603, 261; Connor 2000, 169-72).

In all of this, the operations of parasitism are at work. If beggars' cant is a kind of parasitic language, then the commercial borrowing of it by the denouncers and lexicographers of beggary is a second-degree parasiting of that parasitism. Beggar and bellman each beg and borrow from the other. And this extends forward into the romantic evocations of 'lyric obscurity' and the ' "inner emigrants" of infidel society' celebrated by Daniel Tiffany (Tiffany 2009, 234).

Work for Idle Hands

One of the key pressure points in the simultaneous figuration and non-figuration of begging in the aversive images of beggary and the beggar is the question of work. Everywhere we hear of idleness as identical with and even definitional of beggary. All of this requires it to be held self-evident that begging is not labour, indeed is the active antagonist of labour, though that antagonism is of a curiously and conspicuously active kind. This may be one reason for the strange but insistent effacement of the action of begging from the figuration of beggary. For it is clear that begging is itself in fact a very exacting kind of labour, requiring the ability to endure privation and humiliation, and the development of professional skills of self-presentation. The scandal of beggary is not in fact that the beggar is idle but rather that they are so industrious in the determined maintenance of their idleness. The counterfeit of not working requires considerable investment in the labour of counterfeiting – a work that we might well call counterfaction. The sneering phrase 'sturdy beggar' proves accurate, for there is something markedly strenuous about everything concerned with beggary. Even the term vagrancy is an indication of the restless kinesis of the beggar's existence, an existence that beggars and their dramatists are joined together in forming and maintaining. The demise of the praying-mills that medieval monasteries had been gave way to a sort of outdoor mendicity-industry, which elaborately and indefatigably contradicted the fantasy ideal of productive work, with begging as the opposite it was designed to teach. At the heart of the new doctrine of work were the paradoxical thermodynamics of beggary, which threatened constantly to reveal the scandal that it was no longer possible to say quite what work was.

A key part of this imposture of indolence is the quasi-industrial organisation of beggars into what were commonly known as fraternities or companies. It is not very easy to see how beggars might benefit from such forms of organisation. Even if petty criminals and tricksters must often have benefited from working in consort with others, the act of begging seems essentially a solitary one, with much more advantage deriving from monopolising sources of profit than holding them in common. Despite this, beggars were routinely imagined to live and work in large groups, with clear hierarchies and distribution of roles. As William Carroll suggests, the popular understanding of the collective nature of begging means that '[c]riminal vagrants are thus seen to be essentially just another craft-guild in their organization' (Carroll 1996, 38). Beggars' assemblies were also described as regiments, colleges, parliaments and other sorts of organised corporations.

Once again, and as many have noted, the beggar who makes a profession out of his professing, of hunger, want or sickness, comes to resemble that other dubious Renaissance profession, of play-acting. The resemblance between beggar and actor may lie most essentially not in the fact that both make a living from imposture, but in the uncertainty that is thereby brought to bear specifically on the nature of the work that either might be said to do. The beggar is not pretending to do work that he is not really doing, but is really and in truth at work in the pretending in which he is engaged, an occupation in the business of idleness, and a vanity that is far from being in vain. The consternation of the beggar is not that he is seeking gain from idle dissimulation rather than recognisable and respectable work, but rather that his dissimulation so obviously consists of the same kind of work as that performed by actors. In the cases both of beggar and actor the work is an occlusive *labor celare laborem.*

Samuel Rid's *Martin Mark-all* includes a speech given in defence of beggars, unfairly condemned as people 'that liue by the sweat of other mens browes', which articulates the view that their work differs little from that of other trades, all of which involve forms of pretence and deception, such that 'he that cannot dissemble cannot liue' (Rid 1610, sig. B2ʳ). Rid's preface in fact toys with the possibility that the theatrics of beggary may indeed be a kind of idleness, in the sense not of unemployment, but wasted time, for all concerned:

> for mine owne part, if the inside of my labour cannot winne your content, let the outside of the subiect shew his authours intent. … Indeed Gentlemen this I doe confesse, I shall bring vpon this great Stage of fooles (for *omne sub Sole vanitas*) a peece of folly; if such as count themselues wise dare venter the reading of it ouer, I cannot let them, but when they haue perused it, and finde therein nothing but folly, let them reprehend neither the worke nor workemaster, but rather themselues, in that they would spend their time so foolishly, being before warned of so foolish and idle a subiect. (Rid 1610, sig. ¶2ʳ)

By 1652, Richard Brome's *The Jovial Crew* could make the analogy between the lucrative vacuity of the beggar's work and that of literary writing fully explicit. In his dedication to Thomas Stanley, Brome reminds him that 'we all know, *Beggars* use to flock to great mens Gates' and quibbles about the relations of work and debt in which the play involves him:

> I dare not say (as my Brethren use) that I present this, as a *Testimoniall of my Gratitude or Recompence for your Favours:* For (I protest) I conceive it so far from *quitting* old Engagements, that it *creates new.* So that, all, that this *Play* can do, is but to make more *Work;* and involves me in *Debts,* beyond a possibility of Satisfaction. (Brome 1652, sig. A2ʳ)

Brome goes on to represent his own formal act of meta-petition, by way of excusing it, in what is simultaneously a request and an offering:

> All the Arguments I can use to induce you to take notice of this *thing of nothing,* is, that it had the luck to tumble last of all in the *Epidemicall* ruine of the *Scene;* and now *limps* hither with a *wooden Leg,* to beg an Alms at your hands. I will winde up all, with a *Use* of *Exhortation, That since the Times conspire to make us all Beggars, let us make our selves merry;* which (if I am not mistaken) this drives at. Be pleased therefore, Sir, to lodge these harmlesse *Beggars* in the *Out-houses* of your thoughts; and, among the rest, Him, that in this

Cuckoe time, puts in for a Membership, and will fill the *Choyre* of those, that *Duly and truly pray for you*, (Brome 1652, sig. A2ᵛ)

Sophisticated Beggars

The dynamics of indigent display and the display of indigence always allow for a secret measure of affluence, if only in the belief in the ethical pedagogy that is always at work in the figure of the beggar. One of the most notable scenes of mendicant exposure and encounter embodies a higher-level set of reflections on the nature of ethical reflection itself. The story of Diogenes and Alexander, told so briefly by Diogenes Laertius, has been retold many times: 'When he was sunning himself in the Craneum, Alexander came and stood over him and said, "Ask of me any boon you like." To which he replied, "Stand out of my light" (Diogenes Laertius 1925, 41). The story dramatises the redistribution of worldly and spiritual wealth in the confrontation between the beggar and the ruler. A variation of the story of the meeting with Alexander has Diogenes counterposing imperial majesty and canine abjection: 'Alexander once came and stood opposite him and said, "I am Alexander the great king." "And I," said he, "am Diogenes the Cynic" [κύων, dog]' (Diogenes Laertius 1925, 63, 62).

Diogenes tells Alexander that the only gift he can give him is to get out of his light, 'ἀποσκότησόν μου'. As the beggar, Diogenes should give to the giver the gift of being able to display his wealth in giving, but in fact withholds that gift. Alexander puts himself in the place of the sun, capable of pouring out splendour without stint: but Diogenes's reply identifies him with the shadow obstructing the gift of light that is otherwise given everywhere for nothing. Diogenes here turns Alexander from the source of light into a photographic negative, all his power and wealth merely a sunspot or black hole. The thematics of light and shadow recur through the anecdotes told of Diogenes. Reproved for haunting unclean places, his reply was that 'the sun too visits cesspools without being defiled' (Diogenes Laertius 1925, 65). Diogenes was famous for the piece of performance art in which he carried a lit lantern around the marketplace in daylight, because, he said, he was looking for an honest man. Diogenes is beggarly not just in his refusal to live for gain, or to respect ownership, but also because his shamelessness is an affront to norms of visibility: like the beggar, the dog-like Diogenes, urinating and masturbating in public, admits no distinction between private impulse and public conduct. The shamelessness of cynicism has been advanced as part of an argument for its 'radically democratic character' (Locke 2016, 52).

Diogenes Laertius begins his life of Diogenes with the story that he fled the town of Sinope, where his father Tresius was a money-changer, after accusations of adulterating the coinage. It is suggested that Diogenes mistook the advice given to him by the Delphic oracle at Delos, in the words παραχαράττειν νόμισμα, 'alter the usages', since νόμισμα, that which is current, means both custom and coinage. παραχαράττειν is constructed from παρα, alongside, beyond + χαράσσειν, to stamp, brand, groove or incise, from χάραξ, a pointed stick, so implies rewriting or, more literally, 'recharacterising'. As νόμος, use, custom, from which νόμισμα derives, can also mean melody, composition, the oracle's advice might also be transposed into another key, as something like 'change the tune'. Diogenes Laertius repeats the story that

> When the god gave him permission to alter the political currency [τοῦ δὲ συγχωρήσαντος τὸ πολιτικὸν νόμισμα], not understanding what this meant, he adulterated the state coinage, and when he was detected, according to some he was banished, while according to others he voluntarily quitted the city for fear of consequences. (Diogenes Laertius 1925, 22, 23)

Diogenes is supposed to have mistaken the advice of the oracle, understanding literally what should be understood figuratively. But, since παραχαράττειν νόμισμα might also be glossed as 'change the meaning of these words', therefore enacting or exhorting the exchange between literal and figural currency in its own advice, it is not clear whether Diogenes has taken or mistaken the advice. As embodied in Diogenes, the corporeal philosophy of cynicism has few of the features that one might expect of a philosophical system. Cynicism is more of a philosophical style or posture than a system of reasoning. We are assured by various authors that Diogenes wrote books, but nothing of his philosophy has survived apart from the quips, retorts and *bon mots* that are assembled by Diogenes Laertius and others. Diogenes's philosophical practice, precisely insofar as it would be a practice rather than a theory of how to live a life according to nature rather than according to custom, may be regarded as, so to speak, a literalisation of the advice to change the metaphorical currency, or change the law of exchange. The exchange with Alexander is then a redoubling of that enactment, through its recharacterisation of the action of giving. Alexander's gift to the philosopher would turn him into a beggar; refusing the gift, Diogenes turns Alexander's offer of alms into an embezzlement of the dazzling benison of light.

Diogenes's inversive ethic of intellectual riches amid poverty is expressed in his saying: ' "All things belong to the gods. The wise are friends of the gods, and friends hold things in common. Therefore all things belong to the wise" ' (Diogenes Laertius 1925, 39). Elsewhere, he is credited with an excellent joke that draws together beggary and philosophy: 'Being asked why people give to beggars but not to philosophers, he said, "Because they think they may one day be lame or blind, but never expect that they will turn to philosophy" ' (Diogenes Laertius 1925, 57). Diogenes's cynicism involves a philosophical antagonism to formal philosophy, which at once harnesses the critical force of dialectic and disables it – this, very likely, being what Plato meant by calling him 'a Socrates gone mad' (Diogenes Laertius 1925, 55). 'To the man who said to him, "You don't know anything, although you are a philosopher" he replied, "Even if I am but a pretender to wisdom, that in itself is philosophy" ' (Diogenes Laertius 1925, 65-7). Diogenes is aware that, even at this early moment in the history of philosophy, a certain antagonism to philosophy is an authentic, and perhaps even inaugural, philosophical gesture. The condition of beggary is an image of the inextricability of philosophy from the many parasitic forms of thought that sit down alongside it. The recurrent gesture of disinfection whereby a philosophical system announces its emancipation from previous infestations of philosophical error or imposture, while inevitably continuing to display its own parasitic dependence on those inherited resources of thought, puts mendicant dependence and pretending at the heart of philosophy.

Though always liable to grandiose dreams of intellectual world-domination, philosophers remained close enough to traditions of religious thinking up until the end of the medieval period to find a more natural alliance with the outcast and the indigent. This alliance was assisted by identification between the figure of the wise beggar and the widespread cult, strongest in Christianity, but with corresponding forms in other religions too, of 'holy fools', whose apparent unworldliness and dedication to the life of the mind or spirit imparted to them a glow of sanctity, and made their witless unworldliness interpretable as a kind of wisdom. The philosophical life is thought of as sedentary, but we have noted already that medieval scholars often in fact lived vagrant lives, with scholars from Oxford and Cambridge being granted begging passports as they travelled to and from their universities. The essentially gratuitous nature of philosophy derives in part from the fact that it requires abstraction from the ordinary world of subsistence. Its dependence on economic surplus makes it an uncanny parallel to the below-subsistence surplus population represented in the figure of the beggar. Both scholar and scrounger are parasites on subsistence, for both depend on gratuity.

Begging is central to the practical wisdom taught in many religions, and perhaps nowhere more than in Buddhism. Zen monks, especially novice monks in training, practice *takuhatsu*, formalised actions of public begging wearing traditional costume. As in Franciscan mendicancy, begging is supposed to constitute a detachment from the pursuit of material well-being, as well as offering to others the opportunity to gain the merit that comes from generosity. Begging is a solution to one problem of asceticism among creatures who are so at home in the symbolic order, namely that ascesis can so easily become voluptuous, and therefore an excessive form of self-centredness. The enlightened one makes himself independent of attachments precisely by not seeking to make himself egotistically independent of them, for example by massing wealth and possessions, and prudently accepting the need for the limited, continually renewed attachment represented by dependence.

At the centre of Buddhist begging tradition is the emblematic alms-bowl, or *pâtra* of the Buddha. A substantial literature has grown up around this stage property, which serves to emblematise the condition of continent emptiness striven for in Buddhism. The legends of Buddha's life recount that the bowl was given to him by four maharajahs. The Japanese *Tripitaka* elaborates an account of the adventures of this alms-bowl after the death of Buddha. Buddha explains to an enquiring follower that, following a period of discord and contention after his death:

> The Holy phantom-dish will change its appearance and become visible; thus transformed, brilliant with the five colours, flying as it goes, ascending and descending, it will change the hearts of the people and bring back the multitudes who behold it to preserve the doctrines (virtues) of Buddha, and let go their folly. (Nutt 1889, 262)

Buddha prophesies that the bowl will in fact start to wander on its own account, visiting different countries in the East and converting the populations to an understanding of religious truth, coming to rest finally at the abode of the virtuous king of the East. But, following his death, discord and disrespect will again break out, and the bowl will be taken by heavenly dragons to a dwelling at the bottom of the sea, whence it can be raised only by further acts of piety (Nutt 1889, 262).

Not surprisingly, nineteenth-century commentators were struck forcibly by the parallel between the wanderings of the philosophical *pâtra* and the peregrinations of the Holy Grail following the death and ascension of Christ. The alternations between discord and enlightenment parallel the oscillations between the visibility and invisibility of the bowl itself.

The alms bowl or equivalent receptacle, whether it be plastic cup, cardboard box, pilgrim's wallet, the sack of the mendicant Friars of the Sack, or the extended pan of the panhandler, empty, or with a few paltry coins in it, remains both the symbol and instrument of begging all over the world. It is a formalisation of the hand, extended in appeal, and cupped to receive charity. It represents the visual paradox discussed at the beginning of this chapter of a vacuity made visible, or the substantial form of an absence. Probably its primary signification is in fact the empty belly of the supplicant. For the follower of Buddha, it signifies the nothingness and non-attachment to earthly things and provides the opportunity to alms-givers to gain merit through charity. The bowl might seem to reverse the conditions of a fetish as defined by Freud, the making positive of a lack through a material substitution, in which 'the horror of castration has set up a memorial to itself' (Freud 1953-74, 5.153), meaning that the fetishism derives its magical plenitude from the very lack that forms and suffuses it. The bowl appears to common sense as a physical object that has had a hollow space of containment scooped out from it. But this is reversible; it may also indicate the positivity of a kind of emptiness made substantial. The empty bowl signifies its own quasi-vacuity, the hollowing out of the material object by ideal non-attachment, and the release from suffering desire it is supposed to bring. But, in its apotheosis, radiating glory and moving about the world bringing about magical effects, the alms-bowl cannot but revert to the condition of fetish, the idolatry of the material made into agent. So, just as a beggar's bowl must alternate, like the human body it sustains, between fullness and emptiness, so the alms bowl signifies the alternation between fullness and absence that is a characteristic of the philosophical beggar, or the act of begging made philosophical. Philosophy represents itself, to itself as well as to others, as a discipline in humility, even as it dreams of a magical transfiguration of humility into moral or intellectual glory.

The figure of the poet also gains admittance to this assembly of parasitical charismatics. In the later work of W.B. Yeats, the visionary beggar is an image of the poet reaching beyond the workaday world of getting and spending:

> 'Time to put off the world and go somewhere
> And find my health again in the sea air,'
> *Beggar to beggar cried, being frenzy-struck,*
> 'And make my soul before my pate is bare.' (Yeats 1950, 128)

Begging, even in the form of the refusal of exchange in the Alexander-Diogenes story, nevertheless forms the bridge between material and intellectual affluence. The beggar-poet-philosopher may aspire to put off the world, but this remains a worldly venture, which must be underwritten in and by the world. Diogenes is paired with Alexander as negative to his positive through his recoil from him. The suggestion of their parallel existence, as potentate and doggy impotent, is embedded in the somewhat dubious tradition that Diogenes and Alexander died on the same day (Dudley 1937, 24). Diogenes's adulteration or revaluation of the currency of petitionary exchange in his encounter with Alexander does not in the least imply that he regards himself as above, or even beneath, the act of begging in general, for his willingness to beg from anyone and everyone who might give him what he needs is a central part of his philosophical performance of unashamed naturalness, in which it is as natural and so reasonable for a human to beg for what he needs as it is for a dog. For the cynic, being without shame is a paradoxical demonstration of the sovereignty of being above and beyond it. Indeed, the performative point is the demonstration of the beggarly dependence of Alexander on the idea of his own magnificence, of which the fantasy of being able with magical magnanimity to fulfil the wildest dreams of a beggar is an essential part. Diogenes's adulteration of the philosophical coinage of economics turns the emperor into the mendicant, begging in vain for the opportunity to prove his wealth and power.

Diogenes is one of many 'sophisticated beggars', to quote the allusion perhaps accidentally made in the title-song of Roy Harper's first album of 1966: 'I'm just a sophisticated beggar living underneath your summer day'. This is itself refracted through King Lear's words to Edgar on the heath: 'Here's three on's are sophisticated. Thou art the thing itself. Unaccommodated man is no more but such a poor, bare, forked animal as thou art' (Shakespeare 2011, 653). It is surely plain that Diogenes is himself as sophisticated and even sophistical a beggar as can be imagined. Like Edgar, he is forked in two senses, the corporeal – a torso bifurcating into two legs below the waist – and the figurative, in that he is costumed in the disguise of a naked indigent. So the sense in which he is a forked animal is itself forked, a word which undergoes interesting bifurcations through the works of Shakespeare (Dorfman 1994). For the intrinsically symbolic creature that a human being is, mendicity must always at least raise the possibility of mendacity, and Diogenes's unnecessary nakedness and poverty may be regarded as a form of open-air theatre, or pedagogic performance. Diogenes is not a dog, but a 'dog' – the claimant to a canine title, along with a power of self-designation, that must obviously and comically be unavailable to dogs themselves.

There is a long, and continuing, tradition that suggests that a certain kind of serenity attaches to the condition of the beggar who does not aspire to riches, but only subsistence. Cicero, in his *De finibus bonorum et malorum*, *On the Ends of Good and Evil*, disapprovingly quotes the view of the Stoic Zeno that the happiness that comes from wisdom is indivisible, and so not capable of being diminished by suffering: 'If poverty is an evil, no beggar can be happy, be he as wise as you like. But Zeno dared to say that a wise beggar was not only happy but also wealthy' (Cicero 214, 487). If Diogenes displays serenity, then it is of a notably spiky, irascible and resentful kind. Diogenes does not depend on charity, but his philosophy does depend on the display of his intellectual independence in his apparent material dependence. The regular, or honest-to-goodness beggar depends on his manifestation of dependence on the act of begging; unless I beg, I will be nothing at all. The philosophical beggar depends on the exhibition of his independence from that dependence; I beg in order to show that begging is nothing at all, and thereby to secure my transcendence of its triviality.

The idea that beggary might afford opportunities for the pedagogic display of wisdom takes another form in the stories that are designed to teach that one should always be generous to beggars lest they turn out to be angels or even gods in disguise. Odysseus's return to Ithaca in books 17 and 18 of the *Odyssey* disguised as an aged beggar by Athena is an early narration of this cooperation of inward power and outer weakness. In Ovid's frequently-reworked story of Baucis and Philemon in Book 8 of his *Metamorphoses* (Ovid 1916, 449-57), the two poor cottagers Baucis and Philemon are the only ones to offer hospitality to Jupiter and Mercury, travelling disguised as beggars, for which the entire country is punished by being destroyed in a flood; only

Baucis and Philemon's cottage is spared the flood, and is transformed into a magnificent temple.

In all these cases, the uncertainty that attaches to the figure of the beggar is the source of the uncanny possibility that they may in fact be an embodiment of power, whether intellectual, worldly, or divine. In the course of the modest repast Baucis and Philemon put together for the disguised gods, a miracle suddenly occurs: 'the mixing-bowl, as often as it was drained, kept filling of its own accord, and that the wine welled up of itself. The two old people saw this strange sight with amaze and fear, and with upturned hands they both uttered a prayer' (Ovid 1916, 453). The magic power of spontaneous refilling – 'cratera repleri/sponte sua per seque vident succrescere vina' (Ovid 1916, 452) – is an internal doubling of the old couple's act of spontaneous generosity, which is prolonged into an act of self-engendering. But it is also a mark of the transformation of the currency, which promises to exchange the deficit of giving into spiritual profit. The charisma of the philosophical beggar borrows, or perhaps simply purloins, this promise of magical credit that is embodied in the figure of the angelic-divine beggar, who, it is promised, will give you back your giving tenfold.

Obviously, wisdom is different from wealth, and is often represented as its antithesis; but they can also be seen as equivalent, with the dissimulated wisdom of the beggar being thought of as a kind of opulence in itself. Indeed, one might say that the figure of the philosophically-dissimulating beggar is the very means whereby wealth is supposed to be coined from wisdom, or wisdom construed as a kind of wealth-beyond-wealth.

In a world wrestling simultaneously with the stubborn irreducibility of poverty, and also with the many unsuspected and unaccountable agonies of affluence, destitution continues to have a charismatic power of fascination equivalent to the fascination with kingship of the Renaissance. The gaunt afflatus of this bare life is always available for the philosopher, or rather an ascetic *eidos* of the philosophical, to beg, steal and borrow. The philosopher, in all his embodiments, as saint, poet, artist, borrows from the beggar the art and expectation of living without visible means of support, sustained only by the mystical credit of their unworldliness, our belief in their belief in themselves. At the heart of this enterprise is the magical offer to change the currency, coining sovereignty from dependence.

4
Political Petition

Petitions and petitioning have been part of systems of government in most systems of which we have knowledge, and for much longer than we might imagine. Wherever there are holders of power, protocols seem to arise by which petitioning approaches may be made to it. Lex Heerma van Voss goes so far as to propose that 'petitions seem to be a global phenomenon, stretching back in time almost as far as writing' (Voss 2001, 2). Writing has a large part to play in the social performance of petition, but it would be safe to assume that there are protocols of petition in every society in which there are dynamic divisions of power between the rulers and the ruled, that is, in which those ruled must also be made the subjects of rule. Petition has an essential role in mediating between laws and norms and their applications. Petition prompts adjudication, and vice versa. Any rule which must not only be held abstractly to apply, but needs also concretely to be applied, by imperfect and unpredictable actors, in contingent and mutable circumstances, will allow for and produce the action of petition, arising from dispute or disagreement as to how the law has been applied. So, seen in the largest sense, petition has an essential role in any social arrangement governed by laws, norms or rules which cannot be counted on to be self-applying and self-interpreting, and in which there is consequently room for dispute or discontent; which is surely to say, in any social arrangement whatsoever. No law can legislate for itself; no government can govern its own government. Of course it is possible for a tyrant or tyranny simply to act, violently and arbitrarily, on the basis of pure dominion, but this is not what is meant by law or government, both of which are subject to the condition of internal defect which means that their coherence or self-identity must always be secured by remedial supplements. Petition is both the evidence of that constitutive defect, for petition points to the gap between law and the law of law, and the attempt to make it good.

Gwilym Dodd has argued that a considerable part of the everyday business of medieval parliaments in Britain consisted of the processing of petitions, which were largely private, and of two principal kinds – complaints, relating to injustices, and requests, typically for some kind of royal favour, such as a grant, office or pardon (Dodd 2007, 1-2). This distinction, between 'justice' and 'grace', is a feature of many petitionary systems. Petitions were both requests that went beyond the normal systems of determination and distribution, in the exercise of 'discretionary justice', and part of the everyday workings of government, making for what might seem like, but seem rarely to have been experienced as, a legality of regulated exceptions and anomalies.

From around the beginning of the fifteenth century, the form and practice of the petition began to move away from acts of private and informal begging, supplication or entreaty, typically in the action of religious prayer, towards actions of a more formal and public kind, almost always presented in written form, and increasingly issued by or on behalf of collectivities rather than individuals. Peter Fraser is among those who have identified a move away from private to collective petitions in British politics, a move which may be seen as an absorption of petitioning into the system of democratic representation. Fraser sees this change as beginning during the reign of George III, writing that 'while there were innumerable private petitions to Parliament (representing the grievances of every kind of individual person or institution) in the country before 1779, one has to search hard to find anything resembling political petitioning' (Fraser 1961, 201). However, in the decades following the writing of these words, historians have detected and discussed much more evidence of political petitioning in earlier periods. R.W. Hoyle maintains that, during the sixteenth century, 'there was a constant stream of members of the commons petitioning government for the exercise of its discretion. This was the small change of government: petitions, whether from villages, towns, commercial interests or groups among the commons such as weavers, were read and acted upon as appropriate' (Hoyle 2002, 389). When large groups of people gathered to formulate and deliver petitions, and refused to disperse until they had received an answer, as sometimes occurred, petitioning could edge alarmingly close to sedition (Hoyle 2002, 389). These kinds of gathering mark the characteristic development of petition from individual to collective forms, as well as marking a kind of involution into self-reference, as the making of the petition comes to be as important for the petitioners, or even, in time, more important, than its effect.

As a noun, petition, modelled on Anglo-Norman *peticion*, was used in English from the early 1400s to name both the act of requesting or entreating and, from around 1450, the thing petitioned for. At the beginning of the seventeenth century, petition transitioned (like *transition* itself later on) into a verb, replacing the phrase 'make petition'. Increasingly from this point on, rather than to perform an individual act of begging or entreaty, to petition generally means to present a formal written petition or application to a particular authority, an authority, what is more, that might be specifically required and even constituted to respond to such petitions.

There has been extensive interest among historians in the political work performed by petitions. Many have seen in petitions an opportunity to assess the ways in which ordinary citizens, outside the circuits of power, have been able to articulate their concerns and grievances. Petitions therefore seem to give a sense of the irregular texture of social and political life. Collective petitions seem increasingly to be identified not so much with requesting as with pleading, in the juridical sense of complaining, or asserting different kinds of claim. It is tempting in fact to see the history of petitioning as a proxy for acts of political self-assertion in general, through objection, resistance and proposed reform. In the process, it might seem as though the act of petition, in the sense in which it is under examination in this book, shrivels to a mere framework or formality. Nevertheless, I want to propose that some kind of tension remains in play between the raw or primitive force of petition, as a suspension of legality and the assertion of what is 'due', and the forms of political assertion through recognised channels and procedures, giving to these communicative actions their particular tonality.

At early stages of the law pleading must often have entailed an oral action, in which somebody would bring their appeal or complaint to open court. John Baker maintains that, though oral pleading of this kind had actually been forbidden by the middle of the seventeenth century, oxymoronically enough 'the process whereby pleading was formalised into an exchange of documents occurred without leaving a mark on the face on the record' (Baker 2003, 335). Nevertheless, the plaint, plea, or petition retains some part of the intense, intimate and risky immediacy of their appeal. The essence of pleading, plaint and petition is that they are painful, and they are the enactment of pain itself. The petitioner may, through the very fact of appeal, the calling by name of the one petitioned, invoke their station and reputation, but in doing so they also annul all distance and indirection. The petition always aims in part to borrow the urgency and immediacy of prayer, with its promise of direct access to the merciful and bountiful ear of the deity, in the process cutting through the deceits and delays of worldly existence. We will see that, in the case of the political petition, its force and meaning derived from the short-circuiting of bureaucratic impediment, and the pleat in administrative space it provided through the direct access of the periphery to the centre.

The exercise of the right to petition and, as a consequence, the subjection of the monarch to the duty of entertaining it, is a crucial aspect of kingship. A just king must ensure that laws are applied justly, but that can only be guaranteed if the king is granted the power to set aside the laws he in his person guarantees, and perhaps can only guarantee because of this excessive power and power of excess. It is necessary, that is, that the king have the power to go beyond strict necessity. Just as petitioners are dependent upon the figure of the king, as a court of final appeal, so, somewhat more surprisingly, kingship is dependent upon the exercise of petition, and the exercise of exceptional powers it allows, powers that are both circumscribed by, and yet also uncontained by law. It appears that the belief in the power of the sovereign to grant petitions, as a secular analogy of the power of God, or intercessive fairy godmother, to grant wishes, remained strong, perhaps because the institution of sovereignty itself exists in part to fulfil the wish for there to be a wish-granting authority that goes beyond established or customary authority. This may be part of what George Orwell notes in 1947 as the survival of the 'idea almost as old as history, the idea of the King and the common people being in a sort of alliance against the upper classes' (Orwell 1947, 25).

In England, petitioning of the king seems, if not to have arisen for the first time, then markedly to have accelerated in the late thirteenth century, during the reign of Edward I, from 1272 to 1307. In later centuries, it would often be asserted that Edward formally proclaimed a right to petition at some point during his review of administration he undertook following his accession to the throne in 1272, though no such proclamation has yet been discovered. Nevertheless, it does seem likely that some kind of formal permission-solicitation to subjects to petition parliament must have been issued, or been understood as having been issued, in order to bring about the sudden increase in petitions to parliament that undoubtedly occurred during the later 1270s. Gwilym Dodd suggests that petitioning performed two important, but contrasting political functions for the Crown. First of all, it provided a proof of the willingness of the king to accept the duty of ensuring the administration of justice impartially to all his subjects: prior to his coronation, there had been widespread discontent at the inefficiency and corruption of regional officials. But secondly, it also provided a highly effective way of consolidating the authority and reach of the Crown. Dodd argues that 'large-scale petitioning in parliament represented an important stage in the growth and influence of the late medieval English state' (Dodd 2011, 33).

In fact, it would take centuries for anything like a formal right to petition to be established. During the turmoil of the middle years of the seventeenth century, collective petitioning, and more particularly the action of assembling in order to form and deliver a petition, came to seem threatening. Following a number of royalist petitions in 1648, Parliament issued a declaration 'For the suppressing of all Tumultuous Assemblies, under pretence of framing and presenting petitions to Parliament', which limited the number of persons presenting a petition to twenty. Following the Restoration, this number was reduced to ten, in a 1661 'Act against Tumultuous Disorders Upon Pretence of Preparing or Presenting Petitions or other Addresses to his Majesty or the Parliament'. It was not until the Bill of Rights in 1688 that the formal pronouncement was made that 'it is the right of subjects to petition the King, and all commitments and prosecutions for such petitioning are illegal ' (Knights 2018, 21-2). Nevertheless, there were still obstacles and resistances to be overcome and this right cannot be regarded as guaranteed in practice until the beginning of the eighteenth century.

Nevertheless, the growth in England of the myth of the 'right to petition' turns what was very likely a rather uneven and not coherently intended development into something with mystically inaugural force, inauguration being perhaps the most mystical idea of all in the human imagination, given that no human being has ever been present at their own individual beginning.

Although petition is dangerous because it always in fact gives itself its own right, arbitrarily and necessarily in excess of the ordinary operations of law, it appears that, not only in England, but across Europe, 'petitioning remained, in practice, an unquestionable custom, despite the lack of a positive right to petition', as Andreas Würgler claims (Würgler 2001, 30-1). To lay claim to a right to petition is to recruit for this potentially anarchic force (anarchic meaning lawless because without the legitimating authority of an *arché*, or beginning) a prior legitimation in law. Monarch and commoner both gain from this myth, for the commoner can thereby count on an imaginary permission to diminish to nothing the otherwise infinite distance from kingship, and the monarch can maintain the credit of broaching and sustaining this channel of approach. It is another of the many ways in which monarchy makes itself powerful through imaginary means, subjecting itself to the anarchic provision of a meta-legal right of legal remedy that exists before and beyond law.

The religious dimensions of petition were unmistakable, especially given the fact that the monarch tended to reserve for himself, or to have set apart for him, the power to grant petitions, for mercy or special kinds of favour, that were not based on judgements of equity. As Andreas Würgler observes, writing specifically of a German context but probably with much more general application, '[t]he rulers' power of grace and mercy echoed God's mercy towards repentant sinners and conferred metaphysical legitimation' (Würgler 2001, 15). The most important aspect of the imaginary mechanism of petition is the capacity it gives the monarch to ally himself with the force of pathos, the ambivalent lawful-lawless power to moderate law, or restore law to its proper self-resemblance once it has been corrupted. The power of pathos over law can operate only because pathos can form no part of it, law being unable to operate lawfully on the basis of passion or sympathy. The operation of the infinite and exceptionless mercifulness often confidently attributed to God would have to be identical with injustice itself; when everyone can guarantee that merciful exceptions will be made in their case, no judgement will be possible.

The extraordinary prevalence and persistence of the petition even, and perhaps especially, in the most 'heartless' and abstractly rationalised systems of government suggests its general role in joining administration to affect. Christina Schwenkel, writing specifically of bureaucratic conventions in contemporary Vietnam, offers the phrase 'rule by sentiment' (Schwenkel, 2015, 212). She concludes her essay by asking 'What does it mean for a petition to be effective and to act with agentic capacity?' (Schwenkel 2015, 223), and offers the following affirmation:

> While the petitions submitted by residents in social housing did not achieve their desired results, they did succeed in enabling petitioners to become more visible political actors whose strategies of mimicking the bureaucratic state enabled

a prolonged conversation with local government through the
circulation of documents. (Schwenkel 2015, 223).

The terms of her question make it self-answering: what it means for a petition
to give agency is that it gives agency – or at least the feeling of agency,
brought about through the agency of feeling. But this universal explanation
is itself in need of explanation. What does that feeling of agency mean? Rule
by sentiment in fact depends on particular sentiments, especially those of
compassion and sympathy, which may be summarised with the term pathos.
But what is the agency of pathos?

Pathos belongs to the register of feeling, but is not itself directly a feeling,
like rage, fear or contentment. Pathos is in fact something more like a meta-
feeling, a feeling occasioned by, or urging us towards, feeling. If a story, or
scene or human circumstance evokes pathos, it means that it seems to
demand a kind of compassionate or sympathetic feeling-with. The pathos of a
situation is not anything that one should feel about it, but rather the abstract
impulsion to feel something about it – to be, as we instructively say, 'moved'.
It would make no sense for me to say that I myself felt 'pathos' or 'pathetic' in
relation to the story of an orphaned child, or bereaved mother, because the
pathos inheres in the story or circumstance. The exhortatory force of pathos
explains why it is used to characterise that which in a drama urges or awakens
feeling, rather than a particular feeling in itself. Among social creatures, all
feelings have a tendency and even a kind of implicit intention to move others
to imitation of the feeling, but the complex state known as pathos makes this
injunction to the passage and sharing of feeling much more explicit. Pathos
does the work it does in petition because the demand to feel amplifies the
demand being made by the petition, while also deflecting it from the petition
itself to the state of feeling it may evoke. So the feeling, of sympathy, or fellow-
feeling, seems to be making the demand.

But the power of pathos does not rest all on the side of the petitioner,
because the petition itself also depends upon the power of pathos it attempts
to deploy. This is the sense in which the one petitioned also gains a dividend
from the injunction to feeling contained in the pathos, as it circulates between
petition, petitioner and petitioned. The one who yields to the petition, or
even simply exhibits their capacity for yielding, gathers charisma from this
very capacity to temper, or partly to relinquish power in the face of pathos.

The reason that God can temper justice with mercy without thereby
becoming unjust is because God is outside law, even if he decrees and
indemnifies it. The sovereign or other authority who is the subject of petition
can be because they similarly stand above or aside from the everyday
operations of the law. They cannot modify the law, or create new laws, by
their responses to petitions since their power consists essentially in suspending
laws or setting them aside. This condition of being above the law, or, since he
does not constitute a supreme court or superior authority, beside it, gives hope

and opportunity to the petitioner, just as it confers a gratifyingly gratuitous immunity to the petitioned ruler. Cecilia Nubola explains the implications of this condition of exception in early modern Italian states:

> [T]he prince should not be confused with the body of tribunals, parliaments, and magistracies of any degree. This may partially explain why, in the petitions and supplications, also in moments of serious conflict (e.g. in cases of revolt or rebellion), it is excluded outright that the prince be held directly responsible for the injustices that are the cause of the rebellion. All the responsibility must fall upon persons and positions of lower standing (corrupt officials), while the relationship of trust and of filial obedience with the prince is to be preserved and confirmed. Laws, regulations, and officials can be unjust and corrupt – never the prince. (Nubola 2001, 37)

R.W. Hoyle has shown how, during the reign of James I, who seems to have had a very strong tendency to be generous beyond his means in response to petitions for position and preferment, it proved necessary to establish a set of guidelines to rein the king in, for example through the issuing of *A Declaration of His Majesties Royall Pleasure* (1610), known colloquially as *The Book of Bounty* (Hoyle 2011, 560). Despite the fact that petitions were supposed to be filtered through officers known as 'Masters of Requests', it remained common for petitioners to wait for the monarch on the way to chapel, which was the accepted place to present petitions to him. (Hoyle 2011, 555). Despite, or even on account of, the shared belief in the power of the king to go beyond everyday structures of resource distribution, supplying 'grace' rather than merely the adjustments of 'justice', the tendency was for the king to become 'a "service monarchy" satisfying a range of needs for its subjects, from the granting of legal rights to the resolution of disputes' (Hoyle 2011, 544). But monarchs have often, consciously or not, attempted to resist this reduction to bureaucratic function, through the charisma granted by their power to grant petitions that bypass these mediating channels.

This shared state of anomaly therefore establishes a striking analogy between petitioner and petitioned. By humbling themselves before an absolute power, the petitioner gave themselves the chance of an act of grace that would advance their situation far beyond might reasonably be expected. By subjecting themselves to the requirement of being open to petitions, the ruler themselves attained to a kind of grace, in their very power to render themselves subject to the power of petition. In both cases, petition provides a route to power through unpowering.

However it may seem to go beyond or beneath customary structures, the petition always contains its own forms of mediation. Indeed, there is something paradoxical in all petition, which, in citing or recalling the primary appeals or demands of the child, issued in the form of the spontaneous and inarticulate cry rather than in fully-formed language, simultaneously asserts its absoluteness and compromises it: the *hic et nunc* immediacy of petition is always in fact a repetition of this primary kind of infant demand, and so never absolutely *hic* or *nunc*.

It is this residue that establishes the power of the petition to transform weakness into strength. As one might expect, petition is usually more common and more effective among social groups who already enjoy certain levels of privilege or advantage. At the same time, the particular condition of petition, as Roger Gomm's 'bargaining from weakness' (1975), or the negotiation from, and therefore to some extent with, disadvantage, could give opportunities to groups such as women who traditionally had much less secure access to redress and self-representation. Marcia Schmidt Blaine concludes her study of female petitioners in eighteenth-century New Hampshire, for example, with the judgement that

> Women understood their qualifications as petitioners and their rights before the government. Using societal assumptions of dependence and helplessness in their communications with the government, women were able to use the traditional language of petitioning to put forward their individual needs and demands, all within the acceptable bounds of patriarchy. (Blaine 2001, 77)

But the most important form of mediation at work in petition is the fact that it comes more and more to be expressed in writing rather than direct speech. The fact that literacy has been a minority accomplishment until relatively recent times means that for centuries it was necessary to enlist the service of scribes to draw up petitions. Benjamin Kelly argues for this reason forcibly against using petitions such as those that survive from the period of Roman rule in Egypt of the first century CE in order to provide any kind of access to the voices of ordinary and otherwise excluded people:

> In most cases, it is simply impossible to tell whether we are hearing the 'voice' of the petitioner, or that of the scribe, or whether we are hearing an echo of discourses that were common in scribal and legal culture, and simply repeated through force of habit, without necessarily representing the innermost mentalities of either petitioner or scribe. (Kelly 2011, 38-9)

The constraints of writing have often been used to place limits on the power of the beggar, or to ensure that their petitions are honest and justifiable. But these very constraints can also provide kinds of impetus or advantage to the petitionary act. We saw in chapter 3 that the issuing of licences as part of the effort to control begging and vagrancy in Tudor England led quickly (and, we might now think, predictably) to an industry of forged licences. Similarly

discreditable uses of false accreditation are still in use among those 'on the
knock' in London, going from door to door aggressively selling inferior but
highly-priced household goods.

Clara Devlieger has described an ingenious set of variations on this practice
among contemporary disabled beggars in Kinshasa, in the Democratic
Republic of Congo, which develops the strategy very considerably. These
beggars are known, somewhat sardonically, as '*batu basalaka documents*', those
who 'do documents', or, borrowing some ironic force from the official aroma
of the French term, *documentaires*. Their practice is not to appeal for alms
directly, but to flourish a document of some kind, purporting to confirm that
they are collecting for a particular praiseworthy purpose. Donors are given in
return a copy of the document as a kind of receipt, which may mean they are
immune from being requisitioned for a certain period. The aim, Devlieger
argues, is to take some of the sting out of the petitionary or solicitational
demand by framing it as a kind of transaction, deriving its authority, not
from traditional kinds of moral or religious duty, but from the abstract
distributive transactions characteristic of a secular society that would like to
be seen as dedicated to social welfare: 'Presenting themselves as an NGO,
the "receipt" beggars gave was meant to represent an understanding between
the beggars, the donor, and (implicitly) the government, thus legitimizing the
act of begging by imitating the practices of a state bureaucracy' (Devlieger
2018, 456-7). Such practices exhibit a characteristic alloy of the deflection and
intensification of aggression, in what Devlieger characterises as a mixture of
'force, negotiation, and performance' (Devlieger 2018, 457). If the acting out
of a reciprocal relationship between beggar and donor blunts some of the
offence of a highly invasive and unidirectional personal appeal, it also creates
a framework of expectations that in its turn allows for levels of harassment that
make the petition hard to distinguish from a protection racket: 'A donor paid
their dues, and in return the beggars agreed to leave them alone for a year'
(Devlieger 2018, 465). Documentation is essential to the reconstitution of the
demand into a negotiated condition in which '[o]bligation and debt became
matters of regulation, allowing for a temporally regulated relationship with
a donor, translating the act of begging into mutually acceptable, legitimate
"disability taxes" ' (Devlieger 2018, 464).

David Zaret has pointed to the role of printing in widening the address
and audience of petitions:

> Beyond facilitating greater access to petitions for readers and
> signers, printing transformed the content of petitions by orienting
> their production to ongoing public debates and readers of printed
> texts as devices that constituted public opinion for the purpose of
> influencing individual opinions. Communicative change thus has
> strong implications for the "invention" of public opinion as both
> a nominal and real category of social life. (Zaret 1996, 1526)

Petitions thereby involve ever more complex kinds of addressivity. The petition aims at getting a hearing from the one petitioned, but more and more aims also to be 'overheard' by others. In the process, it aims to make clear to the one petitioned that their response will similarly be overheard by those listening in on, or listening out for, it. Printed petitions 'appeal to an anonymous audience, a public, to whom reasons are given in support of divergent political positions. Political discourse now presupposes a public competence not simply to understand but also to make normatively binding judgments on rival political claims' (Zaret 1996, 1541).

As petitions become more formalised and mediated, their point and purpose can shift markedly; there may be progressively less confidence that the body petitioned will grant the petition, with more and more value attaching to the politically solidifying effects of preparing and submitting it. The purpose of the petition thereby becomes ever more self-referential, eddying backwards from outcome to preparatory process. The purpose of a petition becomes essentially to construct, prepare and exhibit the act of petitioning. Massive petitions like those organised by the Chartists functioned essentially as spectacular forms of demonstration, the petition of 1842 containing more than 3 million signatures, which was six miles long and weighed 6 hundredweight, being formally processed through the streets to Parliament (Pickering 2001, 368). It seems clear that, although petitioning was at the centre of the Chartist movement for political reform, there was little expectation that petitions would bring success through being granted (Chase 2019, 532-3). Indeed, there is a sense in which the potency of petitioning depended on the assumption that the petition would fall on deaf ears. Francis Place wrote of a petition of 1811 to free the radical reformer Francis Burdett from imprisonment

> It was a matter of indifference to a large body of the electors what the House did with the petition ... Many wished the House to reject it, as then another meeting would be held. What was most desired was a wrangle in the House. Everybody knew that as far as the House was alone concerned it was useless to petition it ... But the House was the best vehicle through or by which the people could be addressed, and a wrangle in the House when reported in the newspapers was sure to fix the attention of the people on our proceedings. (BL Add MSS 27850, p. 218, quoted Fraser 1961, 208)

Paul A. Pickering concludes similarly that '[f]or the Chartists petitioning was, first and foremost, part of the dramaturgy of demotic politics where its function and benefits were extra-parliament' (Pickering 2001, 378), and Malcolm Chase agrees about the force carried by 'the visual and moral theater of the petitioning process' (Chase 2019, 546).

Petitioning has often been thought to diminish with the consolidation of democratic processes, such as the extension of the franchise, as though petition performed the function of what democratic institutions are assumed to supply in a more formal or abstract fashion. Indeed, the history of petition suggests that it may have a larger or more general function of opening the way for such functions, and thereby rendering petition itself unnecessary, this being particularly the case when what is being petitioned for are themselves democratic rights. As Paul A. Pickering observes, in the case of petitions which demand voting rights or other rights of representation, as in the case of Chartism or women's suffrage petitions, '[s]igning a petition was an analogue of voting that was often regarded as precious in its own right' (Pickering 2001, 376). This makes the petition a kind of self-granting action – a formalised and aggregated appeal for the right to vote which awards itself what it seeks in the very voting procedure the petition mimics. These growing forms of self-reference in the petition resemble the shift from direct address to reflexivity that we will find in the form of the prayer, and account for the substitute gratification that a petition may constitute, especially if it is refused, for the one petitioned is thereby convicted of having ignored what looks like a popular vote.

The autotelic tendency of the petition is embodied most powerfully in the increasing emphasis on the gathering of signatures, or 'hands', as they were commonly known in the sixteenth and seventeenth centuries. The number of signatories seems to provide a scalable measure of the moral force of a petition, with the very measurability itself adding a measure of force to it. This quantified store, the very quality of being quantifiable I have called 'quantality' (Connor 2016, 20-52), gives to the petition the sense of unanswerable rightness, whatever its actual success, and, like the beating of drums by an advancing army, gives that army a sense of the power of its very undifferentiatedness, a large number of distinct agents surrendering their distinctness in their unified cause. This emphasis on the accumulation of numbers rather than the perfecting of arguments is a particular feature of nineteenth-century petitions in Britain. There was a growing emphasis on the necessity of continual increase in numbers, along with, in the case of Corn Law petitioning in the 1830s and 1840s, the phenomenon of counter-petitions, with rivalry resulting between the different parties (Miller 2012, 890-2). The 'monster petitions' of Chartism, so-called originally, no doubt, because of the magnitude of their monstration rather than their monstrosity, were achieved by the tactic of funnelling together many signatures from different localities in support of the same demand prior to the submission of the petition (Pickering 2001, 372). The size of petitions in the nineteenth century was matched by their numerousness: between 1838 and 1843, the most intense years of Chartist petitioning, 94,000 separate petitions were laid before Parliament (Pickering 2001, 369).

It would be easy to see the history of the petition as a steady and uninterrupted move away from spontaneous and asymmetrical appeal to strongly conventionalised, shared interlocution. As with other kinds of painful or vehement human encounter, we would certainly expect a tendency for petitionary form progressively to soothe and diffuse the force of petition. James A. Jaffe finds in his survey of petitioning in colonial India just such a steady drift from 'supplicatory and submissive rhetoric' (Jaffe 2019, 595) to the 'language of procedural, or adjectival, justice' (Jaffe 2019, 589). He concludes that, by the middle of the nineteenth century, petitions had become 'systematized and bureaucratized', and were 'almost completely shorn of the languages of obedience and deference', meaning that 'the customary language of petitioning had all but disappeared by mid-century and given way to a modern bureaucratic discourse' (Jaffe 2019, 592).

In fact, though, the history of petition is better grasped as an unstable oscillation between asymmetrical, self-inaugurating and self-legislating appeal and the kind of negotiated, symmetrical interlocution in which the needs and benefits of petitioner and petitioned are locked tightly together. Just as collective petitions moved during the nineteenth century toward the condition of the political demonstration, so perhaps the demonstration has taken the place of the petition from the twentieth century onwards. It might seem as though this process has removed the last traces of pathos which lingered in the petition, with supplication giving way entirely to the defiant and determined framing of demands. ('What do we want?'; 'When do want it?') However, the potency of weakness has proved difficult to dispense with altogether, and petitionary elements survive and are regularly revived in the theatrics of the demonstration.

There is first of all the fact of theatricality itself. Participants in a demonstration may well derive huge strength and a sense of resolution from being part of an indomitable army on the march, even if demonstrations are in fact normatively peaceful (a norm that is not always observed), keeping their aggression in check precisely through the exhibition of their being placed on exhibition. The members of a demonstration are exposed to a public and appraising gaze just like the beggars with whom they share the urban streets. Those who participate in a demonstration or manifestation are making manifest, among other things, their compulsion to take this public action, their choice to surrender choice in the face of some commanding cause they are determined to show that they are unable to endure or ignore. The very collectivity of the demonstration is a coercive display of the coercion of each member into collectivity by their cause, their choice of having to be compelled to join the demonstration. Demonstrations, along with petitions, often accompany strikes, and indeed the demonstration displays something of the carnival logic of busily industrious inaction of the strike (Connor 2019, 110-12). When demonstrations provoke reactions from police or security services, the actions of demonstrators, or rather their tendency to the kind of passive inaction that means they have to be dragged into the police van, often seem intended to demonstrate helplessness in the face of brutality rather than coordinated power, thereby demonstrating that demonstrators have a grievance as well as a demand, the former potentiating the latter. The enactment of rightness is always much more forceful when it can draw on and deploy the force of pathos.

The gesture of lying in the path of construction or demolition vehicles recalls the way in which some beggars will sometimes seem deliberately to put themselves at risk of being walked over. In Bombay and other Indian cities, the destitute will often sleep in full daylight in the middle of pavements, though this is partly because sleeping elsewhere than in the middle of crowds is so dangerous for them. Those engaging in sit-ins, lie-ins and other disruptive occupations of social space mimic the mendicant's conspicuous defection from the purposive bustle of urban life, especially when they are designed to impede the movement of traffic. The demonstrators who chain themselves to trees or railings, or superglue themselves to pavements, are similarly making a display of their disability, their choice of choicelessness, rather than their defiant determination to stay in place.

Nudity represents an interesting example of imperative vulnerability, and one that has particularly close analogies with the display of indigence by beggars, public semi-nakedness being as we have seen a recognised feature of 'Tom o' Bedlam' beggars in the sixteenth and seventeenth centuries. In April 2019, protesters from the Extinction Rebellion group stripped off in the public gallery of the House of Commons during a debate on Britain's exit from the European Union, the logic being made explicit by Mark Ovland, one of the protesters, as reported in the *Guardian* newspaper: ' "By undressing in parliament, we are putting ourselves in an incredibly vulnerable position, highlighting the vulnerability that all of us share in the face of environmental and societal breakdown" ' (Elgot 2019). The calm and sensible explication of the meaning and method is performatively dissonant with the action it captions. This is because the action may be seen, or at least aims to be seen, as a corporeal argument for the uselessness of argument, a bodily setting forth which both doubles and stands in place of a verbal 'pro-posing', and so derives its strength from its self-denuding of ordinary rational means. Such a demonstration has particular force in the gallery of a chamber supposed to be dedicated to rational debate. Rescuing the action from irrationality with a head-screwed-on explanation of the kind quoted by the *Guardian* symbolically returns it to the logic of debate, to which it reasserts a petitionary rather than antagonist relation.

The nudity of protesting females, as practised for example by groups such as Pussy Riot, seems to be regarded as particularly potent, because of the voluntary subjection to the danger of 'objectifying' sexual display that is much more likely to come into play in the case of females. This doubles the vulnerability of the naked person with the more particular kind of exposure to a sexually desirous or predatory gaze that a female, or at least an attractive young one, can usually count on. The self-affirming self-exposure of demonstrations like the Slutwalks, in which women dress provocatively in order to neutralise by mimicry the caricaturing of women as sexual objects, is a particularly striking example of the effort to assert strength through the aggressively inversive exhibition of weakness, in order to shame the one who is the wielder of the shaming gaze.

Other aspects of the iconography of demonstrations seem similarly designed to diminish or even demean the demonstrators rather than acting as a simple show of force. Children and animals are commonly in evidence in demonstrations, as signs of innocent and undesigning vulnerability, just as they are mainstays of beggarly display. A demonstration in October 2019 by Extinction Rebellion in front of Google's London headquarters took the form of a nurse-in, with mothers sitting down to suckle their babies, in a demonstration of the threat posed by unaverted climate change to future generations.

Demonstrators' slogans can certainly be trenchantly witty, but the very fact that the comedy of demonstrations can seem to aim at providing some kind of entertainment suggests the pseudo-exchange of the busker, mime or street-dancer, which bid for the onlooker's attention and sympathy. There can be something deliberately clownish in the carnival costumes and comportment of the demonstration. There is a striking rhyme between the improvised and homemade boards and banners carried by demonstrators and the cardboard signs displayed by beggars, both of them being warrants of indigence. More assertive kinds of assault on public attention or territory, like those of football supporters, or sectarian marchers, rarely allow themselves such suggestions of helplessness or inadequacy. In the cases both of the demonstrator and the beggar demonstrating their indigence, the amateurishness of the sign may serve as a guarantee of the unfalsifiable sincerity and spontaneity of the message. And demonstrators will often deliberately dramatise their subordination to the condition of sign-carrier, by marching under banners, or holding aloft placards that lower them while elevating their message. The most arresting form of this dramatisation was seen in the striking sanitation workers in Memphis in 1968, who marched in sandwich boards stamped with the simultaneously bold and piteous slogan I AM A MAN, the effect being to reduce the wearer to a condition of serial anonymity that undermined their defiant proclamation. Demonstrations are usually clamorous affairs, of course, and represent the attempt to take possession of space through appropriative defilement that Michel Serres has analysed in *Le mal propre* (2012). But they can also effect pathetic variations on this, through the voluntary self-curbings of silent vigils, the wearing of gags to indicate that voices are being ignored, or the elaborately staged 'die-ins' of anti-nuclear or environmentalist demonstrations. During the Hong Kong protests of 2019, a woman whose eye was injured by a beanbag round fired by police rapidly became an icon of self-identification among protesters, who wore bandages and eye-patches and chanted 'an eye for an eye' (Kilpatrick 2019).

Demonstrations may have largely displaced petitions, but they continue both to deploy and diversify the sensory and corporeal rhetorics of petition, in which the logic of impotence and the logic of force potentiate each other through inversion. The demonstration replaces the petition because of the growing power of display in societies more and more dominated by different kinds of mass mediation, and the paradoxically mass-mediated parochiality of social media. But, however dissimilar the petition of the solitary destitute and the organised march of the aggrieved multitude may appear, they both draw on the mythical power invested in pathos, the suffering of the one deprived of everything but the power to inflict their suffering, and the claim that is therefore to be made on the basis of their suffering alone.

5

Prayer

The most familiar and widespread form of petition is the act of prayer. Understandably, most of the theological and philosophical literature on prayer concerns itself with trying to square the practice with belief in a just and merciful God. Briefly: given that God is to be regarded as infinitely just, it is hard to see what kind of influence or efficacy petitionary prayer could ever be expected to have. Either the petitioner was going to get what they ask for anyway, or, in a world framed by an omniscient and omnipotent God, they were not, because what they ask for would in fact be harmful, or for other inscrutable reasons. In neither case could prayer seriously ever be thought to exercise any influence in the matter. There is undoubtedly a great deal of thinking to be done on this score, given that the practice of prayer, especially in its petitionary form, leads to so many, and such fiendish paradoxes. Indeed, one might easily conclude that the practice of prayer is the most powerful proof of the fiendishness of orthodox conceptions of divinity, in the literal sense that it introduces into the most essential action and relation of religious life a kind of demonic interference; for it produces a conception of God either as a capricious tyrant subject to human forms of flattery and blandishment, or as a malicious trickster, determined to persuade his creatures to remain in a condition of petition with regard to everything they have or are likely to get, even though the failure to ask for them seems not to have any measurably negative results.

However, such qualms are of metaphysical moment only to theists, even if they can often prove philosophically absorbing even for bystanders. As such, they will not occupy me much in this discussion. But taken at the right kind of slant, the phenomenology of these metaphysical twists and turns has the capacity to illuminate a great deal of the psychological, emotional and epistemopathic kick imparted by the idea of prayer. What seems important to me is not prayer, but the importance, to so many, and to the point of indispensability, of prayer.

Praying structures the daily experience of the adherents of many religions, and may be the last form of religious behaviour to fall away among those lapsing from adherence. It may similarly be one of the religious practices that is most likely to be adhered to in the absence of any other religious commitment. It is hard to imagine what a religion would mean without some action of prayer, or equivalent ritual observance. Those who devote themselves entirely to a religious life may seek to make prayer not an occasional or intermittent activity but rather the leading activity of their lives, so that living becomes ever more identical with praying. Monastic institutions in the medieval world forged a tight link between temporal power and the supposed spiritual power of prayer, or, what amounts to the same thing, the power of that supposition, in which monasteries functioned as votive factories, forming what one historian of Carolingian monasticism calls 'veritable powerhouses of prayer' (de Jong 1995, 651). So central is prayer to religion that I am going here to allow myself to float the suggestion, without seeking to follow through its implications, that what we call religion may exist to create the conditions for prayer, rather than prayer being merely in the service of religion.

Auguste Sabatier wrote in 1897 of prayer as 'religion in act', characterising it as 'not an empty utterance of words, not the repetition of certain sacred formulas, but the movement of the soul putting itself into personal relation and contact with the mysterious power whose presence it feels even before it is able to give it a name' (Sabatier 1902, 28). Consequently, 'a history of prayer would be the best history of the religious development of mankind' (Sabatier 1902, 28). A religion without the acts of supposititious communion and address provided by prayer, along with the rituals that act out the prayer-relation, would be no more than a slightly eccentric set of physical and moral theories. Marcel Mauss agreed that 'the evolution of prayer is in part the evolution of religion itself' (Mauss 2003, 23), subjoining the convincing, if not entirely comfortable suggestion that the vigour of prayer, beginning in vague and rudimentary forms and eventually 'overrunning the whole ritual system' might in fact be that of a kind of parasitic overgrowth: 'prayer has been the remarkable tree which, having grown up in the shade of other trees, has ended by smothering them under its vast branches' (Mauss 2003, 23).

Petitionary, or please-may-I-have prayer is only one form of ceremonial utterance addressed to a deity or deities. Obviously, prayer may also be used for or strongly implicated in purposes of invocation, adoration, worship, propitiation, piacular atonement and the expression of gratitude. Because my concern here is with forms of petition, it is largely only those forms of prayer which may be regarded as petitions that I will be considering. However, though my argument need not stand or fall on this question, I think it is possible to conceive most of the actions of prayer that are distinguished from that of petition as in fact precautionary or accessory forms of it, for example in that they may involve a work of propitiation, a general promotion of a good disposition in the deity and the securing of well-being. Petition may form part of propitiation, in an appeal for mercy for example, but propitiation will more usually function in an accessory function as a means of softening the offence potentially represented by petition. Propitiation therefore assumes a prior or potential condition of anger or hostility in one's addressee, divine or not. The one who is propitiated is rendered thereby more likely to respond positively to a petitionary appeal. Propitiation aims to conserve or restore a previous state: petition aims at bringing about a change in relations. In fact, though propitiation is part of the manner of petition rather than its matter, it may often be highly material. The gift is often a prelude to the petition. So one brings flowers to apologise for being late prior to making one's sexual petition. Intriguingly, propitiation will often depend more on magico-mechanical procedures than petition. The aim may be thereby to mechanise the process of making petition, to make it less risky and more likely to succeed – to make one's petition, precisely, more propitious.

Even in cases where no obvious or explicit benefit is being sought, invocation, adoration, praise and gratitude all put the one praying in a petitionary relation to the powerful deity. This is because prayers of praise or adulation must cope with a version of the embarrassment that attaches to all requests or petitions, namely that they involve an intimate approach, and so will tend to include or imply a request for permission to carry on, or an exculpatory apology for making the first move in such a presumptuous proceeding: 'May I ask?', 'Do you mind if?', 'Excuse me, but'. For, just as in the case of a petition, there is always the hint of insolence or overreach in any kind of address by a mortal creature to their omnipotent and omniscient Creator. The one who lifts up his voice to praise the Lord is indeed open to the suspicion of exalting himself in the process, a self-levitating action for which a certain kind of extenuation must be sought.

Beyond this, the view is possible that every prayer, *qua* prayer, must employ means to defend against the possibility that, to the very degree that it construes Him as addressable, it must reduce the Creator to puppet-like absurdity. This implicit danger in the fact of prayerful address may account in part for the work done by mediations and intercessions of all kinds, whether material (votive objects, beads, statues) or broadly demonic (saints, spirits, angels), all of which exhortings to *ora pro nobis* fence around the face-threatening act that such address may constitute. Latin *orare* means both to argue, or plead a case, and also to entreat or beseech: prayer must keep itself at the beseeching end of things, to protect itself against the danger of becoming courtroom oratory, or oratorio. The very presumption involved in a prayer of praise requires the mitigation of implicit petition.

This interior solicitation of permission to address the deity, even for the purposes of worship, is accompanied by the even more abstract kind of requisition that is involved in any kind of address, namely that the one addressed attend or pay attention in their person. This is what might be understood as the addressivity of prayer, to *ad-dress* having the primary meaning of to cause to stand up, or to bring to its required position. The arguments developed in this chapter will depend on the assumption that any kind of address to an absent addressee must include, as it were structurally, as a condition of its utterance, and whatever its content, an invocation or calling to attention of that addressee. Every vocative is an invocation, every call a calling in and calling on. The impertinence of the 'Hey you' involved in any such invocation is another reason for the prayer, or the one praying, to be sheepish enough about it to bleat an apology for their temerity.

In any case, even if this argument were not to carry through, and it were still to be insisted that prayer may be employed for essentially different kinds of purposes than that of asking for things, petitionary prayer thought of as the most common and representative form of it. This seems to be confirmed by the fact that when prayer is used in non-divine communications, it always seems to be in circumstances involving some form of petition, even if only a mild or precautionary one. When one refers to a prayer in nonreligious contexts, as for example in the common use of 'pray', or 'pray you', to mean 'please', it always seems to imply a praying *for*, or at least *in order to*.

Performing

Whatever their content or intent, however, all forms of prayer must be regarded as performative; communicative actions that do what they say, and say what it is they are currently doing. Prayer must always be the performance of an action, of asking, praising, repenting, and so on, not the characterisation of a state of affairs. You do not usually pass the time of day with a deity, convey information about the condition of your lupins, or offer an opinion about climate change. In fact, prayer is doubly performative. To pray is to perform the action of praying for. But it is also to perform that very act of performance. This stuttering bifocalism is in fact quite a common feature of performatives. If I give thanks for something, I simply perform the action known as thanking. But part of that action is the framing of the action as a recognisable performance, something that I am taking the trouble to show that I am taking the trouble to do. Whenever I say 'thank you', I thereby perform the action of thanking, unless I happen to be quoting, discussing, or 'mentioning' the phrase 'thank you'. But it is also always open to me, under certain circumstances and to various degrees, to impart sufficient song and dance to the verbal act of thanking to clad it in social inverted commas, as though I were mimicking the way in which an actor on a stage might perform the action. This is the sense in which J.L. Austin's principle that seriousness must be a condition of performatives, such that 'a performative utterance will … be *in a peculiar way* hollow or void if said by an actor on the stage, or if introduced in a poem, or spoken in soliloquy' (Austin 1962, 22), may call for qualification.

In fact, however, Austin's very words may lend us just what we need for that qualification. The peculiar way in which a performative may seem 'hollow or void' is also the principle of echo or sonority on which many acts of solemnisation depend, and which attaches to many such acts, for example in reflexive formulae like 'thus' or 'hereby', or simply 'here', as in 'this rough magic/I here abjure' (Shakespeare 2011, 1091). Formalisation of any kind can bring about this doubling of performance. If I warn you that you are making too much of a habit of coming late to work, I may simply be performing verbally the action known as 'warning'. But if I am your employer, or their representative, and I issue a Formal Warning to you regarding your persistent lateness, I am not just *doing* the action of warning, I am acting it out in a way that identifies it clearly as a warning, and so says, not only 'I warn you', but also 'Take careful note of the fact that this is a warning, and that this present action can and possibly will at some later time be taken to constitute a valid performance of it'. In such a case, I am performing the act of performing.

Prayer is perhaps not entirely unique in this respect, but may be unusual in that such double-marking always seems to be a feature of it. Giorgio Agamben associates this kind of performative with the making of oaths: when one says 'I swear that', followed by some assertion, 'the performative substitutes for the denotative relationship between speech and fact a self-referential relation that, putting the former out of play, puts itself forward as the decisive fact' (Agamben 2010, 55). Prayer goes well beyond the simple action of asking (nothing so simple after all, in fact, as this book will carry on trying to show), for which simply asking for something would suffice: it performs the supplementary act of displaying and in the process asserting a certain kind of hopeful faith in the autoreferential efficacy of the action of asking.

Prayer performance is almost always conducted in words. This may seem like a slumpingly obvious point to make about prayer, but the fact that prayer verbalises is extremely significant. For prayer is the performance, not just of the power of wishes, but the special power of wishes once they have been expressed in certain ways. Prayer is one of the most important of the ways in which the power of articulation is repeatedly assumed and thereby assured. The symbolic importance of gesture and posture in prayer is certainly very great, but their importance is to make the body a languaged object rather than to detract from the work of words. Indeed, the power invested in prayer is more than that of a mere instrument: as in the act of 'veridiction' (Agamben 2010, 57) constituted by swearing, prayer involves a recognition and renewal of the constitutive power of language for the human subject. As Agamben explains, the specificity of human language, as opposed to that of other species, consists in the fact that 'uniquely among living things, man is not limited to acquiring language as one capacity among others that he is given but has made of it his specific potentiality; *he has, that is to say, put his very nature at stake in language*' (Agamben 2010, 68). This does not occur only in the act of swearing, which coincidentally will always require some kind of petition, or invocation of some exterior pledge or power; it is also at work in the petition of prayer.

To be sure, oath and prayer seem superficially to be antithetical. In the case of an oath, one attempts to banish uncertainty through the act of assertion; in the case of prayer, one acknowledges and inhabits uncertainty through the act of asking. But the two are linked through their performative nature. In an oath, one establishes one's authority through mediation ('I swear by Almighty God'); in a prayer, one establishes a mediation of one's own verbal authority ('Almighty God, I pray thee'). So oath and prayer are linked through the performance of the fundamental dependence on language that is an essential part of human nature, or the second nature that it is. Along with the promise, a form of self-bondage that only language permits, petitionary prayer depends on language, and in the cases both of swearing an oath and of uttering a prayer, the dependence on language is ritually seconded through performance. The opening of a question in petitionary prayer, and the closing of questions in the oath are only superficially antithetical because they are both variations on the essential condition that belongs to language, of being able to put one's being at stake. Not only are many prayers themselves vows, but, as we will hear later, many forms of prayer, and perhaps especially Christian prayer, feature reminders to God of his prior promise to hear the prayers of the faithful, a promise that he has made us promise to remember.

Adjuration

The appeal of the prayer and the assertion of the oath will both typically depend on the power of naming, which can enact the demand that both God and man keep their word. To beg, entreat or implore is always to adjure, meaning to call to make or observe an oath. The act of begging expresses a state of disadvantage, but it always also assumes a kind of asset or advantage, by virtue of which one may be entitled to make one's appeal. 'Assuming' here has the sense here both of taking 'for granted', as we suggestively sometimes say, and also the sense of taking on, or taking in to oneself, as when one assumes a role. The one who sues, entreats or petitions does it through, or by, this assumption. So one always begs in the name, or through the invocation, of some third state or entity, lying between entreaty and entreated. This can be a deity – 'In God's name' – or a deified abstraction - 'for pity's sake'. Many entreaties are explicitly or implicitly evocations or invocations in this manner, the calling on or calling in of accessory proofs or helps.

Many forms of magical procedure involve invocatory petition, in which supernatural or chthonic entities are enjoined to give their aid, either in protection or aggression, or the fulfilment of positive and negative wishes. Sometimes petition itself takes an invocatory form, as the one petitioned is addressed in such a way, through the ceremonial invocation of third parties, as to make them compliant to the request: by all that's holy, I implore you; in the name of the law I command you. Such invocations may centre on the utterance of names, of deities or demons. But invocation may have a role even in more direct petitions, insofar as they may involve what we call 'appeals', which involve or invoke the force (the force of invocation is always subjunctive, in its invocation of force) of naming.

The cases of appealing and adjuring are parallel. When one appeals, one calls on one's interlocutor in the name of the name they bear, or what they are called, invoking them by means of their very vocativity. Prayers very commonly open with such a vocative, 'Our Father', 'Almighty God', 'O Lord', 'Eternal Rock of Ages', which clears the channel and summons the addressee, or calls them to attention. The vocative 'O' carries a great deal of the force of address in prayer. Address does not require this preliminary vocable, as the beginning of the Lord's Prayer makes clear, but it is very common in English prayers. Even before the specific epithets that may follow, the preliminary exclamation 'O' conveys a kind of preparatory exaltation, enacting a quasi-verbal posture of praise or petition. The vocative 'O' of prayer is usually distinguished orthographically in two ways from other more vernacular uses of the word. The first is that the vocative form is very rarely spelled 'oh'. The second is that the vocative 'O' is usually capitalised, as though to suggest grammatical agreement with the capitalised names that may follow it – 'O Heavenly Father'. The effect of this respectful elevation of the 'O' is to feed a certain ceremonial authority to the act of address itself.

For all their familiarity, vocatives are hard to account for grammatically. They sometimes, as in Latin, form a case in a system of inflections, though in other languages they are indicated by prosodic modification. But the vocative case is different from other grammatical cases, which indicate the function of a verb in a sentence, rather than, as with the vocative, the cast or orientation of the entire utterance of which it forms part. This marks the vocative out as a sort of 'outlier case', which both does and does not belong to the grammatical system of the language in which it functions (Daniel and Spencer 2008).

The vocativity of petition, especially in the form of prayer, may perhaps be seen as a counterpart to what I have elsewhere described as the widespread phenomenon of panophonia, or the tendency to hear voices in the absence of visible agents (Connor 2012). Hearing voices assumes absent but intentional subjects, capable of vocally addressing us: prayer assumes absent but potentially attentive subjects, capable of being vocatively addressed by us. In the one form of hearsay, saying is the product of a certain kind of animising hearing; in the other, hearing is the product of a certain kind of saying, prayer calling into existence the audient ear on which it calls, and relies.

Vocatives are used both to address or to invoke. This is a salient difference in the case of prayers, in which the addressee of one's appeal is usually by definition not visibly present. One addresses an interlocutor who is already there; one invokes one who is elsewhere, or at least whose attention is otherwise engaged, and so is not yet quite in position to be an interlocutor. But prayer wishfully compresses these two alternatives, in its forms of invocatory address. There is always the risk of impertinence in such invocation, given the directive force that is contained in address, the early meanings of which include, as we have seen, to set upright (as in dressing a stone), and to reform, address therefore being close to redress. To address is to induce one's potential addressee to pull themselves together. This potential impertinence is neutralised in the elaborate submissiveness of such invocations. Of course, one has to address one's addressee in order to invoke them, otherwise they would not know that it was them who was being invoked (did he say Mary, or Margaret?), so invocation must constitute a sort of exploratory overture to address. But this pre-address is actually a feature of all vocatives that are part of formal demands or appeals. For one calls on one's addressee not just to indicate that they are the one being addressed ('John, can you pass the salt?'), but also in order to call them into a particular condition, of responsible attentiveness, to which they too must be expected to submit. This accounts for the nervous repetition of respectful vocative forms in the course of what would otherwise be quite ordinary kinds of interchange ('Begging your Honour's pardon', 'Unimportant, your Majesty means, of course'), which protect against the risk of over-familiarity by reminding the addressee that they are being addressed not in their own person but as the embodiment of the office they are currently performing.

Thus one calls on the force of calling itself, the interlocutor's capacity to be called by their name, to authenticate and enforce one's appeal. One appeals, literally, to the name, or appellation, as 'callability', of one's interlocutor, and so also 'in the name of' naming and nameability themselves, both saluting and utilising them. When one adjures, one calls another to oath, as when one summons a juror, a juror being etymologically one who is *iuratus*, called to oath. Appealing need not refer to another's actual name, but rather to the fact of their having a name, by which they may be called, and the honour of which they should wish to defend. The one named is reminded thereby that having a name means being able to be named, and so called upon. Subjects have names in order that they may be subject to naming, subject to the demand that they live up to their name. Perhaps all petitions are implicit appeals in that they attempt to capture or conjure the addressee in the force of the petitioner's fantasy, or the fantasy force and force of the fantasy embodied in the petitionary *dispotif* itself. To appeal to someone is to call on them to accede to being called in to this circle of projections and expectations. To appeal is to call on someone, in the name of their name, to acknowledge the force of appellation, and in the process, this being the grandiose temptation of petition, to invite them to make a name for themselves. To address someone is to make them stand up, in the place that address puts them. Just as to declare is to declare the right to declare, so to petition is to invoke the potency of the petitionary situation. Similarly, adjuring need not, and usually will not, call on another to take or honour an oath, but will always be performed in the assumption, or 'in the name of' the assumption, that they are capable of taking or honouring an oath.

The appeal is essentially to the fact of participation in language, and the specific forms of commitment to the condition of being bound, bindable, or biddable by it. And this invocation, or calling in, of the general human predicament, at once a subjection and a power, of being bound by language is enacted through an utterance that assumes as well as alludes to this bondage. A declaration declares the speaker's right to make a declaration, sometimes, as in Jacques Derrida's analysis of the American Declaration of Independence, inaugurally, behind and alongside the fact of what is being declared (Derrida 2002). Similarly, an adjuration draws its addressee towards the condition of being adjurable, capable of being put on their honour, behind and alongside whatever the particular thing requested may be. This adjuring may for this reason often also be a conjuring, in the sense that it is produced through, and perhaps ultimately from, nothing but, but also nothing less than, the productive force of language itself.

The *iuratus*, or juror, the one sworn by being adjured or brought to the necessity of swearing, is the subject of swearing in the familiarly double sense of being subject and being a subject. She swears an oath, in a free act for which nobody may act on her behalf. But to swear is to subject oneself to a binding force, the force which one simultaneously exerts and submits to. So to bring or urge someone to this condition is to participate in this duality of assertion and submission. One acknowledges the sovereignty of the one capable of binding herself in this way, according her this inalienable freedom of choice; but at the same time, one accords her sovereignty only so far as she undertakes this exercise of sovereign self-submission. This is particularly the case of Christian prayer, which inherits from Judaism a strangely impertinent willingness to remind the Almighty that he is bound by the terms of a contract, to which he has previously freely subjected himself:

> For thou, O Lord of hosts, God of Israel, hast revealed to thy servant, saying, I will build thee an house: therefore hath thy servant found in his heart to pray this prayer unto thee. 28 And now, O Lord God, thou art that God, and thy words be true, and thou hast promised this goodness unto thy servant: 29 Therefore now let it please thee to bless the house of thy servant, that it may continue for ever before thee: for thou, O Lord God, hast spoken it: and with thy blessing let the house of thy servant be blessed for ever., to be attentive to prayer. (2 Samuel 7.27-9)

The close similarity in sound of *adjuring* and *abjuring* can occasionally lead to confusion. And, though abjuring might appear to be the opposite of adjuring, they do indeed have quite important things in common. To abjure is more than to abandon, or give up. To abjure is to swear away, where to adjure is to swear in, or call to oath. An abjuration is a formal announcement of a renunciation, in its earliest senses, the retraction or forswearing of a previously taken oath. Abjuring converges with disavowing, taking back what has been pledged or devoted, which may itself constitute the making of a kind of pledge.

Devotions

Prayer is devotional, or more generally, what is called votive. It may not at first, or even at length, be obvious what devotion might have to do with petition. They may even seem like opposites, since, in devotion, one gives a gift, or gives oneself as a gift, whereas in petition, one seeks, or beseeches, a benefit. *Votive*, from which English *vow* and *avow* derive, is from the past participle of *voveo*, to pledge, promise or consecrate. But this kind of pledging is usually in fact part of a petitionary exchange. F.E.J. Valpy's *Etymological Dictionary of the Latin Language* defines *voveo* as to 'pray for a thing, while I vow to do something to obtain it' (Valpy 1828, 521). Alfred Ernout and Alfred Meillet agree that the primary meaning of *votum* is 'promesse ou offrande solennelle faite aux dieux, en échange d'une faveur demandée ou accordée' 'promise or solemn offering made to the gods, in exchange for a favour sought or given', which leads to the word being used to mean 'souhait exprimé, désir', 'expressed wish, desire' (Ernout and Meillet 2001, 753). This makes sense of the derivation of the word *vote* from this same root. What links giving and anticipatory receiving in a more primary sense is desire, or, more specifically, the pleasure of expressed desire. Desire expressed, we may venture, is always partly the proleptic performance of its fulfilment. The pleasure of self-confirming performance is a pleasure that is itself a kind of magical gift, a gift that gives itself, to itself, or, in that telling contemporary locution, 'the gift that keeps on giving'. One might see in the act of voting for something a kind of wishing, in which the articulation of the wish is also a sort of pledging or dedication of it in the cause of its own granting. In devotion and votive action more generally, one votes for, and thereby in imagination pre-approves, as the credit-card companies say, one's own petition.

Ultimately, prayers of worship and prayers of petition are identifiable through the relation of exchange they both constitute. Not surprisingly, most internalist accounts of prayer by adherents of religious faith attempt to diminish or to deny the idea that prayer might constitute any kind of negotiation. But most of the efforts to assert the pure gratuity of prayer are only themselves part of a transactive routine for bringing pure gift and pure transaction into the impurity of exchange. It is pleasingly unsurprising that Marcel Mauss, the future author of the most influential work in the anthropology of exchange, should have begun his academic career with the doctoral thesis on prayer from which I have already quoted. Though her focus is on ideas about prayer in Anglo-Saxon England, Stephanie Clark surely articulates a principle of more general applicability in her businesslike assertion that 'Like the gift, prayer is inescapably economic' (Clark 2018, 274).

The human tendency to overestimate the powers of one's own requisitory speech is perhaps suggested by the fact that obtaining an audience or being heard is often elided with realising one's desires rather than merely having the chance to register them. How often do we hear that officials or governments who decline requests or demands are 'not listening', or not hearing what we are saying, as though it must be impossible for somebody genuinely to hear a request and yet not grant it? Perhaps the frequently-noticed compliance of *obedience* (Latin *ob* + *audire*) with *audience* exercises its force in the grandiose expectation that to be heard is, or ought to be, in itself to be obeyed.

Precatory relations extend well beyond religious practice, or, better perhaps, extend religious practice into many other areas of experience. I write these words, as I have written almost everything I write, in a votive fashion, in that I give myself over to it, in the hope thereby of deriving from it a yield, of pleasure, the esteem of others, or other sort of profit. Devoting attention to the subject of my writing makes it a kind of offer, in which I simultaneously bid it (entreat and enjoin it) to repay me. I feel happiest writing at a particular time of the day, in my case (like many others) early in the morning, surfing, I am very tempted to think, the cortisol surge than most people experience just after waking, enhanced in many cases by the effect of the stimulant drug caffeine, or just the drug-like elation of breakfast. This pharmacological enhancement assists me no doubt, as I perform my matutinal orison to whatever topic may be occupying my attention, in pledging myself to my devotion, confirming myself in my faith that my faith will be enough to effect a votive attention adequate to its object. Such votive reflexivity may be even more intense among what are known, sometimes mostly to themselves, as 'creative' writers, whose narcissistic faith in their power of making things up out of what seems like nothing must presumably involve much more risk of misfire or narcissistic recession than my kind of writing, that is content to be merely, but reliably, about other things than itself. But the fervour of devotion surely comes in part comes from the concealed rapture of the thought of thereby compelling its deity. The subjects of romantic adoration, especially where it is unsought or unrequited, as in the case of celebrities receiving acts or expressions of devotion, know how frighteningly imperative the demands for reward or response can be in such acts.

Prayer is a dutiful and habitual action, but duties and habits can act as screens for or displacements of more primary kinds of gratification. In order to understand the force of the act of prayer, we should not shy from enquiring into the kinds of gratification it offers. A large part of this gratification may come from simply the sense of allayed anxiety and increased security it may give. There is clearly a kind of conservative reassurance simply in the fact of prayer being a mechanical action, that, like an intoxicant or antibiotic, works to some degree even if your heart is not in it. This reassurance may depend upon the background of inhibition and potential self-reproach that must exist in every form of social organisation. The one who fears punishment or retribution, and may even feel that they deserve it, may find some solace in the fact that a means seems to exist in prayer whereby their fault may be made good, redoubled in the reassuring sense that they have not neglected to exercise it. As a means of purgative confession, prayer can seem to offer a magical power of redemption.

As I have already observed, the reassurance offered by the thought of direct reparative access to a god, or similarly all-powerful agency (the figure of the god usually being the obedient servant of the power they are assumed in fantasy to wield) may have to contend against the suspicion, triggered by an apprehension of the egotism of the desirous demand for satisfaction through prayer, that such an approach to the Almighty may in fact be regarded as arrogant effrontery. For this reason, prayer tends to be construed, less as a resource for the needy than as a duty for the devout. Regular acts of prayer are enjoined in many religions, and perhaps nowhere more emphatically than in Christian scripture and doctrine. The Quran also has God addressing this demand for prayer to his believers: 'I am God; there is no God but Me, so worship Me and keep up the prayer so that you remember me' (*Qu'uran* 20.14, 2015, 196). The idea that prayer is demanded by God, as articulated for example by Søren Kierkegaard in a journal entry of 1848, probably goes a long way to relieve the anxiety attending the presumption of petition: 'The more a person prays, the more certain his final consolation is that God has commanded that we *shall* pray; for God is so infinite that many times a person would hardly dare to pray, however much he wanted to' (Kierkegaard 1967-78, 3.3427). So the act of prayer, even where it involves petition, may also have wrapped up in it a petition for the strength and faith required to enter into the act of prayer itself. Making a demand through prayer can therefore be turned into meeting an equivalent demand for the making of it in prayer.

This reassurance may hold in particular of prayers for forgiveness rather than for more positive favours or benefits. Where the addressee of such prayers is another mortal, prayers for forgiveness tend to magnify that addressee, precisely because the special kind of giving given in forgiveness is such a divine speciality. The one being begged for their forgiveness is being asked for something they not only do not have to give, but can in fact only ever give *gratis*, just as a god gives forgiveness as a kind of grace; for-giving benefits from the unsettled combination of intensity, completion, diversion and undoing that is signalled by the richly mixed prefix 'for-': (forgo, forbid, forfend, forsake). Acknowledging, or what appears to come to the same thing, according, this kind of power allows one to share in it, so that it is not only the one petitioned who is, like the Virgin of the Ave Maria, *plena gratiae*, full of grace, but the petitioner too.

This again connects with the idea that a petition can activate a sort of magical expectation that it is at least in part capable of itself fulfilling. The doctrine that humans have a duty to prayer is balanced by the extraordinary guarantee given in the course of the Christ's Sermon on the Mount: 'Ask, and it shall be given you; seek, and ye shall find; knock, and it shall be opened unto you: For every one that asketh receiveth; and he that seeketh findeth' (Matthew 7.7-8). The doctrine that God has commanded his worshippers to pray to him under the express condition that they will be given whatever they ask for is an extraordinarily frank statement of the lengths to which desire will go to assert its power over logic and reality. And yet, there may also be a hidden impotence in an asking that is assured of success in this way, for such a guarantee deprives the act of asking of any actual power of persuasion. The omnipotent emperor is thereby forced to surrender all his potential for power to his imperial power itself. Wilhelm Stekel sees the practice of prayer as a central part of the dynamic of sexual impotence, embodying a sort of ascetic striving which conjoins assertiveness and submission, so that 'religious ecstasies are so powerfully charged with dammed-up libido that prayer may even become an erotic act' (Stekel 1940, 1.283).

The imperious demands of George Herbert's two poems on prayer seem wittily to exaggerate and parody the doctrine of the unfailing power of prayer over its divine addressee. The sequence of metaphors for the work of prayer that makes up 'Prayer (1)', includes its designation as 'Gods breath in man returning to his birth', a line that is always summoned for me when I hear the phrase 'circular breathing' to describe a particular technique in the playing of wind instruments. This is followed by a sequence of martial metaphors that seem borrowed from the rhetoric of wooing by siege:

> Engine against th' Almightie, sinners towre,
>> Reversed thunder, Christ-side-piercing spear,
>> The six-daies world transposing in an houre (Herbert 2007, 178)

In 'Prayer (2), Herbert focusses less on the irresistible power of prayer than on the unobstructed availability of the divine it guarantees:

> Of what an easie quick accesse,
> My blessed Lord, art thou! how suddenly
>> May our requests thine eare invade!
> To shew that state dislikes not easinesse,
> If I but lift mine eyes, my suit is made:
> Thou canst no more not heare, then thou canst die. (Herbert 2007, 371)

In both poems, though, the idea being dangerously mooted is that of the helplessness, not of the one praying, but the God being preyed on in prayer, unable either to turn his ear away or step aside from the irremissible openness for precatory business to which his immortality subjects him. The aim is of course to intimate the contrary truth of the power of God given to men through prayer, precisely through the conspicuous exaggeration of making God so unable to resist its force. The prayer-poet must trust that he will be forgiven for his witty revelation that God is the helpless object of the all-powerful exercise of prayer, this very fact being the source of the confidence in his forgiveness.

Precatory Technics

It is a striking fact that one usually prays for things for which only the act of praying will do. Ordinarily, one prays in extremity, or at least prays more intently and meaningfully under conditions of want, disadvantage, disrepair, or despair. It would be absurd, or weirdly obsessive-compulsive, to pray for things which one has a perfect right to expect. So 'Give us this day our daily bread', but not 'Please ensure that the baker once again proves willing to accept money in exchange for bagels'. But the one who lives a life of prayer, or the one who, as many adherents of religions are encouraged to do, strives to make prayer a regular part of their lives, thereby tends to the conversion of life itself into a relation of prayer. This can have what may be thought to be the desirable effect of turning almost all the routine expectations we may have of material existence into amazing and improbable miracles ('O Lord, who time and again makest this cup fall to the earth through the force of gravity after it slippeth from my fingers.') Michael J. Murray and Kurt Meyers press a little further in trying to answer the question why the Christian God should in fact enjoin it as a duty to ask for things which, given everything else which is the case, are quite likely to be on offer anyway – air to breathe, intermittent rainfall in temperate zones, the free use of one's limbs. 'Why is it', they arrestingly ask:

> that God, who has at His command all resources and who has the capacity for assessing His creatures' true needs far better than the creatures themselves, would make the distribution of at least some earthly blessings contingent on the creature's recognition of his needs and his request that God make provisions for them? (Murray and Meyers 1994, 312)

Their answer, in part, is that this has the effect of preventing the kind of complacency or arrogant sense of self-sufficiency they call 'idolatry' (Murray and Meyers 1994, 312), and thereby also maintains the believer's recognition of the ultimate responsibility of God for everything that is the case.

Praying may be regarded as a kind of wishing, made executive through stylised forms of articulation. To wish means to want or desire; and it also means to articulate that desire. Petition need not form a part of optative expressions, which merely give expression to a wish, whether positive or negative. Indeed, an optative expression – 'would that I were in a position to help' – may be understood simply as a report on the speaker's state of mind. And yet, optative expressions always seem performative, in that they carry out as well as simply representing the action of wishing, and also seem to implicate the utterance in the wishing. Optative expressions belong to a special mood or mode of articulated longing: as neatly summarised in a Middle English grammatical text, 'Þe indicatif mod is þat þat schewis þe sothe or þe false; þe inperatif þat commandis; þe optatif þat yernys' (Durham Cathedral MS. B.IV.19, fol. 1ʳ, quoted in Thomson 2019, 191).

The difference between a wish and a want, which might seem to mean more or less the same thing, is that a wish is a want tending to an articulated petition. But articulate wishing – 'I wish I could figure out why my Wi-Fi keeps cutting out' – is tellingly different from the action known as 'making a wish'. When one makes a wish one performs a special kind of action, an action that is none other than that known as 'making a wish'. In making a wish I perform the strange, giddy circularity that is characteristic of many performatives, which not only performs an act, but formally performs the act of performing it. There is a strange duality in every performative. Every performative –commanding, declaring, warning, threatening, promising – does something, as well as representing something, in 'the performance of an act *in* saying something as opposed to performance of an act *of* saying something' (Austin 1962, 99). This last phrase neatly distinguishes between a locution (an act of saying) and an illocution (something done by or through the act of saying). But it must be obvious that all illocutions depend upon acts of saying, meaning that there may always be an act of performing bundled in with the performing of an act. Normally the difference between these two things is wafer-thin and of no account, But there are circumstances in which the performing of the performance, the illocutionary force of the locution itself, understood as the performance specifically of an act of saying, becomes prominent and potent. Petition is one of these, along with other forms in which the force of saying seems to be to the fore. In petition, we may often use a phrase which highlights the locutionary act: 'I'm telling you', 'I'm begging you'.

All of these will tend to be what we think of as magical uses of utterance, utterance in which locution and illocution cannot in fact be distinguished: utterance where there is at least a veiled wish that wishes might indeed be horses, so that beggars could ride. This is a wish, not only for a desired object, but a more all-purpose wish that wishing was all it took, that words can fork lightning. As long as we do not think too much about it, we tend to think that the signification of a wish is accessory and incident to the making of it. The view held in magical thinking is the opposite, that the making of wishes is what makes for wishing and itself makes them 'come true', if not in the sense of being granted, then of coming into their particular kind of truth.

Wishing is one of the words which most obviously performs this magical possibility. Of course, one can simply wish or wish for something silently, or as a description of a state of mind, of desire or longing. But wishing as the utterance of a wish, which often requires the specific utterance of the words 'I wish', has become requisite in the use of the word. Wishing is often close to benediction, as in wishing someone good morning, or a Merry Christmas. The sign of its magical propensity is the fact that wishes can take an executive form, separated from their originator or the action of wishing – as when asks 'please send her my good wishes'. Wishes are meant to 'come true', which seems illogical if wishes are taken to be merely the utterance of a desire, since, as such, they are already true. If the utterance of a wish is understood as an effort to alter the state of things through utterance alone, then the fulfilment of a wish is at the same time the coming true of the secret wish that impels all acts of wishing – the wish that it could be true that wishing could work directly on the world.

The generalisation of prayer can sometimes extend to the point of enlarging prayer beyond its physical performance of praying, or liberating prayer from the limitation of its objectification. For Peter Sloterdijk, religions are to be thought of not primarily as matters of belief but rather as matters of reflexive practice, and especially practices of self-formation, in a recoil, that seems to be universal among creatures such as human beings with significant access to symbolic life, from the atrocity of unstyled existence: 'no "religion" or "religions" exist, only misunderstood spiritual regimens, whether these are practised in collectives – usually church, *ordo*, *umma*, *sangha* – or in customized forms – through interaction with the "personal God" ' (Sloterdijk 2013, 3). It is not just an accidental feature of praying that there are techniques associated with it. For prayer itself constitutes an anthropotechnics, a styled way of being rather than mere, unmeaning existence, ambling along any old how.

Strangely perhaps, verbal and corporeal techniques are used, not just to mark off the performance of prayer from other, more natural or unformalised kinds of utterance, but also to perform the generalisation of prayer, just referred to, into a generalised or unformalised condition, in which it is identical with living. This may explain why autonomous machineries of prayer like the prayer flags and prayer wheels of Tibetan Buddhism can successfully perform as a kind of devotion rather than the profane mockery that the practice of purchasing indulgences was taken by many to be prior to the Reformation. The Tibetan prayer wheel, or mill, probably derives from a revolving eight-sided bookcase in use in Chinese Buddhist monasteries by 823 CE, for purely practical purposes of storage and access. By the early 12th century, the device was being used for purposes of what Lynn White calls 'mechanized piety'. Where in China windmills were used for pumping and grinding, in Tibet their use was exclusively in the 'technology of prayer' (White 1960, 518). In fact, neither prayer flags nor prayer wheels are properly so named since what they enact or transmit are mantras rather than utterances (Winder 1992, 25), which are much closer in the first place to spells or magico-mechanical formulae than the psychologised magic of prayers.

Marcel Mauss, for whom prayer achieves its highest form in the devotional individualism of Protestantism, sees the 'materialized prayers' exemplified in 'the rosary, the prayer-tree, the prayer-wheel, the amulet, phylacteries, *mezuzoth*, miraculous medals, scapulars, ex-votos', as a degeneration into fetishism (Mauss 2003, 26). Even when the act of prayer is not displaced from a praying subject into any kind of external machinery, it may nevertheless be marked off by ritualisation from ordinary kinds of propositional utterance or event. For Luce Irigaray this takes the form of cultivating a sense of breath, the most automatic of human actions, and normally thought of as the mere inessential vehicle of prayer, as a mode of prayer in itself. 'Becoming spiritual amounts to transforming our elemental vital breath little by little into a more subtle breath', she promises (Irigaray 2002, 70). Cleo McNelly Kearns (2005) has connected this ambition to Eastern traditions and disciplines, especially that known as *pranayama*, in the phenomenology of prayer. Self-perfecting, especially the imaginary self-perfecting of the body, is the acting out of a continuous prayer addressed to the divine for the self-perfecting of divinity. Rerealising breath as spontaneous prayer requires simultaneously a work of extreme self-discipline, and the achievement of a magical release from any need for conscious action. Styling one's breathing as prayer means (according to the magical logic of performance) that one will be able to be praying whenever one is breathing, and so therefore unable ever not to be praying, one's existence made over into praying without residue, like the miraculously self-winding watches, powered by one's own movements, I remember from my watchfully allegorical youth.

Despite the seeming distinction made between magical incantations, which are presumed to act mechanically, and prayers, which involve the address to an Other whom one cannot count on controlling, prayer is indeed characterised by many of the structural features that are characteristic of magical spells. Prayers are almost always formalised, lifting them clear from quotidian kinds of speech act. They are speech endowed with the magical powers, which is to say powers of performance as well as representation, of art and incantation. The performance of prayers, like the performance of magical spells, tends to require exact observance (a word that has come to mean a prayer) of a formulaic ritual, in a votive kind of exchange in which submitting oneself to an external power seems to give access to another sort of power over the external world. Saying your prayers at night associates praying with the calming rituals of childhood storytelling and lullaby, the gentle lilt of a familiar chant assisting the passage into the safety and repletion of sleep. The trance-inducing effects of poetry, 'hushing us with an alluring monotony', according to W.B. Yeats, 'while it holds us waking by variety, to keep us in that state of perhaps real trance, in which the mind liberated from the pressure of the will is unfolded in symbols' (Yeats 2007, 117) may recall the effects of this kind of sleep charm.

Wishing actions are magical in two contrasting senses. Firstly, they have a prescribed form. One must make a wish according to some formula, often with accompanying actions that must be performed at a certain place or time, in a certain order, etc. It does not matter how ardently one might wish for a sight of one's future lover, or the extirpation of a wart, the wish will not take or work unless the locally-operative rules of wishmaking, arbitrary and therefore absolute, are followed. This mechanism makes for cast-iron cause-and-effect guarantees, as articulated for example in Ned Washington's lyrics in the 1940 Disney film *Pinocchio*: 'When you wish upon a star/Makes no difference who you are/Anything your heart desires will come to you'. Wishes have the power they do because they are separated from the self which makes them, as in the meta-wish that Bertram offers his mother the Countess at the beginning of *All's Well That Ends Well*: 'The best wishes that can be forg'd in your thoughts be servants to you' (Shakespeare 2011, 91).

Oddly, the fact that purpose must be obedient to prescribed process in wishing also means that the act of wishing can be performed accidentally, as in folk tales of the type known as 'the Foolish Wishes' (Aarne-Thompson-Uther 750A), a sequence of wishes which first cause unintended damage and then must be used up to return things to normal. There is, for example, the story of a couple who are granted three wishes. First the wife sees a pudding, and incautiously wishes she had one; her husband, vexed at her frittering away a wish on something so inconsiderable, wishes that the pudding was hanging from the end of her nose; which, being granted, requires him to blow his final wish on wishing it away (Anon 1932). The story of Niels Bohr's horseshoe shows magical accident working in the other direction. A visitor to Bohr's house saw a horseshoe hung above the entrance and enquired incredulously of the Nobel prize winning physicist 'Are you really that superstitious? Do you really believe that the horseshoe brings you luck?' 'Of course not', replied Bohr, 'but I'm told it works even if you don't believe in it'. In the version of the story given by Werner Heisenberg, the efficacy of unbelief is actually ratcheted up a notch: Heisenberg reports Bohr as replying ' "Natürlich nicht; aber man sagt doch, daß es auch dann hilft, wenn man nicht daran glaubt"': 'Of course not: but they say it helps if you don't believe in it' (Heisenberg 2012, 113; my translation). This means that the horseshoe works not just *even if* you don't believe in it, but *especially* if you don't.

Wishes are usually in fact numbered, or incorporate forms of counting procedure. Thus, the compulsive handwasher must perform their votive action a certain number of times, or, as British handwashers were exhorted during the COVID-19 epidemic, sing a wishing song like Happy Birthday, or God Save the Queen, a certain number of times to ensure thorough washing of the hands. Indeed, numerative affordance is perhaps one of the reasons that obsessive-compulsives are in fact so drawn to handwashing rituals: for there is no bodily apparatus more apt for digital-decimal variation than the hand, or indeed ('this little piggy') foot. The subjection of thought to number, or defined procedures, like the 'algorithms' that have long been a staple of exopistemopathic magic talk (Connor 2019, 322-4) is another aspect of the mechanisation of desire in wishing.

If wishing magic is mechanical, it is also true that it is driven by Freudian 'omnipotence of thoughts' (Freud 1953-74, 13.84), that is, the belief that, subject to certain disciplines and procedures, thoughts are capable of acting and intervening directly, and therefore nonmechanically, in and on the world. (The very thought of the omnipotence of thoughts may in this respect be thought of as self-instancing.) And yet the point of wishing-magic, like most forms of magic, is precisely that it is not really any kind of thinking, but rather the delegation of thought to formal procedure, thinking, as it were, by acting's attorney.

So, though they may seem to form a stark contrast, the mechanical and mental aspects of wishing are in fact closely confederate. When you close your eyes to make a wish, you allow and assert the priority of the inner world of thought over the outer world of matter. When closing the eyes is associated with closing the hands ('hands together, eyes closed', as I was daily enjoined in school assembly), or in fact, with precisely the same effect of countermanding manual action, the opening of the palms in the Muslim posture of prayer, one similarly asserts the metamanual efficacy of thought. The secrecy attaching to magical procedures, and the prohibition on telling others what you have wished for seem to work (or 'work') in the same way. This reveals that, when it comes to the optative actualisation of desire in the action of wishing, subjective self-relation in fact takes the form of an imaginary machinery, rather than any numinous principle of 'soul' or 'spirit'. So wish-fulfilment is not the opposite of the material reality embodied in scientific mechanism, it is a modulated form of that mechanism, which I may live to regret having called a psychotechnography (Connor 2017, 14), that is, simultaneously an imaginary mechanism and projection of imagination itself as a kind of machinery. A wish is therefore a very particular kind of quasi-object, an object impregnated with subjective force: '[This] quasi-object is not an object, but it is one nevertheless, since it is not a subject, since it is in the world; it is also a quasi-subject, since it marks or designates a subject who, without it, would not be a subject' (Serres 2007, 225).

Objects are of great importance in wishing procedures. Such objects are often known as 'votive'. Things that you 'wish on' are things you wish at, or, as we will see later, by: petitory proposals seem to be prepository through and through. There are wishing wells, wishing boxes, wishing lamps, wishing-trees, wishbones, candles, buttercups, dandelions, ladybirds and rosary beads, each one choreographing a particular wishing song and dance. As I have observed, magical objects and procedures are also associated with the kind of acted-out wishing known as 'casting a vote', as one casts a spell. Indeed, the word bead itself derives from Old English *bede*, prayers or devotion, the word here passing, in the late fourteenth century, not, as is customary, from the object to the action it enables or accompanies, but from the action to the humble object it employs. Thus 'to bid a bead' is to offer a prayer. The action of praying, as *beden*, has been secularised into German *bitte*, please, Greek παρακαλῶ, please, you're welcome, and English 'I bid you (good day, farewell, etc)'. To bid has also become more imperative, in naming an action of commanding. Bidding is one of many words in which asking rises to requiring, and maunding (begging) becomes a kind of mandate or commanding.

Wishing depends on and deploys the mechanical, which is to say, computational capacities of words. A pocket version of Grace in Peterhouse, Cambridge, spoken when no students, but only fellows, are present, is, at the commencement of the meal, 'Benedictus benedicat', may the Blessed One give blessing. At the end of the meal, it modulates to 'Benedicto benedicatur', may there be blessing from or (if Benedicto be taken to be dative rather than ablative), to the Blessed one (Dixon 1903, 182). The circuit of vicariance carried by these active and passive subjunctives (benedicat, benedicatur) makes it clear that blessing is something that is requisite for, imparted to, and derivative from, the source of all blessing, who is already benedictus, blessed, or, in its more exaltedly magico-poetical form, blesséd – or even, we might say, in the ambiguously active-passive expression used by women of my mother's generation, 'well-spoken'. In the burbled chiasmus of the Peterhouse Grace, the one who gives blessing is given the power to give blessing by being capitalised as the Blessed One from whom the power to give blessing proceeds. In prayer, one invokes the power one gives oneself to evoke the power of another. Once again, petition is a secretly imperious power, which depends on what depends on it, the petition for power giving power to its own petition.

Imprecations

Kenneth Burke is among those who have seen a particular connection between the work of prayer and the paradoxically spiritualised mechanism that is at work in what is known as poetry. Burke rather strangely associates poetry with the work of prayer, on the grounds that they are both not just the expression of a wish, but also the communication of that wish, and therefore the expression of the wish to communicate. These remarks, which occur in an essay of 1939 on the Freudian analysis of poetry, attempt to enlarge the Freudian idea of literature as wish-fulfilment into the idea of poetry as a kind of wish-transmission, which seems a strange, but perhaps suggestive way of thinking of prayer.

> Prayer would enter the Freudian picture in so far as it concerns the optative. But prayer does not stop at that. Prayer is also an act of communion. Hence, the concept of prayer, as extended to cover also secular forms of petition, moves us into the corresponding area of communication in general. (Burke 1939, 409)

For Burke, the formal devices of poetry are associated with 'all that falls within the sphere of incantation, imprecation, exhortation, inducement, weaving and releasing of spells; matters of style and form, of meter and rhythm, as contributing to these results' (Burke 1939, 410). Intriguingly, Burke also draws into association with these prayer-like actions some things that he sees as their opposite: 'Here, as the reverse of prayer, would come also invective, indictment, oath' (Burke 1939, 410), and repeats his claim, without explicating it further, in a footnote: 'Dream has its opposite, nightmare; prayer has its opposite, oath' (Burke 1939, 411 n.8). Burke's emphasis appears to be on the ways in which poetry offers a secularised form of the magical operation involved both in petitionary prayer and in execration, but it might be possible to see something of the erotic pleasure of drawing one's listener into the circle of incantatory power at work in the act of prayer.

Petitionary prayer is usually positive. But there are negative forms of prayer as well, maledictions as well as benedictions, in the form of curses, comminations, and the hostile kind of praying known as imprecation, which, for a brief period from its introduction in English in the late sixteenth century could mean to pray or supplicate to a lord or deity, but by a century later has been used almost exclusively to mean the calling down of evil or calamity on a person. The votive link between the curse and the blessing is suggested by the Greek equivalent, the *anathema*, which is derived from ἀνάθημα, an offering, or something set up for the gods, from ἀνά up + τιθέναι, to place. The use of anathema to mean sacred, devoted to or set apart for divine use, survives as long as 1608, when Edward Topsell tenderly denominated a spider's web as 'the very patterne, index, and anathema of supernaturall wisedome' (Topsell 1608, 262). Anathema here reechoes the well-known ambivalence of the Latin *sacer*, both consecrated and condemned.

The petitory-invocatory aspect of cursing is suggested by the fact that the curses of beggars, also expert in elaborate benedictions in thanks for offerings, have long been regarded as dangerously potent (Waters 2020). For my mother, nothing could be more reckless than to refuse to buy the withered grey sprig of 'heather' offered for sale at her door, which was 'lucky' only through the protection money handed over to forfend bad luck. Although curses often involve, as the *OED* characterises it, 'invocation or adjuration of the deity', they also usually assume for the curser or for the curse itself the power of affecting their victim by direct *fiat*, a command which itself has the form of a precatory imperative. Occasionally, the righteous may call upon the deity to punish the wicked, though this is much rarer, given the prohibition against wishing ill upon others (for among those who are said to be cursed are the 'unmerciful'). The Anglican service of Commination only implicitly calls upon the Lord to punish sinners: rather it gives warning of what lies in store if they persist. The closest to a prayer comes in what may be heard as an implicit optative in the series of cursings: 'Cursed is he, that curseth his father or mother', and so on, which may perhaps be read as 'cursed be he', or 'may he be cursed', or even just 'cursed is he, and quite right too'. Indeed, the second half of the service of Commination quickly provides reassurance against what has been colourfully threatened in the first half of the ritual, several times guaranteeing God's 'endless pity' and 'infinite mercy', and promising purging with hyssop and various other conveniences for those who turn away from sin in time (Anon 1559, sig. U8ʳ).

Cursing is much more in evidence in the truncated or implicit forms of swearing, and indeed this is the usual signification of cursing or cussing in the USA: 'damn you, sir!', implying 'may you be damned', and 'blast this useless sellotape', implying 'may this sellotape be subject to blasting'. Blasting is particularly interesting, since it invokes a pernicious breath breathed out upon an object, causing death or shrivelling, which is itself a magical, or optative operation, depending on the magical belief in the power of the breath both to vivify and putrefy ('Breathe on me breath of God', in Edwin Hatch's hymn, that always imparted a waft of disgust when I sang it). Presumably there is a special link between this kind of magical action, and the action of invoking it in speech, given the participation of breath in the latter. In such utterances, the prayer is internalised, hence the term 'imprecation'. I was darkly warned as a child not to use the expression 'blimey', or 'Cor blimey', since I was said 'really' to be saying 'May God blind me, if...', and, as noted already, magic is magic precisely because it works mechanically, whether or not you can spell out the spell you are unknowingly purposing.

In fact, the curse is more magical than the prayer, in that it seems more obviously to assume and wield the very power that is being wished for or invoked. A curse can mean both an utterance designed to encourage God to produce ill effects, or the ill effects themselves, as in the phrase 'the curse' used of menstruation. The *OED*'s remark on *curse* is the familiar miracle of dry derisiveness: 'It may be uttered by the deity, or by persons supposed to speak in his name, or to be listened to by him.' It is as bizarre that God should go in for cursing as it is that he should bless, for from whom might his act of cursing invoke assistance but from himself? Again, this may give a particular potency to 'blasting', as swearing, since it contains the idea that God's curse is the blasting gust of his very utterance, a doubling which is itself shadowed in the mortal curse.

Cursing is matched by blessing. Blessing was regularly used to translate *benedicere* and εὐλογεῖν, to speak well of or praise, but in fact probably derives from a much more physical practice: Old English *blóedsian*, *blédsian*, *blétsian* meant to smear with blood, as a form of consecration, or magical protection. In blessing, often accompanied by an action, such as the making of the sign of the cross, a special kind of violence seems to be invoked. This is reinforced by the later association of English blessing with French *blesser*, to wound or injure.

Blessing, like cursing, is a powerful action performed by symbolisation, whether verbal or physical. So powerful is it, indeed, that God himself, who must be presumed to be the source of all blessing, and therefore himself unlikely to benefit from it, is nevertheless subject to it, as in the miraculous first words spoken by Zachariah, the father of John the Baptist, who has been made dumb for his disbelief that he will have a child with his wife Elizabeth, when his tongue is loosed: 'Blessed be the Lord God of Israel' (Luke 1.68). Some warrant is given for this power of giving blessing by the fact that Zachariah is 'filled with the Holy Ghost' (Luke 1.67) and with prophetic ventriloquism 'spake by the mouth of his holy prophets' (Luke 1.70), but one must suspect that the chain of command is really an effect of the prophetic powers assumed to be possessed by language itself.

And yet, although both benediction and malediction seem to require or implicate the mediating omnipotent agent dreamed up by Rank and Sachs (Rank and Sachs 1916, 71), the curse or malediction often seems more likely to depend on the conjuration or adjuration of mediating powers. Indeed, it is the impiety of this swearing or declaring *by*, which calls for the deprecation (literally the unpraying or praying down) of the profane prayer-magic contained in phrases like 'by God', 'by Jove', 'by Christ' or, in folk etymology, 'by our Lady' (bloody). We may in fact suggest that malediction is essentially a kind of biloquism (an early alternative to the word ventriloquism), or double-talk, which borrows its power from the parody of the divine invocation in blessing it effects. Though both benediction and malediction depend on supplicatory invocation, the proliferation of accessories and adjutants in diabolical wish-making may warrant the supposition that malediction is more essentially a matter of mediation than benediction. Malediction is mediation diversified perhaps, where benediction is mediation dissimulated.

Many maledictions take the form of what was known as a *defixio* or, in Greek, κατάδεσμος, a charm which arrests or paralyses. Often, these charms took the form of strips or tablets of lead on which the imprecations were inscribed, sometimes in backwards writing, reversal being especially powerful computational magic, with the lead then being rolled up. Lead seems to have been used because it was relatively cheap, and quite easily scratched with a stylus (Gager 1992, 3-4). Like writing itself, lead seemed to be ambivalently both durable (cold and heavy as death) and ductile (pliable, inscribable). The defixiones were sometimes themselves transfixed with iron nails (Gager 1992, 18), or enclosed in objects such as the fourth-century lamps apparently thrown into the cistern of the sacred spring of Anna Perenna in Piazza Euclide in Rome (Mastrocinque 2007).

Another of the objects commonly employed for cursing in the ancient Mediterranean and Middle East were magical bowls, which were commonly inscribed with spells on their insides, sometimes in a spiral coiling inwards from the rim to the centre, and buried upside down, in a practical enactment of their power to trap or constrict one's enemy, or a malign spirit (Montgomery 1913, 40-5;). Occasionally, the bowl could be provided by a human skull. As so often, the supplications contained in these inscriptions, whether defensive or aggressive, rely upon supplementation, as Dan Levene explains: 'the insult, injury, offence or theft that was committed against a particular individual was transferred to one of the gods, so that now the god became the injured party and was thus in a position to redress the insult, injury, offence, or theft' (Levene 2013, 6).

The force of the spell, or incantation, is the force of enclosure, or the magical suspending of time and mutability, sometimes by putting things back-to-front or up-ending, in that primary infraction of the irreversibility of things in nature that the symbolic order implies and supplies. At its heart, as it is at the heart of all art, is the principle of reflexive redundancy (Connor 2011), that which turns in, or 'waves back', upon itself. In his final book, which he sent to his publisher on the day before his death, rendering it both final and yet, because he had no time himself to reread it, unfinished, Michel Serres finds in this principle of *relire*, rereading, the principle of the *relié*, retying, relying or religion (Serres 2019).

Gratifications

Prayer power is gratifying in that it seems to hold out the prospect of a considerable profit from the relatively minor sacrifice of freedom involved in observing a ritual. There are many forms of pleasure that are offered by formalised speech, but most will involve at bottom the principle of effort saved, in a way that may resemble the Freudian economics of laughter. A formalised utterance is one that seems autonomic, requiring less of the labour of composition or even recall than the devising of ordinary kinds of utterance, and so in a sense seems to utter itself. This may account somewhat for the fact that impassioned speech, which may similarly give the gratification of spontaneous overflow rather than careful contrivance, is often also rhythmically highly patterned, as though passion were a vehicle that transported itself. Some writers have felt a vague unease at the absence in English of a simple word for the one who prays, since 'prayer' seems already to have been commandeered in the word used for what the act of praying amounts to. Some resort to a term like 'precator' (Houghton 2004, 172; Clark 2018, 11), or 'orant' (Boynton) or a splitting of the action from the actor, in the 'pray-er' (Coleridge 1839, 38). But this coincidence is telling, for the action of praying is an action that aims to consume the actor in their action.

But there is another kind of gratification offered by prayer, that involves a different sense of gratuity, or something for nothing. As I have suggested, the work performed by prayer is a reflexive work, of performing the very efficacy of the performance. Petitionary prayers, whether of cursing of blessing, also require an intermediary, somebody to whom the petition is addressed. Indeed, we may define petition as the mediation of desire, through the turning to, or invocation of another. Often that intermediary will be a god, or a figure credited with power to grant the wish (king, father, fairy godmother, etc). But, in the absence of such an addressee, the act of wishing itself may be all that is needed to provide the necessary accessory. In fact, the addressee may be able so often to be dispensed with in the act of wishing (in blessing or damning and blasting, for example), that one may begin to suspect that addressee of being a sort of stage-property, intended to fill out the performance of the wishing, understood as the staging of the magical wish that wishing could be immediately effective. It is this principle that Dylan Thomas turns into an act of magical contagion at the end of his villanelle 'Do Not Go Gentle into That Good Night': 'Curse, bless, me now with your fierce tears, I pray' (Thomas 1978, 108). The poet-son performs a plea to his father to perform equivalent acts of petition. It is as though being alive is identified with being, or wanting to be, able to believe in wanting.

So the essential principle of prayer is that it must have an addressee, even though it is an addressee that, in order for the act of prayer to make any sense, that is, to make sense as the senseless thing it is, must be invisible and unapparent, and so wholly the creature of the act of prayer, there only in the special kind of not-being-there summoned and sustained by the act of prayer. This makes prayer itself an utterance that is uniquely dependent upon faith and hope, directed at, and dependent not on the addressee, as the content and intent of the prayer might seem to indicate, but on the drama of the address, and the self-fulfilling power of the act of prayer itself. This absurdity forms a kind of imaginary economics that keeps available for the adult the childish gratification of the something-for-nothing of magical belief. The gratification this offers is that of an excess, in the increase of logical complexity, rather than that of a reduction in tension offered by the calming adherence to formula. The pleasures of prayer thus include at the same time the calm of enhanced lawfulness, of a universe made to be adequate to human needs and desires, and the epistemic excitement of what must be the greatest anomaly of all, that there might be any adequation at all between a mote of individual existence at prayer and a universe that is not inattentive, or otherwise occupied, but earlessly incapable of audition.

The excitement, even the sense of exaltation, allowed by this anomaly, makes the usual considerations at work in philosophical discussions of petitionary prayer beside the point. Indeed it may well be the point to *make them* beside the point, by asserting what, following Coleridge, Kierkegaard and Derrida, Christopher Stokes calls the 'negative rationality' of prayer (Stokes 2009, 553). I have argued that to pray for benefit or assistance to a being believed to be omnipotent, omniscient and bottomlessly beneficent cannot be other than impious, since it implies the possibility of changing the mind of God, which could only be possible if God were an impostor. One may, of course, add the common hedge on impiety, by specifying that the benefits applied for should be granted only 'if it be Thy will', though this cannot really be much improvement, since it implies the impossible action of God performing something against his will, or opposing it by mistake, or without meaning to. So opening up the very possibility of God willing otherwise than he will anyway be going to asserts a condition it is impossible to assert, and implicates the impiety it seems designed to protect against. But all such objections, which have provided such copious and rewarding toil for philosophers and theologians concerned to assert the rationality of prayer, are similarly ways of securing the phenomenological essence of prayer, which is to assert the sovereign power invested in the possibility and performance of petition, over against any instrumental purpose they may have. Divinity does not exist in order to grant petitions: petitions exist to make and secure the projective power of divinity. This makes sense in particular of the prayer uttered by the father of the boy possessed by a dumb spirit in response to Jesus's assurance 'If thou canst believe, all things are possible to him that believeth': 'Lord, I believe; help thou mine unbelief' [Πιστεύω; βοήθει μου τῇ ἀπιστίᾳ](Mark 9.23-4), words which amply testify that the addressee, or point of application, of the act of petition is the divinised-divinising act of petition itself.

So it should not be a surprise that the paradoxical nature of prayer, far from weakening it, has often been proclaimed as its most distinctive and valuable feature. For Christopher Stokes, characterising Coleridge's attitude to prayer, 'human language is indeed improper in purporting to hail and name God, and thus prayer must work against the grain of tenable meaning, courting paradox and even impiety as it does so' (Stokes, 2009, 543). The struggle of prayer against the rationality that resists it, and insists that the prayer can only be autistically requisitioning itself, is systematically, and in an extra loop of self-gratification, misrecognised as the struggle of the yearning soul to close the gap between its mortal self and the divine.

At this point, we need to allow an objection that might well be made to the kinds of gratification that have so far been suggested for the operation of precatory petition, which have depended on the accomplishment of more or less successful actions. For prayer is arguably best thought of, not so much as an action as a passion. When not delegated to magico-mechanical procedures, practices of prayer often involve high levels of emotional arousal, and one of the recurrent features of the history of religion is the effort to restore the levels of libidinal investment in prayer that may have diminished through conventional or mechanical forms of repetition. Prayer draws reassurance from ritual, but the open-ended nature of prayer, which must always allow for the possibility of its failure, means that this reassurance is never fully assured. Prayer is often associated with the simultaneous tension and discharge involved in lamentation, and the weeping that may give expression to it. Children learn that the production of tears both produces pleasurable attention from others, and has an intrinsically calming effect – tears produced as a result of emotional stimulus rather than, for example, as a reflex from physical irritation of the eye, have a specific chemical composition, consisting of more protein-based hormones, including leucine enkephalin, which is an endogenous pain-killer (Frey et. al. 1981). The lachrymal narcissism of prayer is in part a narcotic: 'It is a child that sings itself to sleep,/The mind, among the creatures that it makes' (Stevens 2015, 461).

If there is enjoyment in the adult *enfantillages* of prayer, it is characteristically an enjoyment that must combine with or pass through duress and jeopardy. Prayer can only be the assertion of faith because it is also the putting of faith at stake and in question. It is for this reason that prayer is much more commonly associated with tears than with laughter, for tears allow simultaneously for the expression of pain and the partial annulment of that pain through its very expression. Lamentation allows for the shaping of longing into a kind of pleasurably self-relieving liniment. Early Christians in particular tended to emphasise that prayer was more associated with endurance than with triumph, often using the formula, sometimes attributed to Tertullian, *preces et lacrymæ sunt arma ecclesiæ*, prayer and tears are the weapons of the Church. The final section of Tertullian's 'On Prayer' emphasises the passive operativity of prayer, as compared with the aggressive miracles wrought by it in a previous dispensation:

> *Old-world* prayer, indeed, used to free from fires, and from beasts, and from famine; and yet it had not (then) received its form from Christ. But how far more amply operative is *Christian* prayer! It does not station the angel of dew in mid-fires, nor muzzle lions, nor transfer to the hungry the rustics' bread; it has no delegated grace to avert any sense of suffering; but it supplies the suffering, and the feeling, and the grieving, with endurance: it amplifies grace by virtue, that faith may know what she obtains from the Lord, understanding what — for God's name's sake — she suffers. (Tertullian 1885, 691)

Tertullian concludes that the rains of heaven are superior, and indeed more capable of bearing up against God himself, than the fires of rage: 'Is it wonder if *it* knows how to extort the *rains* of heaven — (prayer) which was *once* able to procure its *fires*? Prayer is alone that which vanquishes God' (Tertullian 1885, 691). William Blake articulates the doctrine of the triumph of expressive suffering in 'The Grey Monk': 'The Hermits Prayer & the Widows tear/Alone can free the World from fear/For a Tear is an Intellectual Thing/And a Sigh is the Sword of an Angel King' (Blake 1965, 481). The power that tears may have both to prolong and to dissolve the sense of suffering, learned early and unforgettably by human infants, is sentimentally evoked in Wilfred Owen's 'A Tear Song', in praise of the glistering tears of a trilling chorister, seen as a kind of jewelled prize wrought from the combination of singing and weeping:

> God the boy's jewel took
>   Into His casket,
> Flinging the anthem book

> On His waste-basket.
> God for his glittering world
> Seeketh our tears.
> Prayers show as eyelids pear hath no ears.
> Prayers show as eyelids pearled.
> God hath no ears (Owen 1983, 143)

Some writers find in the state of yearning for the impossible plenitude that seems to be promised in prayer the essence of prayer itself. Such, for example, seems to be John D. Caputo's argument for the religious basis of the seemingly atheist Jacques Derrida's relation to his abandoned Judaism. 'Deconstruction is a passion and a prayer for the impossible, a defense of the impossible against its critics, a plea for/to the experience of the impossible, which is the only real experience, stirring with religious passion' (Caputo 1997, xx).

The assumed divinity of prayer is why there can be such satisfaction in magnifying and multiplying the act of prayer so that it may become, not a passionate episode, driven by desire or desperation, but a whole way of life, a mode of existence in, and as, a ceaselessly renewed posture of petition. No doubt there is something infantile in this, the enactment of the idea of a life lived as an endless series of immediately fulfilled or at least in principle infallible wishes. But there is a subtlety too, that one would have no reason to expect the child to have developed for themselves. For prayer exists to maintain the pulsative faith in the idea of the addressable, in the one able to be petitioned. Praying promises for the prayer a standing reserve, or what we rightly call a *supply*, of the *sujet supposé supplier*, equivalent to Lacan's *sujet supposé savoir* (Lacan 2018, 232), the subject supposed to be evocable and rousable by prayer. This may be another reason why prayer tends to be prefaced by vocative formulations, such 'O God', 'Merciful Father', 'Lord of Heaven' and so on. The phrases that may seem to be making humble acknowledgment of the transcendence of the one addressed must also constitute something of a self-warranting for the petition for which they prepare, especially if they contain a reminder that the addressee of the prayer is not only vastly powerful, but also bottomlessly merciful.

The precautionary adulation found in the vocatives that open many precatory actions are balanced by the 'Amen' that closes many prayers in Judaism, Christianity and Islam. Perhaps no word more work in confirming that a given utterance is, or is to be taken as, a prayer, and, for many Christians, a prayer will remain indefinite or incomplete unless concluded with an amen. At the same time, saying amen in response to any utterance goes a long way to getting it treated or regarded as a prayer. The word doubles the performative of the petition that has preceded it, saying, so be it, let it be that that of which I have said 'let it be that' should be permitted to come to pass. *The Myroure of Oure Ladye*, a fifteenth-century devotional text written for the nuns of the Order of St Bridget in Syon Abbey, takes care to specify the two aspects, affirmation and wish, of the word amen:

> Amen. thys worde Amen ys a worde of hebrew, and some tyme yt ys a worde of affermynge and ys as moche as to say as 'Treuly' or 'Faythfully'. And some tyme yt is a worde of desyrynge and is as moche to say as 'So be yt' (Anon 1873, 77)

In scripture, the word amen in fact appears both before an utterance, and at the end of it, the English word 'verily' corresponding to the former. '[A]s it is prefixed to a speech, it signifies *so it is*. … [A]s it is added to a petition or request, it signifies *so be it* (E.H. 1864, 266). On one occasion in Revelation, Amen is actually given as a name or title of Christ: 'And unto the angel of the church of the Laodiceans write; These things saith the Amen, the faithful and true witness, the beginning of the creation of God' (Revelations 3.14). This suggests that the role of Christ in relation to the Father may be that of embodying the promise of petition itself. Paul explicates this relation between Father and Son as a yea-saying countersign in the affirmation that 'For all the promises of God in him are yea, and in him Amen, unto the glory of God by us' (2 Corinthians 1.20). This makes petition, or the simple, empty, reduplicative speech-act that seals it, identical with the Incarnation.

The reverberation of petition in the amen is encouraged by the fact that it is often literally echoed back by a congregation to the preacher who has intoned or articulated a prayer on their behalf. It is as though the amen which emphasises or underwrites the petition were also enacting in advance a magical answer to it, simultaneously 'please let it be' and 'right you are then'. The female participants in a food-related Jewish ritual in which amen is intoned multiple times in response to benedictions of different foods suppose that a new angel is created by every utterance of the word, on the grounds that the numerical values in Hebrew of the letters in the word amen are equivalent to those in the word מלאך‎, רְאָלְמָ‎, רְאָלְמָ‎ *mal'akh*, angel (Neriya-Ben Shahar 2018, 158). As one nineteenth-century commentator suggested, 'the joint prayers of a whole multitude of Christians must needs have a kind of omnipotence in them, and secure the richest blessings' (E.H. 1864, 267).

This effect of ricocheting self-potentiation may be at work in all the forms of collective utterance which characterise prayer – as though the greater the numbers of those uttering the prayer, the more likely it is that it will be granted. The strength of this kind of collective action depends upon the tension imparted by the very risk of its loss of impetus as a result of those who decline to join in, for example in the will-to-continuation which keeps a round of applause going, and seems to be trying to drown out the apprehension that its force depends upon its own powers of self-reinforcement.

Prayer is often delegated to persons invested with special kinds of power by communities of believers, such as priests and monarchs. The history of royal prayers in particular seems to be characterised by an interesting effect of augmentative reflexivity: as David Baldwin's history of royal prayer indicates (2009), monarchs are both the subject of prayers for their longevity and health ('God Save the Queen') and the privileged spokespersons for special kinds of petition, in times of stress or war. Shakespeare seems to offer us in the final words of Prospero in *The Tempest* an insight into the helplessness of the one caught up in this dream of omnipotence:

> Now my charms are all o'erthrown,
> And what strength I have's mine own,
> Which is most faint. Now, 'tis true
> I must be here confined by you,
> Or sent to Naples. Let me not,
> Since I have my dukedom got
> And pardon'd the deceiver, dwell
> In this bare island by your spell;
> But release me from my bands
> With the help of your good hands.
> Gentle breath of yours my sails
> Must fill, or else my project fails,
> Which was to please. Now I want
> Spirits to enforce, art to enchant;
> And my ending is despair,
> Unless I be relieved by prayer,
> Which pierces so that it assaults
> Mercy itself, and frees all faults.
> >   As you from crimes would pardoned be,
> >   Let your indulgence set me free. (Shakespeare 2011, 1094-5)

This is the second of the two gestures of renunciation that Shakespeare allows us and himself to pretend he is enacting through Prospero at the end of *The Tempest*. The first is a giving up of his 'so potent art', the power to raise storms and make the dead walk, which he grandiosely abjures, in the breaking of his staff and drowning of his book. I have already alluded to the twinning of abjuring and adjuring; when Prospero declares 'this rough magic I here abjure', the ceremonial 'here' indicates that the abjuring is itself a kind of conjuration, or magical proceeding. This second is a renunciation of the very potency claimed by that renunciation. It is a reminder that Prospero has been dependent all along on the elves, the 'demi-puppets' that are themselves 'weak masters'. It asks for, and in the process exemplifies, the frail and failing mastery of prayer. Prospero reminds his audience of the way in which he has held the characters of the play pent and 'spell-stopp'd' (Shakespeare 2011, 1091) by his magic, in order to suggest that he too is dependent on being set free by those who hold him captive in the rough magic of their imputed and imputing belief.

But what Prospero's inversion of supplicator and supplicated also prays for is to be released from the fantasy of potency; he prays to be freed from the confinement of being the one assumed to be able to grant prayers, on the 'bare island' of his supposed so-potent art. He supplicates for release from the servitude of being the granter of play-prayers in the wish-fulfilment of art and magical thinking. In his prayer to be allowed to shuffle off the burden of his art, he reveals the last workings of its weak, wishful ministry, as he begs the audience to lend their hands to the making of that happy ending he, or his deviser, has taught them how to want. The wit is delicately teasing, though its implications are breathtakingly blasphemous: Prospero here masquerades as a kind of God begging his creatures to give him a break, petitioning to be let out of the penitentiary of the divine part their craving pleasure forces him to play.

Shakespeare's play with the solemnity of prayer – even down to the wink in 'by your indulgence set me free' towards the Catholic practice of purchasing in indulgences redemption through prayer – is impish to the point of impiety. Its oscillation between human and divine scenography also goes to the heart of the practice of prayer. For prayer is precisely what makes religion a practice rather than an abstract predication, something lived rather than merely thought. Without the requirement for prayer, the claim that the universe was formed and is governed by an all-powerful supernatural force would be no more than a phantasmagorical kind of physics, that would need to make no claims on us and have no implications for human life beyond the requirement to make some minor adjustments to some high-level cosmological equations. Prayer is the way in which religious believers live out their faith, as well as their doubt, insofar as this may be seen as a struggle for and within faith. Prayer makes it possible for belief not just to exist but to be existed, in becoming a mode of being. Prayer asserts not only that a God exists but also that that existence matters mightily for human beings, that God and man are objects of mutual concern.

This extraordinary claim accounts for much of the power of prayer. But, for precisely the reason that prayer is essential to religious belief, it also represents religion's greatest jeopardy. Perhaps the reason that prayer can come to represent the very arena in which belief is made actual and effective is that it also provides the most powerful indications of the all-too-human needs it exists to meet, in the autistic alterity through which supplication supplies itself with its satisfactions. Prayer is the prescribed path to divinity precisely because it is also the chink through which the tidal ruin of religion threatens to come rushing through. And it is in petition that this extraordinary tension between exaltation and absurdity is stretched to its extreme. Prayer embodies the possibility of a relation, of asking and allowing, beseeching and bestowing, between the divine and the human that is at once its importance and its impossibility. The belief in the efficacy of prayer entails that believers must not allow themselves to believe everything that the relation of petition would otherwise compel them to about the nature of their addressee and its relation to us.

Perhaps the most extraordinary features of prayer are the reciprocal relations of petition that constitute it. For one prays, not spontaneously, but in response to various kinds of urging or injunction, from either a worldly or godly source. One is exhorted to prayer, called to the act of petitionary calling that prayer essentially is. Jesus declares that 'men ought always to pray and not to faint' (Luke 18.1). Paul enjoins his readers to take on the strength of religious faith, 'Praying always with all prayer and supplication in the Spirit, and watching thereunto with all perseverance and supplication for all saints' (Ephesians 6.18). In the first epistle to the Thessalonians, Paul similarly urges 'Pray without ceasing' (1 Thessalonians 5.17). One prays to a God who ceaselessly entreats this entreating act of prayer, the petitioner petitioned by the one petitioned to meet their petitionary obligation. Indeed, in this respect, one may see prayer as the means whereby petition may approach or even seem to achieve its absolute autonomy from its objects and occasions. Construing religion as pure, self-multiplying petition opens the way for a characterisation of religion like that of John D. Caputo:

> By religion I mean a pact with the impossible, a covenant with the unrepresentable, a promise made by the *tout autre* with its people, where we are all the people of the *tout autre* the people of the promise, promised over to the promise. Hear, O Israel (Deut. 6:4), you are the people of a call, constituted from the start by a call, a solicitation. (Caputo 1997, xx)

A life of prayer promises a life lived in unceasing petition, a petition that can never be granted except in the gratification it ceaselessly grants itself, the gratification of meeting the demand for petition. It is perhaps this that finally joins prayers of petition and the prayers of worship, adoration and praise that seem to be their opposites. Just as the object of petition is the act of petition, so the object of praise in prayer is the voluptuous delight of the petitionary relation itself, in its endless exceeding of all occasion or obstruction.

Deifaction

Prayer cannot of course be taken at all seriously, or on anything like its own self-description or self-understanding. The very craziness of seriously wondering about or empirically enquiring into the likelihood of individual petitions from billions of separate persons being able to have any effect on the being to whom they are supposedly addressed may be part of the solemnly delirious diversion from seriousness that prayer constitutes. But this is the very reason for taking it very seriously indeed, though as what it is, rather than what it represents itself to be. What that is, it has been the work of this chapter to try to work free. Human beings, individually and collectively, cannot be fully understood without some account of this extraordinary, wholly inextirpable practice, so singular in itself and by reason of the loyalty it inspires in the hearts of so many possessed. *Homo precans*. Prayer directed at a God, whether avuncularly at hand or ineffably remote, is the proof as positive as will ever appear of the apotheosis of prayer, which, in its power to summon and sustain the idea of a biddable divinity, is the essence of religion; prayer is the deificer. Many have wondered what kind of omnipotent deity could be as clingily dependent on the worship and petitionary oblations as most deities seem to be, but of course it must be the case that prayer is an existential necessity for any god, who must literally depend upon the fact of prayer, in the sense of being its by-product. Only the act of prayer can keep intact the supposition of a being infinitely remote and immediately accessible, through an act of address that is itself modelled on this very duality of intimacy and distance. There should be no surprise in the fact that prayers should themselves so regularly thematise this coalescence of unimaginable magnificence and miserable minimality. The capacity of language itself both to inhabit the realm of ordinary needs and experiences and to reach beyond them into infinities and negativities – the communicability with the Word through the word – matches the capacities of prayer so closely because prayer allows for the misprision of this very ambivalence embodied in the word for the divine. The deificent power of prayer to conjure divinity is verily the apotheosis of prayer.

Noting what was already, by the end of the nineteenth century, an immense body of writing about the efficacy of prayer (James 1985, 471-2), William James protested that 'petitional prayer is only one department of prayer; and if we take the word in the wider sense as meaning every kind of inward communion or conversation with the power recognized as divine, we can easily see that scientific criticism leaves it untouched' (James 1985, 464). And yet, the expanded account of the action of prayer that James offers seems to imply petition, in the form of an articulated demand, even if its addressee is not a personalised deity but a source of spiritual energy:

> at all stages of the prayerful life we find the persuasion that in the process of communion energy from on high flows in to meet demand, and becomes operative within the phenomenal world. So long as this operativeness is admitted to be real, it makes no essential difference whether its immediate effects be subjective or objective. The fundamental religious point is that in prayer, spiritual energy, which otherwise would slumber, does become active, and spiritual work of some kind is effected really.
> (James 1985, 477)

There may well be acts of imaginary communion of this kind, which may be experienced in just the same ways as prayer is said to be experienced, in which the abstract need to invoke an addressee is much less evident. If so, this would constitute an important broadening of the phenomenon of prayer, and evidence that ought to discourage me in my confidence that prayer typically involves invocatory petition. But please to remember that my concern is not primarily with prayer, but with the particular kinds of petition enacted through prayer. So my guiding question will always be, not whether prayer is nothing but petition through and through, but whether the links between prayer and petition are substantial and significant to allow for profitable reflection.

Give us this day

Though prayer is often a kind of demand, one usually does not pray, as we say, on demand, that is *ad hoc*, at the times and in the places where the assistance of God may be required. In most religions, prayer is temporally regulated and itself a means of temporal regulation. Most religions do not go as far as Islam in mandating a set number of acts of prayer at specified times of the day, the five hours of prayer of the *salat*, but many come close, and the most striking fact is probably that there are so few religions in which there is no kind of temporality or scheduling attached to prayer. This might in itself suggest that prayers are not to be thought of as requests for specific goods or benefits, since if they were prayer would only be resorted to at times of particular need. To be sure, praying may be intensified in times of need – war, famine, plague – but for the most part the injunction to prayer is independent of these contingencies. It is an important principle of prayer that one must pray unnecessarily, as though it were maintaining the abstract petitory relation that were important – as it surely is – rather than its object.

One might surmise that the purpose of regulated prayer is precisely to dissolve or weaken the link between prayer and specific need. This may be useful for protecting prayer from the very petitionary forces that seem to drive it. If prayer is to function as reassurance, a reliable source of solace and confirmed faith, it must be protected from the evidence of inefficacy that would otherwise be sure to mount up. The generalising and ritualising of the act of petition serves to make it less potent as an act of petition, and thereby to keep at bay the possibility of disappointment and resentment at the unanswered prayer.

Another of the purposes of temporally-regulated prayer is to create collectivity through synchronisation. And collectivising prayer may itself also help do the work of detaching prayer from need, since it will only be on rare occasions, of earthquake or epidemic, that the needs of a large and diverse community will converge. So recurring time and cohering collectivity will work together, both of them forming nets of precaution to protect precation from the precarity to which it must lead if maintained in its riskily absolute form. The omnipotence of thoughts will need to accept compromises and the social sharing of risk in precatory insurance schemes to maintain its omnipotence. Once again, the condition of synchronicity and quantitative densification that offers reassurance of the efficacy, or at least the utility of prayer, is in fact the demonstration of its deliberate illusion. For what possible God could be swayed by the fact of magnitude in prayer? It is only humans, or anthropomorphic projections that are likely to succumb to the force of numbers.

So it is difficult in fact to resist the suggestion that the regular temporality of prayer exists in order to turn petition into pseudo-petition. The more regularly one prays, and so the more ritualised the act of prayer becomes, the more the difficult and dangerous force of petition is lulled. The here and now petition that might once have broken into or out of earthly time with disruptive effect becomes a social clock that ticks it off. In the periodic interruptions of routine and institutionalised worship by purifying revolutions, such as the Reformation, it is the act of prayer that is often the focus of attention. Purifying, evangelist and inspirational reflexes in religion will often insist that prayer should once again be direct, spontaneous and individual, inspiration replacing and renewing institution. Practices of prayer may respond to the demand to become spasmodic, urgent, demanding, even if they may also paradoxically borrow from the power that Emile Durkheim called 'collective effervescence' (Durkheim 1964, 226), the congregation which amplifies private petition into public expectation and approval.

Sooner or later, though, rhythm and scansion and the force of the already-done will tend to reassert themselves over the ecstasy of interruptive appeal, precisely because this will be the only way to keep the force of that appeal alive. There are two outcomes for the dangerous deificence of precatory insurgence: discharge or decay. Discharge will deflect the passionate and peremptory excitements of expectation into the adjacent satisfactions of acts of wrath or destruction, such as iconoclastic purgings, voluptuous acts of self-sacrifice, or votively-fuelled acts of political violence. Alternatively, spiritual insurgency will be subject to the careful management in which all successful religions are so intuitively and impressively expert, since this is just what it means to become a successful religion, by gently cancelling its tendency to orgasmic self-cancellation, and maintaining the stress of prayer at an optimal level of simmer. In the entropic process of ritual, deificent prayer will have become quietly, decently deicidal, quietly retiring its vocative Other from the scene, and redirecting the petitionary address inwards, into the socialised forms and rituals of prayer itself, in the process making it as clear as may be wished that the only answers to prayers are the ones it forms and furnishes for and in itself.

The moment of greatest need for a religious adherent may be that of approaching death. It may seem obvious that one might resort to petition in such extremity, at a time when no other recourse seems available, though it is often the case that in fact it is not the one dying who prays, but some representative of the church who must pray on their behalf, confirming the principle that petition must always seek out an emissary. The Greek Orthodox 'Office at the Parting of the Soul from the Body' literally provides words of supplication, addressed to the Theotokos, Mary as 'all-holy Birth-giver of God' (Hapgood 1906, 362), for the one approaching death, even as the one to whom the words of the prayer are given must say 'as an organ of speech, I am altogether extinguished, and my tongue is bound, and mine eye closeth' (Hapgood 1906, 363). All is vicariance in this final prayer, as the dying soul is lent a voice by the prayer in which to petition the Angels and Mary to offer their prayers in turn to the Lord God, in a petition-within-a-petition scripted for them:

> Having entered, O ye my holy Angels, before the Judgment Seat of Christ, bending in thought your supersensual knees, cry ye with weeping unto him: Have Mercy, O Maker of all men, upon the work of thy hands, O Good One; and cast it not away. (Hapgood 1906, 364)

At such a time, it may be revealed that the capacity to pray is being identified with life itself, so that one is not praying for life, natural or resurrected, but praying for prayer itself, which has achieved, or recognised, its identification with being alive. In parallel, the prayers for the souls of the dead out of which such a highly-developed and sustained economy was formed in the medieval world seem to make it clear that ongoing petition is identified with a kind of life after death. Here, more emphatically and unmistakably than anywhere else, praying is identified simply with the continuance in being for which one prays. Prayer at the end of life reveals that the need to which prayer gives expression is the necessity for need itself: *egeo ergo sum*.

It is hard to see how one for whom prayer is a vital and committed practice could not feel that their faith is the target of attack, or is at least being significantly devalued, in the perspectives I have developed. However, I doubt very much that the coherence of doctrines and beliefs regarding the personal nature of the transaction between deity and precator is likely to be of very great moment in the religious life of such a person. I have suggested indeed that much that is involved in petitionary prayer is precisely designed to divert attention from such logical considerations. It is not that prayer is irrational; it is that the deflection of this kind of reflection is its very rationality or *raison d'être*. More importantly, I have very little expectation that anything in what I have said could possibly diminish the faith in prayer, and the faith that the practice of prayer is believed to require and sustain. In fact, my suggestion would have to be something like the inverse, namely that *precor quia absurdum*, I pray because it is unavailing, because, unless it were quite useless, prayer could have no utility. There is no way out of the strangeness of the non-self-coincidence of this practice. Prayer is the very principle and enactment of religion, the thing that makes religion a lived rather than merely theoretical reality, even as it is the ruin and ridicule of religion wherever and whenever it is practised. What is more, everything in the practice of prayer depends on its serene immunity to the auto-immune response it should trigger to its own toxic absurdity, and depends too on the very fact that prayer can retain its dignity and ennobling power despite making such a grotesque mockery of the believer, the belief and the believed-in. You cannot poke fun at a practice that so solemnises its own nonseriousness without making yourself look like an idiot. Since prayer is one of the most versatile and abiding of the ways in which human beings exist, and transitively exist themselves, as asking entities or beings-for-petition, then, if specifically religious prayer were ever to shrivel to nothing, its pervasiveness and potency in human life would certainly need to be supplied by other means. And wherever it does show signs of shrivelling there is always indeed an abundant supply of such displaced forms of precatory supplication.

6

Wooing

Where the opposite of theft is ownership or possession, the contrary of theft is purchase. By imperfect analogy, if the opposite of rape is non-rape, in its many forms, love, celibacy, indifference, the contrary of rape is suit or courtship. Such archaic words provide strong hints of the legal expectations and requirements that are part of actions of amorous or sexual solicitation. If, as I suggested in chapter 1, there is a dimension of seduction in every petition, then we may expect the formalised action of sexual solicitation to marry with or form a significant counterpoint to the protocols of petition. Courtship behaviours across the animal world are even more widespread and ritualised than begging behaviours, of which they can represent a reminiscence or modification. This chapter will consider the practices of wooing, flirting, seduction and courting as varied modes of asking, in word and action, or as the ways of petitory putting forward that classically build towards the quasi-contractual ceremony that is known as a 'proposal', and themselves constitute different kinds of bid.

Courting arises from the act of attending at court, a word that derives from Latin *cohors*, an enclosed space, or, by extension, a group of soldiers so enclosed. One attends at court in order to seek favour or preferment, thus one courts the court, construed thereby as a place of courtship. *Hortus*, a garden, is one such enclosed space. The verb *exhort*, along with the rarer Latinate *adhort*, names the act of urging, especially in a military context. Coherence is the quality exhibited by such a cohorted space or institution. The link between the words *exhort* and *horticultural* on the one hand and *court* and *chorus*, from Greek χορός, a dance, provides a suggestive coalition between coercion and consent. Courting is perhaps a delicate or horticultural form of exhorting, requiring as much patience as passion, along with considerable powers of cultivation. Consent, which is taken to be the opposite of coercion, must in fact include and consort with some degree of it. For while one can consent freely, one cannot consent spontaneously, because consent is always agreement to something that is requested or proposed, whether explicitly or implicitly. So, though genuine consent can never be coerced, one can only consent to something that, were it not for that consent, might well be coercive.

Even if it were not otherwise so abundantly manifest, the fact that one 'pays court' ought to make it clear that there is an economics of sexual solicitation. Especially in the animal world, assuming there to be for the moment some other, there must always be outlay or expenditure involved in courtship, often because that outlay is a pledge or proof that the bargain on offer is a comparatively good one, precisely because it demonstrates that the proposer can amply afford to make it. You would want to keep away from a mate for whom courtship represented any kind of sacrifice of vital powers. In this respect, the petition of courtship appears different from petition in the case of need or deficiency, as in the assumed case of an honest beggar, or the 'honest begging' that has been the preoccupation of biologists. Petition for what one needs offers neediness itself as an earnest of what is being requested. In the case of sexual or romantic solicitation, the suitor displays what they possess rather than what they lack – physical strength, symmetrical features, high nutritional condition, strutting self-confidence, song-making prowess, GSOH. Where the beggar bargains from, and therefore on, their weakness, the romantic suitor bargains on and with their strength, imposing rather than imploring. Perhaps we should therefore regard the hopeless lover's petition as a classical instance of mendicant mendacity, the assumption of need in the service of greed. We are, however, going to see that amorous petition represents just as complex a mixture of weakness and strength as other forms of petition.

Passion

In the form in which it has been nourished and itself flourished in literary and artistic forms since classical times, romantic love has been characterised as a passion, that is a hungrily assertive form of sacrificial subjection, which makes up the condition of joyful desperation that seems to be mandated in the case of passionate love. Andreas Capellanus begins his *De amore*, written towards the end of the 12th century, with the bald statement 'Love is a certain inborn suffering [*Amor est passio quaedam innata*]' (Capellanus 1969, 28; Capellanus 1892, 3). The leading signification of passion, from Latin *pati* to suffer, is undergoing, or the condition of being acted upon. Oddly to modern ears, the word passion could be used neutrally to signify simply a way of being acted on considered as a feature or property, as in the definition, in John Dee's preface to a rendering in 1570 of Euclid's *Elements*, of astronomy as the concern with the 'naturall motions, apparences, and passions propre to the Planets and fixed Starres' (Euclid 1570, sig. B1ʳ). In his *Dictionary* (1755), Samuel Johnson defined Latin 'common verbs' that can be both active and passive, such as *aspernor* I despise/am despised', as 'verbs as signify both action and passion' (Johnson 1755, n.p). But given its strong inflection, from its first uses in in Old English, by the religious Passion of Christ, the idea of passion as being acted upon begins itself to be impassioned, implying that being acted on is a kind of action in the passive, which carries the possibility of a glory and inversive exulting in one's affliction. Indeed, passion used as a verb could be used to mean both to excite passion, in oneself or another, or to show passion, sometimes reflexively, as in William Sharp's remark (quoting Prosper Mérimée) of Shelley's yearning for the unattainable that 'There can be few of us who … so passion for this passion' (Sharp 1887, 98).

From the beginning of the 12th century, the word passion starts to be extended to violent or vehement emotional states, especially attaching to sexual love. Strikingly, the other leading emotional state to which the word passion is commonly applied is anger, in which the compounding of assertion and surrender is similarly palpable. Indeed, one might define anger precisely and functionally in these terms, as a yielding to what overcomes one, and as a way of overcoming some obstacle or opponent through that very force of being overcome. The fact that one cannot so readily entertain a 'passion' of fear, or of happiness, suggests that the idea of passion tends to be attached to reactive conditions, in which the subject, in the sense of the one made subject, bears up against some kind of action brought to bear on it. It is as this kind of counterforce that the suffering of love manifests, in the varieties of protest, lament, complaint, exhortation and so on, that operate across the petitory spectrum. More generally, this active passivity is the essential change of valence made available, and in fact irresistible, to all creatures of symbol, and subject to the insistence of the letter.

Desire and anger seem also to be alloyed in the fact that wooing is often imagined as a kind of combat, requiring strategy, siege, sally, and surrender. 'Love is a kind of warfare [*militiae species*]; avaunt, ye laggards!' writes Ovid in his *Ars Amatoria*:

> these banners are not for timid men to guard. Night, storm, long journeys, cruel pains, all kinds of toil are in this dainty camp. Oft will you put up with rain from melting clouds of heaven, and oft will you lie cold on the bare ground. (Ovid 1929, 82-3)

Such antagonism often takes the form of a dissimulated verbal contest, a principle that had already become a cliché by the time of the sparring Beatrice and Benedict in Shakespeare's *Much Ado About Nothing*. Wooing often presents itself as an argument, or parodic disputation, with the varieties of petitory speech act providing the catechistic prompts and demands for response. The agonies that animate imploring and plaint are part of the agonistics of love, which typically amount to the reciprocal play of attack and defence, alerting us to the fact that wooing and seduction are often related also to the activity of gaming. John Wilmot points up the paradox of amorous conflict: 'Twixt strifes of Love and war the difference Lies in this/When neither overcomes Loves triumph greater is' (Rochester 1984, 25). Wooing has been implicated in the psychodynamics of the heightened form of gaming found in gambling, for example by Ralph R. Greenson, who concludes that compulsive gambling 'is based on an unconscious attempt to regain the lost feeling of omnipotence by fighting and/or wooing Luck or Fate' (Greenson 1947, 75), with the father figured in the fate to which the gambler is subject, and the mother in the 'Lady Luck' whom the gambler tries to win to his cause (Greenson 1947, 70). Given that sexual solicitation must always be a kind of gambling across the natural world, it is perhaps not surprising that gambling should present itself to humans as a kind of wooing.

The words 'I love you' imply that love is understood to be a state of feeling. But the manifest differences between such a statement and statements that might report other feelings, like 'I am bored', or 'I could use a coffee' are strong indications that love is not a feeling of which one is expected simply to take note. The duress and consequence that are exacted on and through such a declaration make it clear that really love is to be understood, as Niklas Luhmann maintains, not as an emotion but as 'a code of communication, according to the rules of which one can express, form and simulate feelings, deny them, impute them to others, and be prepared to face up to all the consequences which enacting such a communication will bring with it' (Luhmann 1986, 20). A medium of communication both imparts and itself implies forms of behaviour, and, from the early seventeenth century, people had become aware that 'despite all emphasis on love as passion, they were dealing with a model of behaviour that could be acted out and which one had in full view before embarking on the search for love' (Luhmann 1986, 20). As Edgar Landgraf, among many others, has observed, '[t]he evolution of Romantic love took place first and foremost as a literary phenomenon' (Landgraf 2004, 30). If there were nothing else, the fact that amorous love is commonly known by the name of a literary genre, *romance*, would on its own be strongly suggestive of this link between emotion and medium. The literariness of romantic love both ensures and accounts for its familiarity.

But the other important feature of romantic love, almost always overlooked, except by cynics and satirists, because it stands in such plain view, is that it is fantastic. A romance originally referred to a tale of marvels and the extravagantly improbable adventures of a chivalric hero, usually, from the twelfth century onwards, in vernacular languages, but sometimes translated from Latin originals, such as Geoffrey of Monmouth's *Historia Regum Britanniae*, which may account in part for the designation 'Romance'. From the late sixteenth century onwards, the word romance takes two separate paths, the path which concerns love-relations, and the path which concerns unreal narratives. But they come together in the fact that truth, proof, testing and demonstration are at the centre of love stories, and the acting out of such stories in processes of wooing and seduction. The question that activates and animates all love stories is essentially whether they concern true love, even as, and largely because, the love relation in question can never in fact be straightforwardly true, but always under arduous deliberation.

So, it has been clear, at least from Ovid's *Ars Amatoria* onwards, that 'love' has been 'an art to be practised rather than a passion to be felt' (Dodd 1913, 3). In the later sixteenth century, the phrase 'making love' arises to express the formative and performative work required in love. It seems still to have been novel enough in 1580 for John Lyly to mock it gently, by transposing the courtly arts of love into artisanal apprenticeship:

> A Phrase nowe there is which belongeth to your Shoppe boorde, that is to make loue, and when I shall heare of what fashion it is made, if I like the pattorne, you shal cut me a partlet: so as you cut it not with a paire of left handed sheeres. And I doubt not though you haue marred your first loue in the making, yet by the time you haue made thrée or foure loues, you will proue an expert workman: for as yet you are lyke the Taylours boy, who thinketh to take measure before he can handle the shéeres. (Lyly 1580, sig. K2^r)

In fact, the contrast of art and passion cannot itself easily be sustained, given the intense symbolic work performed in the latter. We speak of labours of love, perhaps, in recognition of the affective-symbolic laboriousness of the amorous relation. Petition, accompanied by the varieties of supplicatory pity-tickling in lovers' lamentations or 'complaints', is at the heart of the communication of passion, and, just as importantly, the passion of communication that necessarily accompanies it, not least because it exhibits the same intense alliance of agency and passivity as the state of love itself. Affection represents a cooler version of the same double condition: a strong feeling of being affected, in which one feels affection *for* that which one is affected *by*. Petition expresses the urgency of amorous desire, because petition is characterised by the same urging of one's helplessness. We will see later how wooing behaviour often implicates agency, or action in the simple, direct sense, with agency in the oblique or substitutive sense, of the one who acts on one's behalf in love.

The kind of romantic love which seems to have developed from the twelfth century onwards, in what became formalised as 'courtly love', enacted a particular economy of intimacy and distance. The feelings of love demanded and promised a sense of closeness, to the point of absolute assimilation, or the desire for it, to the object of one's affections. At the same time, the development of the state of love as a communicative medium required the loved one always to be held at a distance; one can only declare one's love under such a condition of distance, which makes all love in a sense reliably 'hopeless' if what is meant by success is the simple closing of the gap. According to Joseph D. Kuzma, summarising a long critical tradition, 'the protagonist of the courtly drama ultimately seeks neither the full possession of a desired object, nor the realization of some felicitous outcome; but rather, only the ceaseless amplification of desire itself' (Kuzma 2016, 3).

The development of romantic love required a modification of prepositions. Now, rather than transitively loving somebody, such that one might affirm, simply 'I love you', one is said to be 'in love'. This phrase seems first to have been used as a parallel to the animal 'in heat', for example in John Trevisa's 1398 translation of the *De Proprietatibus Rerum* of Bartholomaeus Anglicus, which describes the behaviour 'Whanne þe swan is in loue' (Bartholomaeus 1398, f.146ᵛ), translating 'in amo' (Bartholomaeus 1505, sig. Q3ᵛ). But Stephen Batman's 1582 edition adds the marginal remark, as though to fend off the anthropomorphic suggestion that had attached to being 'in love', 'A fond fayning that a svvanne singeth, vvho hath but a naturall voice, as other birdes haue' (Bartholomaeus 1582 sig. Ki2ʳ). This phrase was then supplemented to bring about the curious notion of 'being in love with', and its variation being 'enamoured of', in which a tripartite relationship, involving the two potential lovers and the ardently dynamic state they inhabit, takes the place of a duet.

Petition occupies the middle passage in the communication of passion, kindling in every passionate petition a passion *for* petition, and therefore for its repetition. The secrecy of the lover who dares not declare his love, or the love that dare not speak its name, are internalisations of this vitalising remoteness. Slavoj Žižek's Lacanian reading of the function of the ideal lover's unattainability rests on the argument that '*external hindrances that thwart our access to the object are there precisely to create the illusion that without them, the object would be directly accessible*' (Žižek 1994, 94), an argument that Žižek hopes will take us beyond the familiar Freudian argument that inhibition intensifies desire, but seems simply to spell out its implications. What matters, for present purposes, is what articulates, in the senses simultaneously of splitting and connecting, that impassioned gap between the accessible and the inaccessible, namely the executive forms of desiring action, in appeal, plaint and petition. Petition, which I would like to be understood as more than one particular kind of speech act in amatory discourse, but rather as its essential form and last instance, always, no matter how humbly or despairingly, makes what we call an advance, reaching out through and into the code of love, in order to close the distance which its very advance opens up before it.

The difference between the solicitation of the beggar and that of the lover is this: where the beggar pleads for a gift, that is, some good that will, however minimally, deplete the giver and make more replete the recipient, the amorous petitioner by contrast, makes an offer rather than a request – that is, they tender a bid. Their aim is not to induce from their intended donor a gift that will assuage their desire, but to induce in that donor an equivalent state of unfulfilled desire. Rather than a remedy for lack, they seek a redoubling of it in the one petitioned. Their aim is not to induce a gift that will ameliorate their beggarly condition, or not that only, but to reduce the one being solicited to a mimic condition of indigence. This is possible because of the curious status of sexual or romantic love as an oxymoronically self-feeding hunger, a famishing gift of desire, at once starving and bloating, that to many will seem well worth the having. It may be for this reason that sexual solicitation, which, among humans as well as animals, involves the giving of mediatory gifts, attempts thereby to constitute itself as the giving of a gift rather than the demand for one. This duality is in fact, not entirely absent in other kinds of petition. The beggar may offer as a side-inducement a gratitude (God bless you, your honour) that imparts and permits a moral glow of self-congratulation. The gifts given as part of courtship among certain animals, the drop of sweet fluid exuded by the male fruit fly, the eye-pleasing scheme of exterior decoration assembled by the male bower bird, the begging cries of female magpies to indicate fertility and reproductive readiness (Ellis et. al. 2009), reverse the relations of begging behaviour among adults and young. Where the hungry, helpless infant begs the parent to feed it, the hungry, helpless would-be lover begs by taking on the role of the parent providing for its begging infant. The action of amorous petition is the attempt to stimulate a shared condition of neediness.

Flirtation

Even in the absence of flowers, chocolates, compliments, and so on, the principal form taken by this gift is in the performance of the stylised seduction itself. What seduces in the seduction is in large part the gift of its style, along with the solicitation it offers to participate in the seductive play. Hence the importance of flirtation, which renders the serious work of sexual pairing and reproduction trivial and playful. This too enables a kind of immunising infantilism, in which both parties may play at parenting and being babied. This kind of adult play intimates and imitates the costless or self-gratifying transactions of childhood, in which pleasure is simply to be had for the asking. Many kinds of public petition speed and concentrate time, the beggar often exploiting the fact that the one petitioned will usually wish the encounter to be over with as quickly as possible. Flirtation by contrast turns petition into repetition, which at once draws out the process and diffuses the danger, of humiliation for the petitioner, and of face-threat or offence for the petitioned. Because the petition is never quite consented to, it is never quite refused either. It is, so to speak, the uncompleted mourning of Freud's melancholia in the future tense, in a precautionary mourning for what has yet to be lost. An important role in flirtation is the prolonging of petition through meta-manoeuvre: thus the lover may be enjoined, or will pretend that he is, to ask permission to 'renew his suit', or carry on asking permission.

It is often assumed that women, or whatever people might have in mind when using the placeholding term 'women', will or even should take the lead in flirtatious leading-on, with men, or rather their semantic lieutenant 'men', acting out the desire to speed things to conclusion. But the petitioning male can also find himself seduced by the very fore-play or entr'acte of his own seduction, and will most likely be unable to play his part unless he has some cultural pre-acquaintance with this fact. The many hours children spend in teasing play may help provide this preparation. Teasing, which refers to the combing out of fibres, is a toning down of Old English *tǽsan*, to tear or draw to pieces, even as teasing also implies a kind of ravelling arousal, this itself alluding perhaps to the primary action of grooming which is so powerful a composer of social time in primates and has recently been reinjected into sexual relations in the use of the word 'grooming' to signify the predatory soothings of a paedophile or other sexual abuser. The earliest meaning of groom in English is simply a boy, or inferior servant, who typically would tend to horses, Shakespeare apparently being the first to separate it from the word bridegroom, in the phrase 'bride and groom' used metaphorically of friends by Iago in *Othello* (Shakespeare 2011, 955). Male or female, the teaser may tease themselves into preferring deferral to dénouement. This is a further example of the petition which begins to turn to itself by way of granting its own suit.

Wooing can involve seduction, but it need not, and there is a distinction between them as regards what they solicit, and how. Wooing solicits acknowledgement and acceptance on the part of the one wooed, through all the modes of urging, persuasion and petition it may employ. So wooing does things like asking, begging, bidding, proposing. Seduction asks nothing, but rather provokes, though in a passive fashion. It does not seek, stalk, pursue, or plead its case, but sits, unresisting, and irresistibly, still. If it exercises anything, it is not petition but fascination, which is not an action, but an affecting or infection. Wooing differentiates its object from all others and devotes itself to its selective attention. Seduction thrives on its apparent indifference. That which seduces does so because it is not meant for us, even if it does not exclude us either. Wooing expends energy, conspicuously and as an argument in its own cause; seduction sucks energy in. There are male seducers and female wooers, but the differences between wooing and seduction programme a certain conventional difference between the actively pursuing male and the condition of female attraction, an active condition which performs no actions. One woos by performing recognisable actions of wooing, but one seduces by being seductive, for which wooing provides no equivalent, since one cannot apparently be 'wooish', 'courtative' or 'suitical' in English. Wooing may adopt postures of weakness through its acts of petition and pledges of service and surrender, but seduction is, as Jean Baudrillard has evoked it, a more contagious and erosive kind of weakness, which does not conceal or suspend its strength, but rather makes strength and weakness entirely equivalent: 'To seduce is to appear weak. To seduce is to render weak. We seduce with our weakness, never with strong signs or powers. In seduction we enact this weakness, and this is what gives seduction its strength' (Baudrillard 2001, 83). Wooing seeks the submission of its object: seduction seeks its own metastasis through its host. If I try to persuade you, I have to imagine you giving up your own position in order to adopt mine; if I seduce you, or provide arguments which prove seductive for you, I furnish you with the conviction that you have never had any convictions but mine. Seduction manifests not just and, for Baudrillard, it seems, not even essentially, in sexual relations, but in practices like adornment and the kind of ritual performance in which one can see

> an ostentatious ceremony for mastering signs, and a cycle for seducing meaning, where the signs gravitate irresistibly around each other so as to reproduce themselves as if by magnetic recurrence, resulting in dizziness, a loss of meaning, and the sealing of an indestructible pact among the participants. (Baudrillard 2001, 89)

But the distinction between wooing and seduction is not a permanent one. For wooing can itself become a kind of seduction, or narcissistic self-enticing, the wooer wooed by their wooing, in petitions that start to seduce, that is, to induce mimesis and self-similarity, rather than to win over or persuade. Alternatively (unless I mean similarly), seduction can be tempted to become directional and projective, fixing its sights upon a particular object.

Georg Simmel's essay 'On Flirtation' sees in the actions of the flirt a demonstration of the essential oscillation between, on the side of the suitor, having and not having and, on the side of the flirt, concession and refusal:

> the distinctiveness of the flirt lies in the fact that she awakens delight and desire by means of a unique antithesis and synthesis: through the alternation or simultaneity of accommodation and denial; by a symbolic, allusive assent and dissent, acting "as if from a remote distance"; or, platonically expressed, through placing having and not-having in a state of polar tension even as she seems to make them felt concurrently. (Simmel 1984, 134)

Simmel's essay is governed by two serenely uninspected assumptions. First, the flirt is always supposed to be female, and second, the suitor is always supposed to be male. Not only is the pursuer always male, the male can be assumed always to be in pursuit of his suit (a tautology that we will investigate soon), or in readiness to resume it. This, says Simmel, is because flirtation is 'the consummation of the sexual role that belongs to the female throughout the animal kingdom: to be the *chooser*' (Simmel 1984, 140). It is because of this in turn, Simmel believes, that women exhibit an interest in suitor males as individuals, whereas males are merely 'disposed to pursue the woman as woman' (Simmel 1984, 140). Men must be chosen, whereas women just need to be women (and, as Balzac's 'Sarrasine', or Wilder's *Some Like It Hot* will hint, perhaps not necessarily even that). However, the reasoning here is not entirely perspicuous to me. One might just as well say the inverse, that, if men are apparently always being appraised in relation to other applicants, actual or potential, for the role, it is males who are in principle interchangeable, and the female object of pursuit that is, at least for the nonce, nonpareil. In the switching of pursuit into accountancy, it is the elective woman who is supposed to play Maxwell's demon to the hot-or-not molecules swarming about her strait gate.

The assumption that courtship patterns, combed and corrugated by flirtation, are in the interests of selection, also assumes that males can be relied upon to be in a steady and continuous condition of pursuit and petition. Men must be ready at all times for sexual essay, in order to be available for female assay. Indeed, we must assume that such a constant state of pertly alert pre-petition, upright on its own Marvellian precipice, with the competition with other males for selection by females, is supposed to be the state of maleness as such. Of course, females must also compete with other females for the attention of males, but, on Simmel's account, what females desire in that attending is the condition of petition to which desire ought to, or is thought to, dispose the male, ever-ready to be rallied. Petition proves and requires a standing reserve of unorientated appetency which is given shape and scansion by the not-so-playful incitements and rebuffs of flirtation, which we might say plays at being playful.

However, there is a danger in the delaying and assaying tactics of flirtation, a danger that, being the very thing that flirtation fences with, is what flirtation is also in the long run for. The logic of flirtation is, as Simmel observes, one of minor concessions given in the interests of maintaining interest, in the financial as well as the psychological sense, since one must be persuaded through the process of courtship to pay considerably more than the recommended retail price. The danger lies in the fact that the anticipation of delight can begin to produce a side-effect delight in anticipation. This is because, as Simmel puts it in a flirtatiously formalistic expansion, 'the sequence of experience oriented to a final feeling of happiness radiates a part of its eudaemonistic value onto the moments of the sequence that precede this final moment' (Simmel 1984, 142). The suitor becomes seduced by the minor satisfactions found in promissory concession, and may even, not even entirely realising it himself, begin to prefer the fluttering bird-in-the-hand, or feather, or chirrup, to what is waiting in the bush. 'The man with whom the woman flirts already feels the somehow allusive charm of possessing her' says Simmel (Simmel 1984, 142). The male petitioner is kept in the 'possibility of the Perhaps' in which 'the passivity of submitting and the activity of succeeding form a unity of enticement' (Simmel 1984, 143). In this respect the dynamic of courtship resembles the tendency of all petitory practices toward auto-fulfilment. In the well-attested logic of inversion that becomes possible whenever symbolism and sexuality converge, libido-driven petition produces the libidinisation of petition itself, so that, instead of, and indefinitely ahead of, delayed gratification, there is the spun-out gratification *sine die* of delay and (even if, as the spoilsport *OED* warns us, delay is 'not immediately cognate with Italian *dilata*') dilettante dilation.

If the aim of the sweet cheat is to teach the petitioner how to want his wanting rather than what he thinks he wants, then the achievement of that aim can also be the ruin of her own strategy, since she too will become an accessory to that puppet play, just as much as he, for her prolonged act of choosing will always offer more satisfaction than the results of her election. For Simmel, the play in question is isomorphous with the play with forms that is characteristic of all art, so that it is 'less the art of *pleasing*' that matters in courtship than 'the *art* of pleasing' (Simmel 1984, 144). Both suitor and pursued depend upon the renewed repetition of petition, which is neatly expressed in the lalling, lullaby, echolalic formulations to which love lyrics are drawn: the Beatles' 'Please Please Me' (1963), or Lulu's self-naming 'Love Loves to Love' (1967).

The petition involved in courtship is of a notably oblique and diffused kind. Courtship is petition implied in action rather than the formalised action of applying. The most important thing about the act of solicitation involved in courtship is that it is almost bound to fail if it advances too early to an explicit asking of sexual favour. The ceremony known as 'proposing', a word which itself seems to represent a deflection of the crudity or threat involved in actually asking for what is desired, occurs by convention at the end of the process of wooing, and ideally at the point at which there should be very little need to ask. According to the contemporary mythos of the decline of romantic myth, the point of all myth being to be already in the past, it is the proposal which represents the last remnants of the courtly asymmetry of pursuit and succumbing, as the denial of the possibility of symmetrical contract. Even if it occurs in the presence of a tax advisor, one of the parties must propose, in order to seem to give the other the freedom to defer or foreclose. Courtship is conducted as solicitation through the deterrence of petition, in which one may ask only for things that are accessory to what is in fact wanted. One of the things that the ceremony of seduction seems intended to demonstrate is that the pursuer would scorn an act of direct solicitation as a disrespectful vulgarity. This is why proposing is so closely allied to postponing ('propose' is almost exactly the same word as 'postpone'), such that the petition involved in seduction and flirtation is really a huge and sustained effort to make petition entirely unnecessary.

There is more than affective economy in courtship. Courtship aims not just at the striking of bargains, and assignment of portions, but also at the forming and enforcing of judgements. When one sues for love, one makes promises, the breach of which used to make men liable to be sued in a different and more directly pecuniary sense. The courts of love, often presided over by women, that were set up in the medieval world, literalise the metaphorical association between law, power and love at work in the idea of courtship. Peter Goodrich makes the case for seeing these courts as a separate system of jurisprudence, based on 'a law of emotion and a corresponding jurisdiction concerned not with individual rights or passions, but rather with a space in between lovers and independent of any recognised right, property, or established propriety' (Goodrich 1996, 30-1). Even if they are to be thought of as playful or ironic just-imagine sorts of jurisprudence, Goodrich argues that 'the history and law of such courts can be used as a way to think through certain strictly contemporary concerns with the rights of sexuality as well as the sexuality of rights' (Goodrich 1996, 31).

All of this might suggest that the entreaty and imploring of the lover are just part of the pantomime, a decoration or hors d'oeuvre, meaning that sexual solicitation is not to be regarded as a serious example of petition at all. And yet there are reasons to see the case in just the opposite way. For the examples already discussed of petitory behaviours suggest that seductive play may be a surprisingly common feature in them. Petition is an instrument of seduction, to be sure, but there is seductiveness in petition *tout court*. In fact, we may see wooing and courtship, not just as specialised forms of requesting, but as implicit in all acts of asking, stylised as these almost always are in human affairs by some form or other of mitigating or deflecting courtesy, that draws its subject in by abstitutive drawing away from aggression or the audacity of direct approach. Given this attraction through detraction, all asking must therefore be seen as a kind of wooing. This includes the blandishments of the advertiser, and the public solicitations of politics: Denis de Rougemont wrote in 1938 that 'The masses respond to the dictator in a particular country *in the same way* as the women of that country respond to the tactics of suitors' (Rougemont 1983, 269).

Loathly Love

To ask for something, in whatever modality, whether enquiring, inviting, invoking, urging, demanding, is always to incite discourse. To ask, for anything, is to ask for a reply, whether or not that reply is positive with respect to what is requested. But if asking is the opening of discourse, it must always be open to the possibility of its closure too. There may be no answer, or the answer may be no, in the countermanding to which every demand must lay itself open. In fact, you can only petition for something to which the answer may be no: refusal and denial are given as possibility in all petition. Part of the seductive economy of petition is that it makes the one petitioned the gift of being able to say no, a freedom previously unavailable to them. Indeed, it is this potentiation of the negative, of negativity as such, that puts petition at the heart of all discourse. There is no negation in nature, unless and until nature includes language, which furnishes the only way for nature to turn itself down. Refusal is from *refusare*, formed from *refusum*, the past participle of *refundere*, to pour out, or give back. At its foundation, generosity must always be capable of returning no for an answer. Refusal, as an interior modification of the refund, displays the same ambivalence as redundancy, which is similarly both plenitude and waste.

All the tension and excitement of courtship behaviour depends upon this possibility of refusal, flooding back and threatening to inundate the opening question of any amorous encounter. If that question is refused, it is the aspiring lover who is turned down, not just their request. This is because the petition involved in seduction and courtship is not a simple request for a benefit. It is a bid, to invoke again that simple word, of such not-so-simple potency, moment and reach: it is a request that is at the same time an offer, and therefore a petition to accept an offer. This raising of the stakes adds considerably both to the tension, constituted as the coefficient of reward and danger, in wooing behaviour. No should always, we are piously encouraged to think, mean no, and be taken to mean it; but amorous or sexual solicitation is precisely designed both to prolong and therefore hold at bay the final decision of what Samuel Beckett calls 'no's knife in yes's wound' (Beckett 2010b, 53).

To the possibility of refusal one must add the curious phenomenon of the unwilling seducee's disgust. To be the subject of flirtatious address might be thought to be an advantage or gratuitous pleasure, whether or not the address was welcome or itself solicited. In fact, however, much of the tension involved in initiating a courtship advance comes from the fact that there seems to be such a fine, but absolute distinction between tolerant encouragement and violent rejection. For reasons that are hard to understand, the unwilling subjects of seduction are much more likely to feel disgust than indifference at the prospect of unwanted advances, however oblique and courteously unthreatening they may be. It may be that this is a sign and effect of the seductive power of seductive behaviour itself that, precisely by seeming to defer the act of decision, in fact implicates both parties in the decision to undertake this work of variegated deferral; not saying no will always risk seeming like a kind of yes. The only alternative is to cut the play short in its tracks, and to represent the seducer as having offered an insult by daring to presume that their advances might for a moment ever be entertained. Needless to say, this revulsion may itself be drawn into the play of dissimulation, which is all the most reason for it to take a cruelly absolute form.

There are in fact two cooperating negativities in the work of seduction. There is first of all the void of desire. This provides the impetus for petition, which aims to ease the ache of lack. But this negative void meets and breeds with what might be called the plenary void of the petition-system's capacity for absorption in itself, in the terms evoked by Jean Baudrillard:

> Any system that is totally complicit in its own absorption, such that signs no longer make sense, will exercise a remarkable power of fascination ... The attraction of the void lies at the basis of seduction: not the accumulation of signs, nor the messages of desire, but an esoteric complicity with the absorption of signs. Seduction begins in secrecy, in the slow, brutal exhaustion of meaning which establishes a complicity amongst the signs; it is

here, more than in a physical being or the quality of a desire, that seduction is concocted. And it is what accounts for the enchantment of the game's rules. (Baudrillard 2001, 77-8)

Despite the conspicuous deployments of wit in wooing communication, wooing is a serious business, which accounts for the prominence of ordeal and probative procedure in it. Nowhere is this more demanding than in the ballad 'King Henry'. It opens with some requirements for wooing:

> Lat never a man a wooing wend
> That lacketh thingis three;
> A routh o gold, an open heart
> Ay fu of charity (Child 1882-98, 1.299)

We are, it seems, never to learn, unless the ensuing narrative is intended obliquely to teach it, what the third thing is. As the ballad begins Henry seems much more intent on hunting than seduction (he 'lay burd alone'). He is about to make 'beerly cheer' in his hunting lodge at the end of a successful day in the field when, with theatrical wind and thunder, a 'griesly ghost' bursts her way through the door, and, 'stapping i th fleer', begins to demand food and drink to satiate her gargantuan appetite. The giantess is reduced, or magnified, into a monstrous maw, able only to howl 'More meat!', in response to which Henry serves her in turn and without demur the bodies of his horse, his greyhounds and his goshawks, all of which she cartoonishly devours, leaving only hide, hair and feathers. This is followed, understandably enough, by a demand for wine, of which Henry provides a barrel-full, sewn up in the skin of his horse. The last demand is for Henry to slake the ogre's amorous appetites, in a bed he must make up of heather. Day dawns to her miraculous transformation into a fair and well-spoken maiden, and her congratulation of him for his courteous hospitality:

> When night was gane, and the day was come,
> And the sun shone throw the ha
> The fairest lady that ever was seen
> Lay atween him an the wa.
>
> 'O well is me!' says King Henry,
> 'How lang'll this last we me?'
> Then out it spake that fair lady,
> 'Even till the day you dee.'
>
> 'For I've met wi mony a gentle knight,
> That's gi'en me sic a fill,

> But never before wi a courteous knight
> That ga me a' my will.' (Child 1882-98, 1.299)

This is altogether a very strange, wholly nonconsensual kind of wooing, in which the lustily homosocial Henry has to be educated into the desire for desire by hysterical coercion. All the 'wooing' is conducted on the fiend's side, in her shrieking demands, Violet-Elizabeth-Bott-wise, to have her appetites satisfied. There is in fact a vein of grotesque comedy in 'King Henry' that comes to the fore in the ballad that Francis Child placed next in his sequence, 'Kempy Kay'. In all the versions presented, Kempy Kay is 'a wooing gane' (Child 1882-98, 1.304), and is presented by a father with the fearsome hag who is his daughter, expressively designated a 'Fusome Fug' in one version. No transformation occurs, but instead there is a progressive matching of Kempy Kay to his intended, for 'His teeth were like tether-steeks,/His nose was five feet lang' (Child 1882-98, 1.304), leading to a carnivally nauseous 'happy ending':

> When thir twa lovers had met thegither
> O kissing to get their fill,
> The slaver that hang atween their twa gabs
> Wad hae tethered a ten year auld bill (Child 1882-98, 1.304)

King Henry's uncomplaining, and smoothly unintimidated solicitude in response to the grisly ghost's comedy-horror demands seems to amount to a successful wooing through the endurance of being forcibly wooed, which releases the fair maiden from her fiendish form and, presumably, ensures her happy-ever-after availability to Henry's no longer merely dutiful caresses. Here courtesy is not far away from perversity, dramatising the principle that you can only get what you don't yet realise you want through setting aside your disgust. Instead of a fair maiden whom one woos from the force of one's desire, here is an ugly monster who demands that you woo through (in both senses) your indifference or disinclination.

This is an extreme version of the common convention of probative petition, in which the suitor makes a request that will only be granted if he himself acquiesces to a series of requests from the one he desires, typically of increasing outlandishness and difficulty, sewing shirts without seams, reaping crops with a leather sickle, and so on. More specifically, it deploys the motif of the 'loathly lady', in which a man disenchants a loathsome woman by embracing her (Garry and El-Shamy 2005, 130), as well as, often with gender reversed, the 'frog-prince' pattern, in which tolerance of ambivalence leads to success in love (Coulston 1890; Daunt 1971; Zipes 2008). King Henry does not need literally to slay a dragon to win his maiden, but must instead neutralise the draconian form of her rawly rapacious demand through the magical power of his courtesy. The entire point of the ballad seems to be to show the power of hospitable acceding to quell the menace of appetitive exceeding, thereby modulating the immoderate and transfiguring the formless horror of bestial demand into the stately dance of courtly request and response. As in many other exercises of magic, number is part of the tempering of insatiable appetite in Loathly Lady stories. The hero must perform a particular action, for example giving a kiss, a specific number of times, usually three, this marking out a kind of measure in contrast to the formlessness of the Loathly Lady, whose gigantic stature often seems to stand for immeasurability itself, like the exorbitant ghost in 'King Henry': 'Her head hat the reef-tree o the house/Her middle ye mot well span' (Child 1882-98, 1.299). The potentially disturbing force of petition is tamed in repetition, which is isomorphic with the wait-for-it wish-fulfilling apparatus of the narrative itself. In such tales, desire and petition change their order; where petition would normally arise from unfulfilled desire, here petition and its granting give rise to the simultaneous constitution and consummation of an entirely unexpected desire. It is the workings of the wooing contest that arouse the suit, and pursue the arousal. Wooing is thereby the domestication of desire through refraction into structure.

Something similar happens in the milder form of the Loathly Lady romance that forms the substance of Chaucer's *Wife of Bath's Tale*. The story begins with the rape of a young girl out walking, sardonically introduced by the Wife's reflections that in the times since King Arthur, young girls are no longer at risk from elves, but only from the cadging infestation of 'lymytours', or licensed begging friars, thronging their assigned districts, 'As thikke as motes in the sonne-beem' (Chaucer 2008, 117). Bureaucratic begging has replaced supernatural jeopardy:

> This maketh that ther ben no fayeryes.
> For ther as wont to walken was an elf
> Ther walketh now the lymytour hymself. (Chaucer 2008,117)

But it turns out that, even in the mythical time of Arthur, maidens were, as in modern times, much more at risk from violently libidinous young men than the hosts of faërie. The Wife's story begins briskly with the rape of a maiden by one of Arthur's knights, for which he is condemned to death, but, for the sake of the story, reprieved by Arthur's queen, who poses him instead a 'neck-riddle': if he does not succeed by the end of a year in giving a satisfactory answer to the question 'What do women most want?', his life will be forfeit. After a year of fruitless wandering, he comes upon a foul old woman, plainly a moonlighting version of the Wife of Bath herself, who says she will tell him the answer to the riddle if he promises to grant her next request. After she whispers the answer in his ear, he is able to save his life by announcing to the court that what women most desire is 'sovereignty', but has, demonstrating thereby the truth of his answer, to accede to the old woman's request that he marry her. Following a long curtain lecture about the unimportance of ugliness and poverty in a bride, she offers him the choice of whether she is to remain old and ugly, but faithful to him, or is to be transformed into a beautiful young maiden, with whom the knight must take his chances of betrayal. Having perhaps by now given up all expectation of coming out ahead, the knight leaves the choice to his wife, who, having achieved her aim of being given mastery over him, is transformed into a young woman who is not only young and beautiful but also faithful, if only to herself.

The story dispenses entirely with any kind of wooing, right from the moment when, we are informed, 'He saugh a mayde walkynge hym biforn,/ Of which mayde anon, maugree hir heed,/ By verray force, he rafte hire maydenhed' (Chaucer 2008, 117). As in other riddle stories, physics must give way to metaphysics, the 'verray force' of corporeality turned into a symbolic game. This is to say that one kind of question, the petition of 'May I?', or 'Will you?', is turned into another, more abstract kind, that allows for playfully prolonged absorption in the game of knowledge for which I have tried ambitiously to popularise the term 'quisition' (Connor 2019, 171-211). In petition, asking is instrumental, a way of getting what you want: in quisition, asking is self-referential, and a way of preoccupying instrumentality. So the answer to the riddle 'what do women want?' might be 'to be asked what they want'. The wooer's petition looks as though it is intended to secure an aim, but this is its ruse, into which wooing is seduced. The important thing is not whether the wooer gets what he or she wants, but that, whatever what they want turns out to have been, they will, as we say, have asked for it.

The formalisation of wooing also makes it vulnerable to comic mockery, nowhere more mercilessly than in Robert Gould's *Satyr Against Wooing* (1698). The furious misogyny of Gould's poem is scarcely diminished by his disgust at the foolishness of the men who waste their lives in courting women, the tone being set by the epigram on the title page from Juvenal's 6th Satire:

> Si tibi simplicitas uxoria, deditus uni
> Est animus, summitte caput, cervice parata
> Ferre Jugum: nullam invenies quae pareat [sic – 'parcat']
>   amanti. (Bould 1698, n.p.)

> If you're straightforwardly fond of your wife, if your heart is devoted to her alone, then bend your head and be prepared to put your neck beneath the yoke. You'll not find any woman who shows mercy to the man who loves her. (Juvenal 2004, 253)

Gould reviews different styles and stages of wooing, beginning with the 'Foppling Sixteen Summers Seen' who 'a Tingling in his Blood does find,/ And thinks he's fit to propagate his Kind' (Gould 1968, 2). Bould represents the act of wooing as an absurd formality which must be gone through for the sake of appearances, after the real agreements have been hammered out between the couple's two fathers, like 'Tradesmen bart'ring Ware'.

> The Match thus made up, (thoughtless of th' Event,)
> The Noddy's next to get the Nymph's Consent
> In order to't he Powders and Perfumes,
> And, three long hours in Dressing spent; presumes
> At last before the Idol to appear,
> Bowing, as if the Deity were there:
> Not more cou'd be the Rapture had she been
> A bright, and just descended Cherubin. (Bould 1698, 2-3)

Bould reflects that, in place of the extravagant petitions and promises offered by the hapless young man, a frank acknowledgement of the transaction of which they are a part would be much better: *'Madam (tho' 'tis a Truth that's something bold) / We here are by our Parents bought and Sold'* (Bould 1698, 4).

Interpetition

Literary and popular arts abound in representations of wooing petition, while the act of romantic petition draws reciprocally on literary and artistic forms, in particular the arts of poetry and song. Simmel sees art as more than merely accessory to flirtation, since flirtation consists essentially of the purposiveness without purpose that Kant found in all art. The flirt 'proceeds in a thoroughly purposive fashion but repudiates the "purpose" to which her conduct would have to lead in the sequence of reality, sublimating it into the purely subjective delights of play' (Simmel 1984, 145). Perhaps the flirt and the one [s]he flirts with are both responding to the new principle of reflexivity which Niklas Luhmann identifies in the code of love, which he explains is more than just self-consciousness:

> Reflexivity of loving is more than just a simple matter of the Ego-consciousness fulfilling a function in love. It is also more than mere awareness of the fact that one loves and is loved. What it involves is a corresponding feeling being affirmed and sought in the realm of feelings. It involves loving oneself as the one who loves and is loved, and also loving the other as one who loves and is loved – in other words, it involves directing one's feelings towards this co-incidence of feelings. (Luhmann 2010, 34)

Courtship, flirtation and seduction are intimate transactions, which tend to take place in private, despite being strongly ritualised. When they become public, an uncomfortable kind of interference can arise, as bystanders perceive more clearly what is going on than the participants for whom the dissimulation of what may be in process is part of the procedure. Hence the popular responses to over-intimate public conduct in cries of 'oh really, get a room!', or the 'Man on a Porch' involuntarily eavesdropping on James Stewart's amorous sparring with Donna Reed in Frank Capra's *It's a Wonderful Life*, who at length exasperatedly exclaims 'Why don't you kiss her instead of talking her to death?'

And yet the overhearing and reporting of acts of courtship is also deeply entwined with its practice. Many songs and ballads begin with a third-person narrator describing how when, out walking, they come upon, or more often overhear, a scene of attempted seduction. One example among many is the ballad 'Love Without Measure', which begins:

> Late in the Country as I was walking
> Viewing the Meadows so fresh and green
> There I was a ware of two Lovers a talking
> Vnder a bush, but could hardly be seen,
> I laid me down and I listen'd a while,
> To hear if the man could the maiden beguile:
> But the maid she was crafty, witty and loyal
> Although many times he put her to th' tryal
> And in the conclusion thus he did her wooe (Anon 1666-8)

At this point in the many variations of this song, the first-person witness dissolves into their narrative of the lovers' exchange, sometimes leading to consummation, or marriage, or even both, sometimes to tragic parting. 'Literature', which I must be pardoned for taking here as the name for all formalised, third-person reportings or enactments of wooing, including in theatre, opera, song, gossip and even jokes, provides the arena in which intimacy and ritual are brought together, providing patterns of courtship behaviour that must be rehearsed, recalled, recognised, and revised, always against the background of the always-already that is itself part of the reminiscential structure of wooing. The love letter is the clearest and most concrete instance of this conjuncture, for this most discreet and intimate form of address must invent new and spontaneous ways to sing love's old song. Traditionally, love letters may in fact incorporate or take the form of love poetry, the borrowing of approved sentiments and usages being regarded as part of the acceptable ritual of courtship.

It must be noted that literary critics since the late 1960s have regularly voiced doubts that courtly love ever in fact existed either as a specific code of sexual and amatory conduct, or indeed as a coherent set of ideas about what such conduct should consist of. The first, and most enjoyable of these debunkings was provided by E. Talbot Donaldson, in an essay entitled 'The Myth of Courtly Love' from 1965, which sets out from the proposition that 'courtly love provides so attractive a setting from which to study an age much preoccupied by love that if it had not existed scholars would have found it convenient to construct it – which, as a matter of fact, they have, at least partially, done' (Donaldson 1970, 155). The essay moves, via indications of the many inconsistencies that exist within what are held to be comparable versions of courtly love and between codes of courtly love and what is known about other aspects of medieval life, but with a special emphasis on the assumed centrality of adultery, to the conclusion that

> at least a part of what is called courtly love was no more real in the Middle Ages than it had been before and has been since. As far as the better part is concerned, which I have been calling sublimation, that was surely real in the Middle Ages, and since then has acquired the added reality of becoming a myth. (Donaldson 1970, 163)

In fact, however, it looks as though a large part of the understanding of 'courtly love' must consist in the fact that it has always been in part a myth, for which we can adopt the definition of George Grote as 'a past which never was present' (Grote 1861, 44). It is not just that modern ideas of courtly love are an effect of the refraction of medieval ideas through late Victorian romanticism, or Romanticism: it is rather that the varieties of courtly love are an effect of refraction, at different angles of acuteness, and involving different transferential effects, throughout its history. So we should not expect to be able to separate out straight or neat forms of courtly love from ironic or adulterated forms, since it is part of the code that in enacting it, one acts out what one imagines to be the actions of others.

Perhaps, then, there is something vicarious in all courting, in which one never stands forth in one's own right or one's own interest except by taking up the position where others have stood. The excitements, incitements and solicitings of romantic discourse are engineered and amplified through citation. Umberto Eco defined postmodernism through this kind of deflection:

> I think of the postmodern attitude as that of a man who loves a very cultivated woman and knows that he cannot say to her 'I love you madly', because he knows that she knows (and that she knows he knows) that these words have already been written by Barbara Cartland. Still, there is a solution. He can say 'As Barbara Cartland would put it, I love you madly'. At this point, having avoided false innocence, having said clearly that it is no longer possible to speak innocently, he will nevertheless have said what he wanted to say to the woman: that he loves her in an age of lost innocence. If the woman goes along with this, she will have received a declaration of love all the same. (Eco 1994, 67)

This is attractively twinkling and gets quoted a lot as a result as a compliment to contemporary cleverness. But all declarations of love have always been of this kind, even if it might at other times have been Catullus or Herrick that were evoked. For nobody in human life can ever make a 'declaration' except in a kind of solemnising inverted commas, just as only medieval knights or, nowadays, people in newspaper headlines can ever 'vow' anything, 'slay' anyone, or be 'stricken' by anything. Declarations – 'I do'; 'this country is at war with Germany'; 'George Bailey, I'll love you till the day I die'; 'I'll kill you for this, Simon Gascoigne' – are things that we mean to be taken to *really mean*, which means we must appropriate the kind of solemnising formulae that are thought appropriate to the situation, and that, precisely because they are formulae that do not originate with us, can therefore bind us in and to the future, whether we turn out to have meant them or not.

There are in any case at least six dramatis personae jostling on the scene in any act of seduction. There is the would-be lover; the wished-for beloved; the lover the would-be lover takes him- or herself to be; the beloved the would be-lover takes his or her beloved to be; the beloved the wished-for beloved takes him- or herself to be; and the lover the wished-for beloved takes his or her would-be lover to be. All are capable of attracting or intercepting addresses meant for one or all of the others.

This is why proxy wooing is so common and has been so unexpectedly successful and acceptable, even if, and perhaps even because, the parasitic deflections and oppilations to which it is subject provide so much matter for comic or tragic complication. Ovid advises 'take care first to know the handmaid of the woman you would win; she will make your approach easy' (Ovid 1929, 37). Shakespeare, writing in a period in which matchmaking and delegated wooing were common practice (Greer 2008, 59) is particularly fond of this dramatic device, with Viola disguised as Cesario wooing Olivia on behalf of the Duke Orsino in *Twelfth Night* being a conspicuous example. In her first embassy, Viola uses the very artificiality of her situation, making it clear how carefully she has learned her part, and pretending to be uncomfortable when forced to improvise outside it, to try to create a kind of intimacy of knowingness between her and her near-anagrammatic target Olivia – were I to be wooing you, this is how I would go about it. Her climax comes with her matey mockery of the absurdities of the devoted lover, as she speculates that she would:

> Write loyal cantons of contemned love
> And sing them loud even in the dead of night;
> Halloo your name to the reverberate hills
> And make the babbling gossip of the air
> Cry out 'Olivia!' O, You should not rest

Between the elements of air and earth,
But you should pity me. (Shakespeare 2011, 1198)

Shakespeare has the two partners to the teasing exchange play with the comings and goings of Cesario's text, such that neither of them know when, or whether, the text has in fact been delivered. The seeming immunity offered by her irony provides the alibi permission for seriousness to be established. Seducers know the suggestive power of the subjunctive that Viola does not, or does not quite know she does.

Shakespeare seems to have been particularly alert to the vicissitude that attends upon vicariance (Latin *vicis*, change, interchange, alternation), as Claudio recognises in Shakespeare's *Much Ado About Nothing*, when he begins to suspect that his friend Don Pedro is wooing his beloved Hero on his own account rather than, as agreed, on Claudio's:

Friendship is constant in all other things
Save in the office and affairs of love:
Therefore all hearts in love use their own tongues;
Let every eye negotiate for itself,
And trust no agent. (Shakespeare 2011, 920)

Even when writers aspire or affect to be writing in their own cause, elements of the detour and diffraction tend to enter into their petition. Guido Cavalcanti forms a petition to the very song he is singing to carry his love to his absent lady:

Deh, ballatetta mia, a la tu'amistatequest'anima
che trema raccomando:
menala teco, nella sua pietate,
A quella bella donna a cu'ti mando
Deh, ballatetta, dille sospirando,
quando le se'presente:
'Questa vostra servente
vien per istar con voi,
partita da colui
che fu servo d'Amore'

Ah, little song, to your friendship I commit this trembling soul. Take it, in its anguish, with you to the beautiful lady to whom I am sending you. Ah, little song, sighing tell her when you are in her presence, 'This, your servant, comes to stay with you, divided from him who was Love's servant.' (O'Donoghue 1982, 270-1).

Another striking example of courting 'by attorney', to adapt Rosalind's phrase in *As You Like It* (Shakespeare 2011, 181), is furnished by Richard Crashaw's 'Wishes To His (Supposed) Mistresse' of around 1634. The mistress of the title is not just imagined, but fully imaginary, since she is the 'Divine/ Idæa' of perfection. Crashaw asks us to imagine with him that his wishes that such a paragon might exist might in themselves suffice to make her actual: 'Meet you her, my wishes,/Bespeake her to my blisses, /And bee yee call'd my absent kisses' (Crashaw 1927, 195). The intercessory wishes that are sent out to appeal to the supposed mistress both call on her and call her up. The poet wishes at once to possess his mistress, and also to be able, incompatibly, to wish to possess her. To be sure, the poem looks to the fulfilment of its wishes, in which 'Her that dares bee/What these Lines wish to see:/I seeke no further, it is shee' (Crashaw 1927, 198). But finally, the poet arrives at the paradox that what he wishes for is a mistress that, being all he could wish for, would leave him nothing to wish for: 'I wish, her store/Of worth, may leave her poore/Of wishes; and I wish – No more' (Crashaw 1927, 198). The last four words may be read both as 'I wish for nothing more' and 'I cease to wish', the first being consummation, the second a kind of consuming desolation, since these are not the kind of wishes that seek the bleak surcease of wishing. We may also read the 'No more' as an abrupt, even slightly panicked breaking off from the line of thinking that would lead to the death of the wishes that keep the poem in being. None of this is wishful thinking in the usual sense in which we might speak of it, for it does not seek the satisfaction but the wistful prolongation of its wishing. In a sense, the wishes that the poem encourages us to think of as the emissaries to the mistress are acting in their own interests. The poet's wishes do not convey the poet's petition to his mistress, but convey the fantasy of the mistress to the poet who wishes to wish for her. She is formed in and from the play of this interpetition.

Amorous petition is an effort to ensure what we nowadays call sustainability, or the long life of longing. The state of love, characterised by continuing desire rather than a settled and contented condition of respectful admiration, is kept alive and alight by renewed forms of petition. But perhaps the real function of the need for ongoing neediness that is romantic love is to sustain the necessity and conditions for the act of petition that seems so essential in human relations. Desire may seem to give rise to petition, but petition is needed to give desire definition and keep it in being. Petition is not made necessary by need: rather petition itself is a securing of the need to need in all communication. Amorous petition affects to say 'love me as I love you', but this conceals and gives on to a greater imperative: 'give yourself to the ludic imperative of amorous petition as I have'.

Wooing may of course occur in many other circumstances than amorous or sexual ones: the next chapter will be concerned with the operations of suitors of different kinds. But there is a particularly telling example of the entry of wooing behaviour into social relations in the concern with wooing to be found in psychoanalytic writing. Margaret Mahler identifies a phase in the 'senior toddler', at around 2 years old, in which, beginning to realise 'that the world is *not* his oyster, that he must cope with it "more or less on his own," very often as a relatively helpless, small, and separate individual, unable to command relief or assistance merely by feeling the need for it, or even by giving voice to that need' develops a kind of 'wooing behavior' towards his mother (Mahler, Pine and Bergmann 1975, 78). Educators more generally are familiar with the variations on the apple-for-the-teacher strategy that are symbolically promised or supplied in the language and behaviour of their students. The child who woos its parent is laying down a pattern for adult, erotic wooing, which, in humans as in many other creatures, as observed earlier in this chapter, consists of a voluntary infantilisation, or deploying of weakness. The senior toddler is unaware of the implied or anticipatory erotics of their behaviour, though its effectiveness may depend upon its anticipatory resemblance to what will at a later stage seem like a recapitulation of this earlier behaviour. The transferential relation between infant and adult wooing makes for another sense in which repetition is an executive part of petition.

Psychoanalysts also regularly describe wooing and seduction behaviour in their patients as an example of what they know as transference – the acting out in the psychoanalytic encounter of attitudes and behaviours that have their source in patients' erotic or familial experiences (Bergen 1958, 419; Atkinson and Gabbard 1995, 178). The reporting of such behaviours is no doubt part of their dramaturgy, in which interpretation and interpetition may be closely allied. At least in the classical or approved forms of psychoanalysis, the analyst is supposed to remain unmoved by the attempted seductions of the patient, even as they seek to derive gratification from them by understanding them better than the patient does themselves. In the case of children in analysis, the attributions of wooing behaviour must defend themselves against their queasy resemblance to the paedophile's conviction that they are the one being seduced by the artful dodgery of their victim.

The courtly traditions of wooing and courting behaviour suggest that they occur in a private and intimate space, set apart from the more public forms of social exchange. But the insistence of forms of mediation, whether in the form of the ambassador, or in the form of the personae that wooing seems to engender, suggests that wooing is to be understood as saturated with the kinds of symbolic substitution that testify to the presence of social relations in every form of amorous behaviour, however secret or withdrawn it may appear to be.

7

Suitage

The lover's suit and pursuit are the erotic modulations of a huge range of actions of seeking and requiring in human relations, actions that we should by now be beginning to see, not so much as a distinct class in themselves, as a feature of almost all human actions. Though these have a different method and aim from the actions of wooing and seduction, they are all variations of a petitory libido (meaning something you want, and something you want to want) of seeking and suitage. Suitage is a word of which only one usage is recorded in the *OED*, in a technical book about land surveys, in which it is specified that 'Confinage shewes to what Lord, Honour, Castell, Manour, &c. the Seruice and Suitage (whereunto the Lands and Tenements are lyable) is due' (Folkingham 1610, 72). As indicated by the common pairing 'suit and service', alternating with 'homage and suit', the word *suit* tended until the sixteenth century to indicate a duty performed rather than a benefit sought. A 1685 history of noble families employs the by-then archaic word to mean a more literal payment, in recording that Walter de Vere, a follower of Richard I, 'paid his Suitage towards Redemption of the King, so he did towards the War of *Normandy* for the Fee of *Robert* the Son of *Aubrey* the Chamberlain. And in the first of King *John* he paid Suitage for half a Knights Fee to another Norman Expedition' (Halstead 1685, 76).

It seems to have been during the first half of the sixteenth century that appetency replaced duty in the word suit, as the sense of appeal, petition, or 'paying court' in a romantic sense began to predominate in uses of the word. Given that it has so meagre a lexical profile, I hope I can be permitted to adopt the word *suitage* to signify the whole range of actions of seeking, soliciting and articulate wanting, along with the responses that may be due to or ensue from them. Seen in this way, suitage is much more various and widely diffused than the more specialised modes of petition, begging, political demand, prayer and wooing considered already in this book. Suitage may be taken as a name for the process observed by Frank Whigham when he remarks, calmly, yet far-reachingly, that '[w]e spend most of our lives trying to get one another to do things' (Whigham 1981, 868). We exercise what we are nowadays pleased to call our 'agency' not, for the most part, in actions that we perform on our own initiative or for ourselves, but in the recruiting of agents to do things for us. In fact all agency is exercised in oblique cases, by, with, through or for, other things: if I walk to the larder I have to employ what we call means, including, for example, my legs, by which to do it. All action is interactive action-at-a-distance, from Latin *distare*, to stand in two places, *dis-* comparable to Sanskrit *dva*, two, *dvis*, twice. This includes the distance from oneself introduced by the idea of acting 'for oneself' or 'on one's own behalf', in which one must divide oneself into two 'halves' (OE *healf*, side).

It would be tempting to think that solicitous and suasive action of this kind is a particularly marked feature of highly symbolic creatures like humans who are equipped with such a large variety of means of communication – were it not for the fact that, as may have been demonstrated by my earlier consideration of begging behaviour in animals, we would be better off seeing all creatures as symbolic creatures to some extent. One might, for example, take the operations of *Toxoplasma gondii*, named after an African rodent called a gundi or 'comb rat' in which it was first found in 1908. It is a parasite of cats which induces behavioural changes in rodents it infects, such that they lose their fear of cats (and even become attracted to feline urine), thereby making them easier for cats to catch. Ingesting the parasite along with the rodent returns the parasite from its intermediate host to its definitive host in the body of the cat, where it is able to reproduce. But estimates of the adventitious infection rate in humans range from 30% to 70%, and there is growing evidence of behavioural changes associated with this infection, for example in various kinds of increased disinhibition, if not necessarily increased attraction to feline urine (Berdoy, Webster and Macdonald 2000; Webster 2007). What are the seekings and consequences of collateral infections in species such as human beings? Is our curiosity about such matters that of the cat, however many times removed? Who, that is, has the 'agency', or what is doing the doing, who or what has precedence or competence, in this shuttling morrice of tendings, appetites and appeals? Suasive rhetoric, from *suavis*, sweet, OE *swete*, the Latin and Germanic words sharing an Indo-European root *swād-* with Sanskrit *svādús* sweet, belongs to a logic of the parasite that extends across semiotics and biology.

The *Toxoplasma gondii* effect is known as the 'manipulation hypothesis' among biologists (Hughes, Brodeur and Thomas, 2012), though it is a concept that is instantly recognisable and abundantly evident in ordinary forms of social existence in humans. The history of the word *manipulation*, deriving from Latin *maniplus*, handful, has strong overtones of magical, disguised or concealed action – whether in alchemy or the provision of sexual gratification. Manipulation always has the suggestion of something going on behind the scenes, or beyond the apparent. The 'one another' in Frank Whigham's 'getting one another to do things' goes far beyond mere reciprocity, in that it always implicates others apart from the dyad of the suitor and the one so to speak besought. Getting another person to do something for you in any way that goes beyond the imperious 'do it or else' will always depend on a literal kind of conjuration, in the invocation of moral norms, social expectations and potential rewards, through allusion to present or non-present others who hold these views and therefore form an implicit auditorium for any actions of urging, nudging, encouraging, steering and other forms of suggestive suasion. Other persons can literally be enlisted in the process of urging as will the invocation of the prospect of what others may think. It is these ways to 'by indirection find direction out' (Shakespeare 2011, 302) that form the focus of this chapter.

Assays of Bias

I observed in chapter 6 that vicariousness is frequently present in wooing; but it is not just romantic petition that is performed by proxy. Literary petitions of all kinds are often substituted or delegated, for example by the action of petitioning another to petition on one's behalf, most obviously in religious devotions, when one calls for saintly intercession. Inversely, literary petitions are often made on behalf of persons or entities assumed to be incapable of framing their own petitions. In such cases, rather than using intermediaries to articulate one's own petition, writers pretend to allow themselves to be used by those intermediaries to articulate the petitions of the latter. Writers will often invent characters or speechless beings precisely in order to perform this imaginary intercession, with the writer invoking an entity in order to be able to undertake their act of petition. Examples here would include William Dunbar's 'Petition of the Gray Horse, Auld Dunbar' (Dunbar 1893, 2.215-16), Francis Hopkinson's 'The Humble Petition of the Docks, Thistles, and Nettles of Hartlebury Farm, to the Lord Bishop of Worcester' (Hopkinson 1792, 3.139-42), Anna Letitia Barbauld's 'The Mouse's Petition' (Barbauld 1994, 36-7), John Clare's 'The Wood Nimph's Petition' (Clare 1989, 1.201-2), Royall Tyler's 'The Petition of the Massachusetts Farmer's Dog to his Master' (Tyler 1968, 78-9), Hannah More's 'The Negro Boy's Petition' (More 1830, 36-7), Alfred Domett's ''The Card-Case's Petition: To a Lady' (Domett 1833, 120), Thomas Campbell's 'The Beech-Tree's Petition' (Campbell 1907, 245-6), Thomas Ingoldsby's 'The Church's Petition' (Ingoldsby 1881, 181-3). This kind of literary interpetition fills out and literalises the interceding ascription that literariness in general itself furnishes, as in the romantic modes of language evoked in the love letter, which help to frame the petition of the lover.

Literary interpetition is often reinforced by the giving of voice to books or items of writing themselves, as in Austin Dobson's 'The Book-Plate's Petition' (Dobson 287-8), which provides an excuse for a book-plate to record its itinerary from hand to literary hand:

> The Fifth one found me in Cheapside.
> This was a *Scholar*, one of those,

Whose *Greek* is sounder than their *hose*;
He lov'd old Books, and nappy ale,
So liv'd at Streatham, next to THRALE.
'Twas there this stain of grease I boast
Was made by Dr. JOHNSON's toast. (Dobson 1897, 287-8)

John Byrom's 'The Passive Participle's Petition to the Printer of the *Gentleman's Magazine*' is a protest against the rise (as it turned out, temporary) of the use of the perfect tense in place of the passive participle, as in 'broke' for 'broken', 'wrote' for 'written', or 'mistook' for 'mistaken' (Byrom 1773, 1.107). Practically the only merit of the squib is the play it makes on the idea of the exchange of active and passive in the granting of the power of protesting petition to a part of speech:

Passive I am, and would be, and implore
That such Abuse may be henceforth *forbore*,
If not *forborn*, for, by all Spelling Book,
If not *mistaken*, they are all *mistook*:
And, in plain English, it had been as well
If what has *fall'n* upon me, had not *fell*. (Byrom 1773, 1.107)

The distancing of this kind of petition often allows for ironic or satirical purposes. John Denham's 'To the Five Members of the Honourable House of Commons: The Humble Condition of the Poets' parodies the many complaints made by members of trades for the protection of their privileges as well as the traditional complaint of the poet:

Though set form of *Prayer* be an *Abomination*,
Set forms of *Petitions* find great *Approbation*:
Therefore, as others from th'bottom of their souls,
So we from the depth and bottom of our *Bowls* (Denham 1928, 128)

But Denham's mock petition is not really on behalf of poets, since his purpose is to denounce Parliament for usurping the poet's traditional privileges of lying with impunity:

But ours is a *Priviledge* Antient and Native,
Hangs not on an *Ordinance*, or power *Legislative*.
And first, 'tis to speak whatever we please
Without fear of a *Prison*, or *Pursuivants* fees.
Next, that we only may *lye* by Authority,
But in that also you have got the Priority.
Next, an old Custom, our Fathers did name it
Poetical license, and alwaies did claim it.
By this we have power to change Age into Youth,

Turn *Non-sence* to Sence, and Falshood to Truth;
In brief, to make good whatsoever is faulty,
This art some *Poet*, or the *Devil* has taught ye:
And this our Property you have invaded,
And a *Priviledge* of both Houses have made it. (Denham 1928, 128-9)

Such proxy or imputed petitions form a sort of opposite to apostrophe, the figure of speech, literally indicating a turning aside from an address to address another, that mostly signifies an address to an abstract, absent, or inanimate entity – 'Hail, Holy Light', 'Tiger, Tiger', 'Thou still unravished bride of quietness', and so on. Jonathan Culler sees in apostrophe a kind of animation of the universe through the act of poetry, an animation that is at the same time a self-glorification of poetry's own animating powers. It is, suggests Culler, 'the pure embodiment of poetic pretension: of the subject's claim that in his verse he is not merely an empirical poet, a writer of verse, but the embodiment of poetic tradition and of the spirit of poesy' (Culler 2002, 143). Proxy poetic petitions by contrast constitute a kind of prosopopoeia, or the lending of voice to normally voiceless entities – *prosopon poein* is literally to 'make a face'. Prosopopoeia has sometimes been paired with apostrophe, since an address to an entity may seem to imply or provoke its capacity to reply. In apostrophe, a kind of appeal, a potential calling into speech, is made to the inanimate. In prosopopoeic petition, this power of appeal is given to the object, as something apparently primary, but in actual fact borrowed; by giving a voice to the petitory object, the poet allows it to seem to have leased that voice from the poet, or indeed from poetry itself. Everything here seems to be appealing to and on behalf of everything else. These reduplicating acts of calling by name (appellation) and thereby appealing to objects to answer by name, and in their own name, peal inwardly and recursively without apparent limit.

Chaucer's 'Complaint to his Purse', one of the latest, if not in fact the very last of Chaucer's poems to be written, is addressed to the newly crowned King Henry IV (Chaucer 2008, 656). The obvious anthropomorphic move might have been to put the complaint into the gaping mouth of the purse, but Chaucer engineers a more oblique petition to the purse itself, enabling a series of links to be suggested between money and sex. 'I am so sory, now that ye been lyght', he complains to his 'lady dere', dear, that is, in the sense both of precious and expensive, as though the money in the purse had been spent on maintaining her light-minded pleasures. The poet is heavy because of the purse's lightness, so heavy that he might as well be laid out as a corpse. In its witty plays on different kinds of lightness and weight – the lightness of the sun and so the fructifying lightness of the heavy gold, the sound of which he imagines weighing down his purse – Chaucer is playing with the seriousness of his position, making his 'supplicacioun' to the King by pretending to be making it to his purse, and therefore pretending to be pretending to be making it. The business of petition was so much part of the everyday life of financial transactions, as routine perhaps as the issuing of invoices and receipts, that, as John Burrow observes, poets 'commonly indulged in a variety of very fanciful departures from the dull business of official *supplicacio*, hoping to interest or amuse the reader from whom they looked for a remedy' (Burrow 2011, 349). The poem reminds us that it is its job and that of its originator to make light of his money troubles, to provide an entertainment that may address them in earnest. Literary petition activates and varies the relations between pleading and pleasing, providing pleasure in its plaint. Much of this pleasure comes precisely from the deflection of the direct demand of the petition through the defiles of apostrophe and imposture.

Witty variations are played on this by an anonymous seventeenth-century pamphlet entitled *A Poor Scholar's Thred-Bare Suit*. Filling out the prompt provided by the word 'suit', which had been used since the fifteenth century to mean a set of matching clothes, from the idea of following or fitting unfolded from Latin *sequere*, the pleasure of the poem lies in the way it spins out as many sartorial puns as possible relating to suitorship and sartoriality: 'I have a *Suit* to you, that you would be/So kind as send another *Suit* to me' (Anon 1668). This pun had already been worn fairly smooth by the late seventeenth century: Shakespeare's Pompey, reviewing the prisoners in his custody in *Measure for Measure*, includes 'Master Caper, at the suit of Master Three-pile the mercer, for some four suits of peach-coloured satin, which now peaches him a beggar' (Shakespeare 2001, 822). The fact that paper was still usually made from old rags allows the physical poem, itself printed on a single, disposable broadsheet, to be scabrously implicated in the interplay of body and text:

> My *Doublet canvasse* worn out quite behind,
> I put a *Poem* there, to keep out wind:
> Two sly Slaves followed me, and *One*, or *both*,
> (Like Boyes in Horn-books) Read it through the Cloth (Anon 1668)

Horn books were school texts which were mounted on wooden bats or 'battledores' and covered with translucent horn for their protection (Tuer 1897, 2, 5-6). The reader seems invited to imagine that they are reading this text through a similarly diaphanous veil of metaphor – a metaphor the tenor of which is however the literal truth of the tenuous protection afforded to the author's dignity by the very text they hold in their hand. The textile metaphor was often employed to imply the scarecrow condition of the player or impersonator, as in Hamlet's characterisation of Claudius as a 'king of shreds and patches' (Shakespeare 2011, 317), later taken downmarket by W.S. Gilbert's Nanki-Poo in *The Mikado*, who proclaims himself 'A wandering minstrel I – /A thing of shreds and patches,/Of ballads, songs and snatches' (Gilbert and Sullivan 1976, 299). The grounds of the petition are the wearing away of the petitioner's person to match their ragged suit, but the exhibitionist opulence of the wordplay of *A Poor Scholar's Thred-Bare Suit* plays with the fact that the act of petition is in fact nothing to its purpose, which is to elaborate from nothing an entertaining petitionary performance. The paper-thin patchwork of the petitioner's suit yields the final plea from the scholar reduced to 'the next degree unto Annihilation':

> To summ up all, 'tis a confused rude
> Ragg, that admits of no similitude,
> So thin, Imagination cannot strike it,
> And so like *Nothing*, that ther's nothing like it. (Anon 1668)

Up to the end of the eighteenth century (but also, in various oblique and disguised ways, well beyond), the textual rhetoric of courtship is matched by the paratextual rhetoric of the suitor that features in the petitionary dedication to an actual or prospective patron. As the name suggests, a literary dedication implies a prestation, the formal making of a gift through the very act of marking it as a gift. The author does not really make his patron the gift of a book, since the whole point of a dedication is that it is read by others, who are the book's actual purchasers. Instead he makes him the gift of the public declaration of his offering and the larger dedication of his fealty and future service to the dedicatee. Sometimes this is presented as the payment of a debt, as when, for example, the poet has been given ease and accommodation through aristocratic generosity, or when the modern-day academic records their gratitude to the trust that has funded their sabbatical. But such apparent clearings of arrears are usually in fact to be understood as downpayments, or loss leaders, made in the hope of future employment, emolument, or other advantage. Petition and patronage are twinned closely, with the act of petition furnishing both the stimulus to the generosity of the patron and a foretaste of their reward. It is one of the features of the dedication that it concertinas past, present and future. Through the dedication, the poet offers thanks for past generosity and, in the present tense of that articulated gratitude, gives expression, more or less explicitly, to the hope there may be more where that came from. We have seen repeatedly that there are very few acts of begging or petition that do not begin with some equivalent act of self-lowering or paying of respect. Despite striving to give the impression that they are entirely spontaneous, dedications in fact imply and accord with the terms of an affective contract. The dedicatee is being wooed with an act of flattery that not only allows them an enhancement of their own self-image but also, through the fact that it is enacted publicly, enriches their social stock.

The literary dedication is only one form in which the seeking of advantage from a patron may be instantiated. As social relations became more complex and dynamic during the later Middle Ages, patronage relations became the means of establishing networks of affiliation, allegiance and reliance, the word patronage making it clear that the relations of trust, favour and protection thus accorded to the newly ambitious were seen as a kind of extension to the kinship system. In the process, such patronage relations formed an intermediary stage between kinship proper and a fully modern society which would, in principle at least, be based on the merit of atomic individuals. In fact, however, apparently modern societies retain many of the features and functions of kinship systems, most notably through the local forms of affiliation and allegiance provided by institutions like the school, the college, the regiment, the academic department, the party, the firm, the profession, or even the troop of social media followers, which continue to provide clan-like frameworks for forms of ambition, and protected cultivation and advancement. A society rarely provides opportunities for advancement except through these buffer zones of internal social striving, which function like courts, or spaces of relative enclosure, within which the energies of status-bidding can be contained, concentrated, coordinated and therefore in turn transmitted. In fact, rather then the abstract and impersonal forms of administration characteristic of civic society simply replacing tribal society, in the normative narrative of political order emerging from what Francis Fukuyama calls the 'exit out of kinship' (Fukuyama 2011, 81), these generalised and impersonal forms provide something like the political currency through which quasi-tribal enclaves, guild and cohort relations, fanbase collectives (especially the followers of what are tellingly called 'bands'), identity formations and other forms of minor but pervasive 'repatrimonialization' may be negotiated, cemented and traded (Fukuyama 2011, 81). Rather than an open, or uniformly laminar field of equal opportunities, civil society is the reticulated coordination of these different alveolae of local kinship.

Though it is in the nature of petition always to be dampened and dissimulated, it nevertheless supplies the electricity, or *vis vitae*, of patronage relations, activating contacts, maintaining and impeding circuits, inducing and discharging currents of social tension and potential. The symbolic seekings enacted in petition turn a collectivity from an inert diagram into a dynamic and variable economy of who's in and who's out, made men and coming men on the make. The name given in classical thought for this particular kind of seeking was thymos, Greek θυμός. The contemporary forms of thymos tend to be centred, not so much on wealth, advantage, or power, though these continue to be the almost exclusive preoccupations of contemporary social theory, as on honour, or the demand for recognition, along with its poignant adversary ague, the crushed and crushing self-reproof of shame.

The exercise of thymos is close to that of will, and indeed has often been translated as 'spirit', as in a spirited horse. But the sphere of action of thymos is more specifically social and political than the assertion or exercise of will, and so more complex and conditional. Where will projects energy outwards from the self, in order to overcome obstacles to the self's freedom or expansion, thymos is focussed on the reflexive sense of the recognition we may feel is due to us from others. Will is therefore centrifugal where thymos, ever seeking the amplifying return to itself via the detour of the esteem of others, is centripetal. This circularity is suggested not only by the seeking or striving signified in the -*petal* of *centripetal*, another sprig from Latin *petere*, but also by the word *ambition*, which derives from Latin *ambire*, meaning to walk round, specifically to circulate like a candidate for office canvassing votes, in which sense it is equivalent to *petere*. One modern equivalent to this kind of ambulation is the practice that has come to be referred to in the cynically brilliant phrase 'working the room', to mean ensuring that one has worked one's way round the room, engaging in the small-change transactions of small talk with those who may be in a position to do one good, equivalent to the dutiful grooming performed by ambitious subordinates in primate troops. The ambivalence of ambition derives from this indirect seeking, which is such an excruciating humiliation to Shakespeare's Coriolanus, as he assumes the white toga of the candidate to solicit votes: 'Why in this wolvish toge should I stand here,/To beg of Hob and Dick, that does appear,/Their needless vouches?' (Shakespeare 2011, 229).

In that its strivings and rivalries are often focussed on one's likes rather than one's unlikes, thymos is not only essentially social, it is often hotly homosocial. The reason for this neighbourly near-sightedness, which makes one attentive only to one's similarity and difference in relation to those who are semi-identical, is that one does not seek advantage alone, but specifically the advantage of the recognition of that advantage, from those whose opinion counts. As Francis Fukuyama explains

> Human beings do not just want things that are external to themselves, such as food, drinks, Lamborghinis, or that next hit. They also crave positive judgements about their worth or dignity. Those judgements can come from within, as in Leontius's case, but they are most often made by other people in the society around them who *recognize* their worth. If they receive that positive judgement, they feel pride, and if they do not receive it, they feel either anger (when they think they are being undervalued) or shame (when they realize that they have not lived up to other people's standards). (Fukuyama 2018, 18)

The widespread restriction in many societies of opportunities for females to achieve positions of public power and standing tends to make them much more expert, attentive and inventive in the strategic arts that relate to the creation and maintenance of status, as opposed to power, status being definable as the appearance or assumption of power in the eyes of others. This accounts for some of the acridity of the competition between sisters and in mother-daughter relations. Like the rest of us, highly-paid sportspeople and TV presenters seem to care much less about the absolute levels of their remuneration than the insult to their self-worth offered by marginal differentials between their usually considerable salaries and those of their peers. Most people care much less about being better off than they once were than they do about being slightly worse off than comparable people currently are. During the conditions of confinement of the 2020 COVID-19 epidemic, when traditional examinations were not possible, all students in my university were given 24 hours rather than the usual 3 in which to write their answers at home. Almost immediately, students who had successfully applied for extra time under the old system, typically of about half an hour, as compensation for the various certified disadvantages under which they were suffering, began petitioning for extensions beyond the already taxing 24 hours, to preserve their advantage, like prisoners applying for an extension to their sentence. There seems good reason to suspect that social-political convulsions arise at least as often from these lateral resentments as from the insurgent rage from below of the dramatically dispossessed.

Thymos is often associated with anger and irritable resentment, but the advantage of the concept is that it can also be expressed through may different affective tonalities, including those that are associated with the meeker and self-lowering expressions of petition. Thymotic energies were strongly apparent and indeed came to be energetically diversified in the petitory culture that formed as patronage relations became more complex in the enlarging courts of the medieval and Renaissance worlds. It may seem like an unexpected reversal for such ambitious striving after reputation and recognition, desiring this man's gift and that man's scope, to take the form of petition rather than simple assertion or demand, but readers of this book know that they will not be allowed to forget for long the survival of the root *petere*, to seek, in words like appetite, petulance or competition. Petition is the dominant expression of a culture characterised with the zero-degree term *petitive*, a useful word which, somewhat surprisingly, had to wait until a discussion of prayer by Julian Huxley for its first appearance in print (Huxley 1923, 297). The refractive and reflexive trajectories of the thymotic drive go some way to explaining the 'frantic seesaw' (Whigham 1981, 878) of grovelling and self-aggrandisement that has already come frequently to notice in this book. For most people in a complex, tightly interlinked society, characterised by fluctuating social fortunes, without the opportunity to amass vast wealth or command a usurping army, gaining standing requires trade-ins and buy-offs that make the cat's-paw mediation of one's ambitions through the use of others inevitable. This means that esteem-craving appetite, so seemingly irrepressible among humans, and ever more imperious the more symbolic modes multiply, must fulfil itself in very large part through petitory negotiation. Petition replaces conflict because enforced esteem costs and seemingly counts for so little, compared with injury or death, but it replaces it by diversifying it into new, subtler forms of agonistic relationship. Civilisation replaces risky and expensive forms of conflict with the survival-optimising rituals of abstition, but this deflects rather than dismissing conflict, so that social life remains a busy battlefield of begging.

As in the thermodynamics of gases, the compression of a relatively closed space like a court, college or company induces higher energetic states, and the development of intricate forms of involution. Frank Whigham characterises the patronage relations of the Elizabethan court as just this kind of pressurised circuit-diagram-in-the-making, with petition as the efficient force of that making. At the source of all bounty and privilege was the monarch, but she was not the radial centre for all members of the court, which was a complex and shifting interpetitory network of courtiers and administrators 'who formed a many-layered matrix of mediation and themselves demanded wooing, from below as well as from above' (Whigham 1984, 12). This means that we should think, not in terms of fixed positions in a static hierarchy, but patterns of renewed action between the temporary occupants of those positions, as Whigham explains:

> Most actions of self-presentation flowed between individuals of adjacent ranks, seeking and awarding patronage at all levels of intimacy and degrees of distance from the throne at the heart of the court. When we think of suitors and patrons, we should emphasise the activities that defined them, not the reified roles they occupied permanently. Courtiers of all ranks were by turns (even, in a mixed three-tiered group, at once) suitors to their superiors and patrons to their inferiors. (Whigham 1984, 12)

Whigham notes that the rhetoric of supplication for favour and benefit crosses over with the two other leading registers of supplication, the erotic and the religious, and proposes that 'politic petitions may teach us new things about the congruent realms of erotic and religious desire' (Whigham 1981, 878). Linda Levy Peck pleasingly amplifies this suggestion with the argument that

> in a divine-right monarchy in which the king himself and many other contemporary writers employed the metaphor of God, the free dispenser of grace, the court patron or broker might see himself as similar to the saint who intercedes with an all-knowing God to bring salvation and favour to the supplicant and himself. (Peck 1993, 17)

The literariness of petition comes to the fore in the sixteenth century because it begins to be channelled more regularly through the exchange of letters. This view is no doubt encouraged in large part by the fact that the most eloquent and intimate survivals we have of the process of petition are in fact in the form of letters. The rich tradition of Renaissance drama makes the importance of personal contacts and more or less formal kinds of conversation – in what was known as the 'audience' with a monarch superior for example

– very clear, and we should remain alert to it. But, as the means both for extending and binding together an increasingly inclusive (and so ever more inconclusive) set of relationships, the letter, along with what Frank Whigham describes as its 'human machinery of secretaries, teachers, stationers, and couriers' (Whigham 1981, 867), took on a new importance in the work of negotiating relationships. One might linger for much longer than I have opportunity or stomach to here on the richly shimmering history of the word *stationery*, deriving from *stationarius*, and meaning at various times a sentry, postman, policeman, bookseller, copyist and, from the 1650s, a supplier of writing materials (Pollard 1937, 2-5). Letters impose the duty of reply more than other forms of request, and formalise thymotic exchanges – we still speak, to be sure, of 'paying our respects'. Just as money fixes relations of owing and owning (which could mean the same thing in the early seventeenth century), so the formalised flattery and solicitation of the 'letter petitory' constituted the primary kind of thymotic coin in which to conduct adjustments and exchanges of esteem.

One of the commoner requests made in petitory letters was for the recipient themselves to furnish their support either to the writer, or to a third party, in the form of another letter. Letters produced in response to such epistolary petitions prolong and proliferate the petitory work. Such letters, in the familiar form of letters of reference, recommendation or support, are one of the ways in which networks of petitory patronage survive in the contemporary world, albeit adapted to more bureaucratic and seemingly neutral mechanisms of appraisal and appointment. The word 'reference', meaning a testimonial from a previous employer, came into use in the early nineteenth century. Deriving from the 'letters of credence' or 'credential letters' used to confirm the identity and status of diplomatic representatives from the fifteenth century onwards, references belong to the era of professionalisation that developed during the nineteenth century. Nowadays the ritual of reference-writing may seem to be almost entirely subsumed in the legal and bureaucratic procedures that regulate the processes of advertising, appointment and promotion in the labour market, but it also provides evidence of the survival and even, in certain quarters, the limited flourishing, of patronage relations and expectations. The forms and forces of petition continue to play a large part in the operations of competition. One may of course simply name a referee as part of a job application, in the process thereby 'referring' a prospective employer to them for their opinion. But, in almost all cases, the applicant will have the tact or manners to ask their potential referee if they would be willing to be so named, with the strong implication that the opinion supplied will be a favourable one. This is strongly inflected by the fact that, as in many other petitory circumstances, there are pay-offs for recommenders. First of all, they themselves must be regarded as having an interest in the success of their protégés rather than those of their colleagues. Secondly, they obtain a complement of status in being paid the compliment of being regarded as one whose good opinion is of account. The two combine in the performance of probity, whereby the referee undertakes to supply a balanced and neutral appraisal of the applicant's qualities, unswayed by any of these inducements, a performance which supplies its own small yield of esteem.

In fact, however, references are not for the most part supposed or expected to be neutral assessments. The expectation that an employee has a default right to a positive reference has become a strangely routine feature of the communicative system of professional life – to the point where it is regarded as good behaviour on the part of a potential referee to give warning to a potential subject of a reference if they would not feel able to provide a wholly positive evaluation. Although letters of reference remain indispensable in many forms of competitive selection practice, it is obvious to all that, as one recent assessment solemnly and unastonishingly avers '[c]riterion-based validity studies indicate that reference letter content often has a relatively low association with performance' (Loher et. al. 1997, 340). A letter of reference has a certain kind of gratuitousness, in that it is not only an appraisal, but also an appreciation of the qualities of its subject, one that therefore puts up their price. The potential conflict between assessment and puffery, which is positively incited by the fact that such texts are often in fact referred to as 'letters of recommendation', is indicated by the fact that, when an appraisal is asked for, it is sometimes also asked that it be 'frank' or candid'. As with many ritualised forms of communication, meta-ritual forms evolve for indicating that one is not merely or mechanically depending on ritualised forms: 'No letter of recommendation could be easier to write than this one'; 'I recommend her for this scholarship entirely without reservation'. Such forms constitute a formal verification that the solicitation constituted by the letter is an act of spontaneous generosity, prompted entirely by appreciation of the qualities of the subject, even as it is perfectly clear that it is a piece of professional drudgery. It is this duality – meaning that it is easier to say 'I love you' on demand to someone one does not really love – which can make the writing of such letters so psychologically and emotionally demanding. These ambivalences are intensified by the growing expectations of what is sometimes called 'transparency', whereby the one petitioned for a proxy act of petition on the petitioner's behalf knows that the subject of their encomium may be able to access and monitor any letter that refers to them – which in its turn means that they come under pressure to waive their right to do so, in order to demonstrate that the recommendation is in fact being framed without any kind of duress. An alternative approach is the kind of collusion reported by one researcher, who writes that 'it is not uncommon to hear of professors asking their graduate students to write "drafts" of the letters, which the professor then revises and signs' (Williams-Jones 2012, 2). It is not unknown even for senior professors, when requesting job references from even more senior professors, to provide a helpful checklist of the qualities they would expect to be spontaneously exalted.

Aerial Coin

For many centuries, and in many places, flattery has come under suspicion as a preparation for petition, or more generally as an avenue of parasitism. In the case of the micropolitics of the reference syndrome just discussed, the referee is flattered into agreeing to perform the act of flattery represented by the letter of reference. 'If you are ever approached by flattering words, rest assured the person using them wants something', advised the author of a warning against flattery in 1890 (Orr 1890). 'A *Flatterer* is a Man wholly guided by Self-Interest' affirmed Francois Bruys in his frequently-reprinted guide to the faults of women, 'and is inexhaustible in the Praises of him whom he professes to esteem. As we are not in the least obliged to flatter those we converse with, so it must generally have some Tincture of Guilt in it' (Bruys 1730, 131). Deprived of the expectation of *quid pro quo*, there seems nothing to distinguish flattery from simple praise, while honest praise becomes flattery as soon as there is suspicion of an interest or expectation of a pay-off. Flattery is therefore the silent twin of solicitation. Hamlet defends himself against the suspicion that he may be flattering his friend Horatio by observing that his friend has nothing to give him in return:

> Nay, do not think I flatter,
> For what advancement may I hope from thee
> That no revenue hast but thy good spirits
> To feed and clothe thee? Why should the poor be flatter'd?
> No, let the candied tongue lick absurd pomp,
> And crook the pregnant hinges of the knee
> Where thrift may follow fawning. (Shakespeare 2011, 311)

Flattery is characteristic both of wooing behaviour and of patronage relations, and is indeed one of the most palpable proofs of their cousinship, and shared scope for cozenage. Flattery has the reputation of being devious or subtle. But in fact flattery is not only usually obvious, its obviousness is actually part of its strategy. It is perhaps like the exercise of ventriloquism, which enlists the observer into the creation of the illusion. Perhaps it is in very fact a species of ventriloquism, in which the flatterer offers to stand in for or speak up on behalf of one's self-love: as Richard Stengel sharply remarks, '[i]f flattery were a crime, the recipient would always be an unindicted coconspirator' (Stengel 2000, 17).

The subject of flattery is caught in a characteristic double-bind. Their narcissistic instinct to self-preservation cannot but give credence to the high estimate in which the flatterer seems to hold them. Even if guile is suspected, it is very hard for the subject of flattery not to feel that the flattered has at least got things accidentally right. And the one who believes themselves immune to flattery flatters themselves in that very fact, making them vulnerable to the pretended admiration of the parasite, as Brutus notes of Julius Caesar: 'when

I tell him he hates flatterers,/He says he does, being then most flattered'
(Shakespeare 2011, 342). What seems to matter is not that the flatterer means
what he says, but that he says what the subject of flattery is tempted to
believe he ought to mean. This means in turn that the subject of flattery is
likely to feel not merely gratification, but also gratitude. The sense of a debt
incurred, and the desire to incur further debts of the same kind in order to
earn further increments of narcissistic reinforcement, is what creates the
subject's dependence on his supplicant-supplier. When flattery is contracted,
the parasited willingly becomes the parasite of their own parasite.

The figure of the flatterer has been a staple of literary and dramatic
production in Europe at least from classical times, and, seeing how widespread
tactics of ingratiation are even among social animals, probably in most other
cultures besides. It is often assumed that the flatterer and the parasite are one.
Thomas Aquinas makes no bones that flattery can be a mortal sin (Aquinas
1922, 126). The author of *The Art of Tickling Trouts* (Anon 1708) goes a long way
towards affirming that without the assistance to narcissism provided by the
arts of flattery, human existence would be too hard to bear, affirming that the
art of flattering is

> a great Accomplishment to an *Orator*, a greater to a *Physician*, and
> the only one to a *Poet*: In fine, it is the best *Sweetner*, and gives a
> true *Relish* to the otherwise insipd *Enjoyments* of our whole Life.
> Ay, but say some, to *Flatter* is to *Deceive*, and to *Deceive* is very
> harsh; no say I again, just contrary, nothing is more Welcome
> and Bewitching than the *being Deceived*. (Anon 1708, 7)

The author of *The Court of King James*, a guide to courtly behaviour
published in 1619, included a round condemnation of flattery: 'so is flattery an
inueterate and venimous euill, both to the Court and Common-wealth, yea,
this euill (if we will beleeue *Curtius*) is perpetuall, it doth oftner more priuate
harme, to the well-fare of a Prince, than a war-like open enemie can doe'
(A.D.B. 1619, 75). The author acknowledges the difficulty in distinguishing
strategic flattery from the civilised arts of adaptability that are necessary
to a courtier:

> But peraduenture thou wilt obiect and say, a Courtier must haue
> a cloake against euery winde that bloweth: Indeede I heare it,
> and it griues me that I heare it, yet I can hardly, and in truth very
> hardly, denie and gainsay it. For Courtierrs had neede to apply
> and confirme themselues, to all occasions, and to the conditions
> of them with whome they liue; to bee subtill and craftie both in
> their *Genius* and disposition, and more mutable and variable than
> *Proteus* himselfe. (A.D.B. 1619, 76)

It is precisely this imposture of civilised flexibility that gives the flatterer his opportunity and makes him so difficult to detect:

> who is hee that knowes not that there be those in a Court, who at the first sight doe seeme to haue in them much grauity, literature, and singular humanity, and yet for all this being deepely diu'd into, and narrowly obserued are knowne vnder these beautifull, and spetious outsides and vales of vertue, to couer and keepe secret the deadly poyson of flattery? And with good reason, for the Court is the flatterers stage or *Theatre* wherein hee still doth practise, to adapt and fit himselfe to all assayes excelling *Polypus* farre, yea and the *Cameleon* in change of coullours & mutability of conditions. (A.D.B. 1619, 76-7)

Flatterers are to be guarded against because they are so good at turning social virtues into vices, so good at showing how much acting there always is in the performance of every sincere action. It may be for this reason that, though flattery has been condemned for centuries, it is not usually, Aquinas aside, as any kind of sin or infraction: rather it is as something that provokes disgust, the feeling we reserve for things that are closer to us than we would like. Why disgust, rather than the outrage, sadness, or fear we might typically feel at the thought of a wrong? Perhaps it is because flattery is not so much a transgression, as a contamination, which muddles the moral apparatus that allows us to distinguish right from wrong. As Ian Miller has suggested, '[i]t is very hard indeed to extract praise from the system of reciprocities in which it is embedded and by which it is in part compromised' (Miller 2003, 103). This is why the fact that flattery appears to make praise 'tainted' seems to matter so much:

> flattery can be sincere and can be true. Then what could possibly distinguish it from praise, which is also both sincere and true? Might it be that flattery does to praise what hypocrisy does to all virtue: infects it so that the real thing can never be trusted? (Miller 2003, 98)

Flattery is as disquieting, and disgusting, as it is, in part because it is so close to things we might find admirable – the flatterer depends on at least one person thinking that her blandishments are sincere praise. Another of the queasy uncertainties of flattery concerns its relation to honest work. The flatterer appears to get something for nothing, like the beggar, even though, again like the beggar, one cannot say that their gains are entirely unearned. Flattery, like begging, is not idleness, so much as a deprecated or unsavoury kind of work, like prostitution. Indeed, it resembles prostitution in seeming to stand in the place of – *pro-stare* – some putatively spontaneous or unstrategic kind of action – true love, sincere praise, fair exchange – which it simulates. One might even say that the need with which the flatterer transacts in their subject is something like the need for love of the prostitute's client, where love means the need to be acknowledged.

What is most intolerable about flattery for its victim and so intoxicating for its practitioner seems to be the deceitful inversion of power relations it brings about. All acts of petition must involve some degree of abstitution, self-lowering or standing aside, before the one petitioned. But flattery works by assisting the one flattered to overcome the inhibition of narcissism in which social creatures are schooled, thereby turning the encouraging balm of praise into the luscious poison of self-love uncountermanded. The flatterer makes himself or herself the purveyor of an addictive substance. The aim is that the one who succumbs to the flatterer's blandishments should begin to hang on the words of their hanger-on. As Thomas Gordon wrote in 1741, 'by shewing that we think we are what we are not, [we] court the Deceiver to court us' (Gordon 1741, 189). Thus the flatterer is the very type of the one who tops from below, in the argot of BDSM. One of the reasons that human beings are so bad at defending themselves against flattery is that, even if one is capable of setting aside the content of what the flatterer imparts, the mere performance of the flattering act constitutes a compliment: to be flattered means that one has been recognised as someone who is worthy of being flattered, or at least worth going to the trouble of flattering.

In Christianity, the arch-flatterer is Satan. In *Paradise Lost*, Satan's words to Eve are a masterpiece of flattering strategy, with the devil representing himself as the one who gives the subject eyes to see herself as she would be seen:

> Fairest resemblance of thy maker fair,
> Thee all things living gaze on, all things thine
> By gift, and thy celestial beauty adore
> With ravishment beheld, there best beheld
> Where universally admired; but here
> In this enclosure wild, these beasts among,
> Beholders rude, and shallow to discern
> Half what in thee is fair, one man except,
> Who sees thee? (and what is one?) who shouldst be seen
> A goddess among gods, adored and served
> By angels numberless, thy daily train. (Milton 2008, 222)

Traditionally, the power of Satan was all supposition, since he was supposed to have no power in himself except the power that he could persuade the weak, wicked or deluded to ascribe to him. The temptation that Satan offers is the temptation to believe that another may share the magical belief one has in one's own powers. Milton's word for Satan's verbal performance here is 'glozed' (Milton 2008, 222), a word that benefits from the convergence, from the middle of the sixteenth century, of Latin *glossa*, and Greek γλῶσσα, a word needing 'glossing' or explication, with Middle High German *glos*, a glow. Satan's glozings hold the gleaming glass up to Eve's suppressed will to self-love. Satan first asserts a surprising but pleasing fact, that 'Thee all things living gaze on … and thy celestial beauty adore'. But he then removes the gift he has just given. For it turns out that 'all things living' under the circumstances of Eden, oxymoronically characterised as 'this enclosure wild', does not amount to very much, being limited to the beasts of the field, who are 'Beholders rude, and shallow to discern/Half what in thee is fair'. The lethal dose is injected by the question that torments and energises every human from the beginning of awareness to its end: 'Who sees thee?' The answer is the answer always given by the flatterer: it is Satan who is the mirror, mirror on the wall, offering the guarantee of recognition, the ruse that narcissism depends on to ensure its dominion. The imaginary circuit of recognition allows one to imagine oneself as seen and known again, even though that recognition is in fact inaugural rather than repetition. The flatterer allows one to suppose that there is another, who sees me as I really am, which is to say, sees me as I never yet thought to see myself, as beyond my own imagining, thereby fulfilling the hope of glory that every human must crave, through the daftly bitter paradox of heterautonomy.

Harvey C. Mansfield has suggested that 'modern liberalism with its allegiance to self-preservation [and] distrust of sacrifice' has mounted a 'calculated campaign against *thumos* [as Mansfield renders θυμός]' (Mansfield 2006, 228). The Nietzschean assumption of Mansfield's *Manliness* is that this campaign has something to do with the move away from strong gender differentiations in modern liberal societies, so that recognising the continuing force of honour-seeking means acknowledging the continuing force of manliness. In the Jefferson lecture given in 2007 in Washington, Mansfield seems to generalise the operations of thymos, in defining it as 'a part of the soul that makes us want to insist on our own importance'. Mansfield argues that a politics that understands 'the importance of importance' will be better placed to recognise that '[p]olitics is about what makes you angry, not so much about what you want' (Mansfield 2007), pointing to identity politics as the proof that honour-seeking is in fact potently alive in modern liberal societies. Francis Fukuyama concurs in seeing thymos as 'the seat of today's identity politics' (Fukuyama 2018, 18).

Peter Sloterdijk has also proposed a revival of the idea of thymos. Sloterdijk's focus in his book *Rage and Time* is on the 'moral domestication of rage' (Sloterdijk 2010, 23), in 'the *thymos* that has been conditioned by civilization' (Sloterdijk 2010, 24). Most of his book is devoted to an explication of the ways in which institutional politics has tamed, administered and instrumentalised the principle of rage or righteous anger that manifests in thymos, through processes that persuade the enraged to delegate their anger to political institutions – in particular the revolutionary states of twentieth-century communism. We may bring Mansfield and Sloterdijk together if we posit something like the generalisation of thymos into administered and predictable forms. The most important feature of thymos is that it arises under conditions in which a gap arises between self-esteem, or the wish for it, and the esteem accorded to others. This is to say that thymos characteristically takes the form of a demand, which we should see as at the extreme end of the petitory spectrum that runs from entreaty to insistence. Thymotic petition, in the form of the many petulant claims for honour, respect, dignity, and recognition – bristlingly assertive in their demands, but whimperingly parasitic in their dependence on recognition, and perhaps resentfully enraged by the fact of that dependence – seems everywhere at hand.

I noted earlier that one of the most important drivers of the petitory-patronage complex in the early modern period was the growth of communication, primarily in the form of letters. The huge expansion of communicative media in the last century may be encouraging a similar intensification of the action of getting one another to do things noted by Frank Whigham (Whigham 1981, 868), and the transformation of broadcasting media to media of lateral communication means that we have more ways than ever of effecting these mediated urgings on and through one another. What we seek – honour, respect, prestige, standing, recognition – has the same refracted form as the ways in which we seek it, for both are heteronomic, that is, dependent on external sources.

If flattery is an anticipatory offering of esteem, used both to create indebtedness and to instil a need amounting to addiction, which will give subsequent petition for favour or advantage a greater chance of success, it may be helpful to ask about the quality of the need that it supplies. George Devereux has pointed to the analogy between the forms of flattery conventionally supplied in male courtship of women (and sometimes in the inverse) and that supplied to powerful rulers. Courtship flattery of women, suggests Devereux, 'is often worded in a manner which, through the use of diminutives, reaffirms that which the flattery itself seeks to deny: the smallness, infantilism ("baby") and inadequacy of the person who is seemingly being praised so extravagantly. ("Tiny ears like shells," etc.)' (Devereux 1960, 8). The flattery of rulers similarly offers them a kind of power which allows

> an acting out, in adult life, of infantile-dependent fantasies of omnipotence; it implies the "baby-ing" of the exalted personage, who demands that tasks which men ordinarily perform for themselves should be performed for him by others. … It is this distinctive "power" aspect of the status of the "lady" and of the well-served exalted personage which justifies our analogy between the flattery meted out to women and to rulers. (Devereux 1960, 9)

The fragile and spasmodic anger prompted by the lack or loss of esteem seems to confirm the essentially childish condition of fantasy-omnipotence sought by the flattery addict. The principle of strength in weakness that is actualised through every instance of petitory charisma is apotheosised in the condition of the one who does not even have to beg for the privilege of being made helpless; and yet such a condition of omnipotence in impotence also deprives the infantilised tyrant of the opportunity of overcoming weakness or impediment that is characteristic of real strength. The actualisation of fantasy leaves the flattered tyrant with a kind of simmering, inchoate rage that they will be held forever in fantasy's grip, with the omnipotence of humiliation always a hair's-breadth away from the humiliation of omnipotence. This may be why modern despots so often resort to bare-chested displays of equestrian skill or phallic hole-in-one prowess in golf, even though they will remain infuriatingly dependent upon the lickspittle reporting of their superhuman achievements in cringing media outlets.

If technology has produced a generalisation of the infantilisation of the ruler, who has no need to walk, prepare food, change fuses, or maintain friendships, then communications technology may be producing something like an epidemic of thymotic need, expressible both as anger, and in the need for flattery. So, where for generations, the flatterer would employ their wiles in order to prepare the ground for their petitions, we now see on every side a kind of exhibitionist petitioning for the narcissistic confirmation that flattery offers.

Though commentators are unified in their certainty that flattery is an accessory to begging, or the inducement of gifts, favours or advancement, a singular feature of this kind of begging is that it not only prepares the way for petition, it aims to make it unnecessary, by inducing spontaneous gifts from the subject of the flattery. In this it resembles the potentially aggressive form of begging that consists of performing an unwanted service – clipping your hedge, say, or cleaning your windscreen at a set of traffic lights, or, in a revenge tragedy, knocking off a troublesome courtier – then seeking recompense for the unsought service.

However, the subtlety of flattery consists in the fact that it diffuses and autonomises the act of begging, which accordingly need never rise to a visible or audible condition, or precipitate an explicit act of petition. The sponging of the parasite is designed to be effected relationally rather than discursively. The parasite is a beggar through what he gets, not through what he asks for. He does not need suddenly to risk reversing the flow of benefit from patron to parasite, because his entire mode of operation is solicitative. The need to give back is somehow given in the operation of ingratiation, which aims to make the act of giving gratuitous, by putting the receiver in the way of the gift, rather than in the position of having to ask for it. Where all begging can appear parasitic, flattery is the means whereby parasitism can avoid the taint of mendication, on the part both of the giver and the prospective, prospecting recipient. This dissolution of the more obvious kinds of link between flattery and the begging for advantage may account for the difficulty we may have in recognising how widespread patronage-driven relations of self-seeking dependency remain in modern societies, whether they appear hierarchical or more democratic.

One of the first moral philosophers to view the exercise of flattery approvingly, and to admire and respect its civilising effects, rather than seeing it as corrosive of social life, was Bernard de Mandeville, in his *The Fable of the Bees: Private Vices, Public Virtues* (1714). Mandeville argues that '[t]hose that have undertaken to civilize mankind', lacking the wherewithal to provide real rewards for good behaviour, discovered the utility instead of the imaginary reward 'that as a general Equivalent for the trouble of Self-denial should serve on all Occasions, and without costing any thing either to themselves or others, be yet a most acceptable Recompense to the Receivers' (Mandeville 1924, 42). This imaginary reward is, simply, the gratification of self-love provided by praise:

> They thoroughly examin'd all the Strength and Frailties of our Nature, and observing that none were either so savage as not to be charm'd with Praise, or so despicable as patiently to bear Contempt, justly concluded, that Flattery must be the most powerful Argument that could be used to Human Creatures. Making use of this bewitching Engine, they extoll'd the Excellency of our Nature above other Animals, and setting forth with unbounded Praises the Wonders of our Sagacity and Vastness of Understanding, bestow'd a thousand Encomiums on the Rationality of our Souls, by the Help of which we were capable of performing the most noble Atchievements. Having by this artful way of Flattery insinuated themselves into the Hearts of Men, they began to instruct them in the Notions of Honour and Shame; representing the one as the worst of all Evils, and the other as the highest Good to which Mortals could aspire (Mandeville 1924, 42-3)

For Mandeville therefore, 'the Moral Virtues are the Political Offspring which Flattery begot upon Pride' (Mandeville 1924, 51). This need not be taken as merely a cynical trick. As Daniel Kapust explains, for Mandeville, 'flattery is both a mechanism of socialization and moral education; a form of exchange deployed in an economy of esteem, it is a type of language uniquely capable of manipulating humans into behaving in ways they would not ordinarily choose' (Kapust 2018, 133). William Ian Miller concedes similarly that flattery is too bound up with actions of approbation more generally for us ever to be able to do without it:

Our desire to be flattered will make flatterers of our friends out of kindness, of our underlings out of fear and desire for getting a leg up on the competition, and of our superiors out of a desire better to get us to do their bidding. There is no getting rid of the vice, and a good thing too, or many more of our days would be ruined than already are. (Miller 2003, 108)

The contemporary economies of esteem, given and demanded, offered and expected, which require that we issue praise and commendation in all directions and on so many different occasions, to friends, family-members, associates, clients, co-workers, teachers and subordinates, are closely interwoven with forms of structural mendicancy, a mendicancy that need never speak its name, since it will represent the real recompense for the 'imaginary reward' given in advance by ingratiation, in what Mandeville calls 'the Aerial Coin of Praise' (Mandeville 1924, 55). The generalisation of this currency in democratic societies, means that 'in a democracy, if every man is a king, we are all courtiers as well' (Stengel 2000, 22), and all of us depend upon the engineering of gratuitous favours and advantages throughout life in advance investments of flattery. Just as there are rage-banks, as suggested by Peter Sloterdijk, social life constitutes a kind of stock-exchange of esteem, characterised by complex and fluctuating patterns of investment and return.

The gratifications of praise seem to go far beyond its likely benefits in kind. The most conspicuous inflation of the operations of praise has taken place over the last three centuries in the development of advertising, which both autonomises and anonymises the act of flattery, in products that therefore appear insistently and immoderately to recommend themselves, for consumers who are congratulated in advance for choosing them. It is assumed that we are encouraged to buy products by puffs and endorsements because we may trust the judgement of those doing the endorsing, and because of the drive to conformity with the judgements of others. Of course, one can readily regard these ubiquitous blandishments as mere commercial mendicancy, which is aimed at the pay-off of purchase. But the exorbitance of this universal endorsement seems to become increasingly independent of this kind of purpose, as the gap between deposit and pay-off becomes ever longer.

I am often nowadays approached by publishers to ask if I would be willing to read a soon-to-be-published academic book, with a view to possibly providing an endorsement for the cover and accompanying publicity material. Quite often, even evidently highly-reputable university presses will suggest that I need do no more than glance at a chapter or two of the book in order to frame my pocket panegyric. No payment may be offered or accepted for this service to scholarship, but it represents a significant local variation on the academic esteem economy – a kind of peer-puffery to accompany the allegedly alert and balanced critical verifications provided by peer review. It is in fact one of the longest-established practices in advertising, which was familiar even in the seventeenth century. What used to be known as the Puff has given way to the 'blurb', a term evidently invented by the writer Gelet Burgess for a book jacket he had designed in 1907 for his book *Are You a Bromide?* The jacket is headed 'YES, this is a "BLURB"! All the Other Publishers commit them. Why Shouldn't We?, and shows a young woman with the caption 'Miss Belinda Blurb in the Act of Blurbing' and text that promises 'This book has 42-carat THRILLS in it. It fairly BURBLES' (https://www.loc.gov/resource/rbpe.24203600/?sp=1). It is astonishing how entirely unashamed publishers are using this term when requesting these kinds of cloudy commendation.

The practice may have some market utility in pushing certain books up the recommendation lists, but its most interesting feature is the circuit of flattery-gratifications it actually involves. Since financial payment for such praises would be unacceptable, one is paid in the aerial coin of the intimation that one's opinion might be worth seeking out, and the esteem-inflating exposure they offer to their authors. Contrary to what one might think, the more of such cumulonimbus endorsements one writes, the more authoritative one's judgement may seem to be, and the less debased one's personal laudative currency. In a modification of the principle that even if one disbelieves a flatterer, one is flattered to be thought to be worth flattering, the practice of soliciting and supplying endorsements flatters the flatterer with the possibility that their flattering opinion might have value. A soapy kind of delirium can overtake one in the performance of such a commission, in the sense of the immunity that any such comments one might frame will have from accusations of absurdity, mendacity or self-interest.

It may even be that some part of the desire to give credence to such judgements is the desire to share in the swelling sense of omnipotence that unrestrained flattery can suggest. The more dubious the superlative, the more the flatterer seems to prove, if only to themselves, the South-Sea Bubble power of rootless superlation as such, to seem to put the world in its unpayable debt and in the process pile up petitory credit. This is of a piece with the other autogratifications of petitory practices, such as the act of prayer, and the child's faith in the powers of seduction that their very weakness lends to them, all amounting to the logic of the Ponzi pyramid, of a faith that one has in the powers of one's faith, or the power of others' faith in that faith. A world of goods and services recommending themselves to customers through flattering pre-approval of their choice of them is like the world of constant, and widely-delegated prayer characteristic of some highly religious societies, in which we may by now assume that the apparatus of religious belief is driven by the need for the act of prayer, rather than the reverse; advertising ensures a universal diffusion of prayer, in which, instead of the universal call to prayer, there is a universal call of praying, in which everyone can constantly be preyed upon by being prayed to.

8

Service

A society that exports more and more of its work of solicitation and blandishment to mediated rather than proximally corporeal forms will be able to effect very considerable variations in the forms of its petition and reward. Our pride in our modern immunity from the machinations of the parasite, and our alertness to the dangers of prejudice and privilege and bias through the principle of equal opportunities, dulls our awareness of the continuing shifts of the parasite in the autonomised petitions and prestations at work in the variations of social security and welfare provision, whether financial or medical. The parasite is squeezed out, not through abolition, but through a multilateral generalisation of parasitic relations that aims to make the parasite invisible. The displacing of the value of equality by the desire to achieve 'diversity', whether represented as a benign quotaism, or the means of effecting significant shifts in the distribution of resources, is a telling example of how the opportunities to achieve marginal advantage through indirect means will tend to arise and be seized.

This unstable relation between reparation and advantage becomes clear in the periodic eruptions of outrage in welfare states at those who are said to 'sponge' on the social security system. The word 'sponge' came into use in this negative sense in the 1670s, though 'sponge' had been previously used of the victim of squeezing in the early 1600s, a double sense deployed in Hamlet's interchange with Rosencrantz, whom he describes as

> a sponge … that soaks up the King's countenance, his rewards, his authorities. But such officers do the King best service in the end: he keeps them, like an ape, in the corner of his jaw – first mouthed, to be last swallowed. When he needs what you have gleaned, it is but squeezing you and, sponge, you shall be dry again. (Shakespeare 2011, 318)

The sponger is singled out as a deprecated exception, one who cynically seeks and exploits the gifts and benefits made available by the state rather than gratefully receiving them. This disguises what would otherwise be the uncomfortable fact of the almost universal dependence of every citizen on complex networks of benefits and allowances, all of which are to be had, not as of right, but on application, a word which has become entirely separated from the work of charity, but is still an autonomisation of the actions of asking and granting. The denunciation of the individual sponger who 'makes a living' from the state, even though all of us who earn 'our own' living are permitted to do so only on terms licensed and regulated by some state arrangement or other, means that a polemical generalisation of parasitic relations such as that offered by Peter Sloterdijk in his essay 'The Grasping Hand' is bound to be seen (as it is of course intended to be) as an absurd and cruelly provocative outrage:

> In an earlier day, the rich lived at the expense of the poor, directly and unequivocally; in a modern economy, unproductive citizens increasingly live at the expense of productive ones – though in an equivocal way, since they are told, and believe, that they are disadvantaged and deserve more still. Today, in fact, a good half of the population of every modern nation is made up of people with little or no income, who are exempt from taxes and live, to a large extent, off the other half of the population, which pays taxes. (Sloterdijk 2010)

The outrage at the figure of the sponger arises from the transfer of moral feelings that seem apt at the level of the individual to the much larger scale of a society. The charge of parasitism can only be laid under circumstances where the parasite is an exploitative anomaly, outsider or exception to a normal order of collectively-sanctioned distributions. When parasitism is general and symmetrical, as, for example, in the forms of symbiosis at work in the individual organism and even in the individual cell, it becomes a system of mutual assurance and so tends to vanish from view.

Parasites

The principal means whereby what would otherwise be regarded as parasitism is regularised and made systematic in contemporary societies is through the relation to what are known as 'services'. A highly hierarchical society based on large-scale slavery displays a very simple and obvious structure of parasitism from above, with a small proportion of the population served by the coerced labour of its majority. In such societies, the monarch, court and aristocracy can, and in fact must, depend upon various kinds of attendant, who yield up their service in relations of loyalty and fealty. The idea of service played from earliest times a leading part in religious conceptions, with a 'service' meaning, from the twelfth century onwards, the particular form taken by a religious ritual. Later, it moved by transference from these religious uses to courtly understandings of sexual-romantic devotion. In time, these relations were gradually abstracted into various kinds of office, most notably military service, later distinguished into the different 'services', and into administrative agencies. Among these were the Civil Service, which was originally the name for a department of the East India Company the personnel of which were not military, but by the middle of the nineteenth century had become the name for the coordinated system of state administration and public policy in general. It also provided a name for a new class of agents employed first of all 'in secret service' and then, by the middle of the nineteenth century, as part of 'the Secret Service'.

The slow and uneven move away from structural coercion to contractual or semi-contractual relations both loosens and generalises those relations of service. Almost a quarter of women in employment in 1851 were in what had by the middle of the eighteenth century become known as domestic service (Field 2013, 249). This expansion of domestic service was seen by historians for a long time as an expression of an aspiration to status, through the mimicry of gentility among a middle class growing more affluent. The impetus imparted by feminist perspectives has assisted a growing understanding of such work as a significant part of economic production, rather than part of the secondary symbolic structures of social relations. Edward Higgs suggests that the beginning of what would come to be known as service industries in the later nineteenth century should be seen as a movement outside the home of the domestic labour previously performed by servants inside it, which might often in fact have meant commercial production in homes that were also the sites of businesses. The replacement of domestic labour by such services as restaurants, laundries and board schools may have provided opportunities to perform what had previously been regarded as domestic labour outside the home. Higgs maintains that 'the commercial "revolution" of the late nineteenth century, especially the rise of the service industries, was not the development of new types of work in society, but merely the performance of existing work in a new setting' (Higgs 1983, 209).

During the late nineteenth century, the word 'service' broadened to encompass agencies providing various kinds of amenity to the general population rather than the State, including the postal service, the transport service, the broadcasting service, notably the BBC 'Home Service' which broadcast through the Second World War, utilities, health services and so on. The word 'service was used to denote the means used to connect individual consumers to general utilities; so the pipes that ran off the main water or gas pipes to individual houses were known as 'service-pipes' from the mid-nineteenth century, while 'service roads' are similarly those that give access to individual clients or dwellings, similarly to service stairs and service lifts. From the beginning of the twentieth century the word began also to be used to signify the work of maintenance and repair that came to be ever more necessary with the extension of different kinds of apparatus and infrastructure. Such practices, according to Chris Otter, arose from, and were a constant reminder of, 'the need to regulate large technological systems that, despite the best intentions of engineers, failed to regulate themselves' (Otter 2008, 172). It was not only utilities that required maintenance. The diversification of industries devoted to meeting various kinds of consumer need, as opposed to producing goods, many of them for kinds of 'personal service', from nail-bars to psychotherapy, that might previously have been due to a lord or sovereign, established the economic importance of what came to be known as 'service industries'.

In one sense this process is another part of the autonomisation of the work of expressing and meeting human needs, and the resulting systems of distribution of goods and benefits. It involves a replacement of the intimate, personal and often uncomfortably direct functions of domestic service with abstract functions. Put simply, instead of having to give orders to one's domestic staff, one is enabled under the new service dispensations simply to 'place an order', whether for a meal, or for various kinds of household goods. The arrival of widespread computing in the 1970s brought about the need for automated mechanisms which provided access to shared digital resources, mechanisms which themselves aptly became known as 'servers'. The process of calling up a document or resource became a matter simply of clicking on a link, with no need for any formalised command. With the huge growth in online shopping, such servers became the principal intermediary in the provision of physical goods to consumers. But, despite the fact that their aim and effect seem to be to reduce the intimacy and intensity of need-provision, the psychosocial implications of this shift are considerable.

It is usual to see the relations established by service industries as involving 'commodification', though this term is very approximate. 'Contractualisation' seems preferable in many ways, for what one buys when one buys a service is not a commodity like a dishcloth or a double-scotch, but a temporary agreement from another person or persons to act in such a way as to serve one's needs. In fact, this is a partial reversion to earlier meanings of the word commodity, which was used to refer more generally to a benefit or convenience (such as a 'commode') rather than simply a physical product until around the end of the eighteenth century. Service industries systematise the work of procuring attendance or tending to one's needs that would previously have been provided by attendants. We are popularly supposed to be enslaved by the need to acquire, but on closer inspection it may seem that what we most crave are not acquisitions but requisitions, that is, the power to demand and consume, in the sense of diverting to one's use and, perhaps more importantly, putting beyond their own use, others' time. Humans do not produce large litters, and young humans require huge amounts of tending and attendance over many years. They consume resources, no doubt, but the most important resources by far are not food and material necessities but the social-symbolic resources of service and attendance, that is to say, person-time and what has come intelligently to be known as 'emotional labour'. The arrival of a baby in a room full of adults makes it impossible to pay attention to any other subject. It may be that the lesson this teaches is that, having been the thing that guarantees one's survival into the condition known as a person, the ability to command the attendance of others remains the guarantee of personhood. Perhaps no observance expresses and confirms this more extraordinarily than the institution of birthday celebrations, which institutionalise the performance of a fantasy that the world is gathering round to pay grateful court to the one whose birthday it is. The need for attention is the need for the capacity to keep others in temporary, attentive detention. Attention and retention come together in the antique term 'retainer', which originally meant, as it still does, a sum of money paid to secure and keep available certain kinds of service (one might still 'retain the services' of a lawyer), but was applied in parallel to the person so retained.

We like to think, or at least we speak as though we did, that we do incalculable wrong to a person if we 'objectify' them. In fact, however, what every human originally needs and what becomes an overmastering kind of obsession for many humans, is the need to be an object of concern, what in Latin was known as a *res*, which shares an Indo-European base with Sanskrit *rayi*, riches, as in the name for the collective, cohering object of attention known as the *res publica*, the republic or the public thing, which is held in common by the public and keeps the public able to hold itself in common. To be taken up in objects, animate, material, or psychological, is to lose yourself, or to become able to do so. The function of objects is to give a subject the possibility of projection beyond itself, followed by safe return, in a kind of interrupted interruption of one's self-concern. To be oneself an object of concern is to be reified, and made real, regal, a Ding-an-sich, the thing-to-itself that can only subsist in the light of others' concern for it. To be an object for another is to appropriate their power of forming projects. Human beings are limited to one life, yet cannot but strive through social-symbolic relations of service to assimilate and amass the life-time of others. This regal privilege of being made real through the power to demand and command the attendance of others, exercised, in Freud's tenderly sardonic phrase, by 'His Majesty the Ego' (*Seine Majestät das Ich*) (Freud 1953-74, 9.149; Freud 1991, 7.219), has become the prerogative, the prior mandate or privilege of being able to ask, diffused, and thereby dimmed in danger and intensity, and made reciprocal in the web of social services. So, far from being the object of moral dread, the need to be taken as an object of attention is the primary demand and requirement of every aspirant subject.

The relevance to this enquiry of the growth of what have become known as service industries, the original oxymoron of that phrase steadily fading out of view, comes from the demands attaching to the requirement to ask for different kinds of service. All services, including the ones that are provided 'on demand', which has really come to mean without the need for any demand, put one in the position of a solicitor or petitioner. The residual need for these gift-solicitations can be made out in those strange phantom-exchanges that accompany the ordinary transactions attaching to the accessing and provision of different kinds of service. In my profession, as university academic, one may be admired and rewarded by promotion, not just for fulfilling the requirements of one's post, teaching, course-design, participation in administrative functions and so on, but also for what is formally and rather coyly called 'academic service', which refers to actions which belong wholly to one's customary duties and responsibilities, and yet also seem excessive to them, since they seem in some sense voluntary and delivered out of the goodness of one's disposition. The word suggests that, rather than merely performing services as required by one's contract, one has willingly made oneself a servant, or established a relation of service to one's occupation. In order to be adequate, service must also always be able to be represented as gratuitous, and it is the gratuity of service which puts the consumer of services in the symbolic position of the petitioner. A 'service contract' with a supplier may attempt to spell out precisely what is required from a service relation, but when one complains about the service in a restaurant one is complaining about the absence of the certain indefinable surplus of attention that seems to signal what is due to one over and above that for which one has paid.

And this is nowhere summarised better than in the institution of what has itself become known as the 'gratuity'. It would appear as though all the power, privilege and prerogative belongs to the one giving the gratuity. The 'tip', the vernacular alternative to the gratuity, in fact seems to derive from canting and beggars' slang for a gift or a handout: in Gay's *The Beggar's Opera*, the Newgate jailer Lockit asks his daughter Lucy, whom he suspects of helping Macheath escape from prison, 'Did he tip handsomely? – How much did he come down with?' (Gay 2013, 48).

Gratuity begins as a kind of grace, either divine or, in hopeful or grandiose imitation of the divine, that of the sovereign. But it seems that a gratuity might also often have been given as a kind of inducement or proleptic favour, meaning that it is not gratuitous at all, as, of course, no gift ever can be, except to one possessed of perfect and infallible knowledge of the future and the returns it may bring. The king seeking to secure loyalty or seal allegiance through the giving of gifts, seeking through gratuity to ingratiate himself, has been generalised into the contemporary practice of tipping, which allows commoners across the social spectrum the miniaturised imitation of regal magnanimity. It is therefore a pretence of what is itself often, and perhaps usually, a pretence in the first place. What is important is not to be served one's omelette, but to be treated as one deserves to be in performing that action. It is not unknown however for a gratuity to be offered in advance, more frankly as an inducement to good service ('Here we are Henry: I know you will look after us as well as always'), which is to say service that goes that little bit further than service, and recognises the right of the giver to be treated as more than a mere customer. In a world that is assumed to be governed purely by transaction, the gratuity is prompted by those unnecessary gratifications provided to the customer that suggest that their server is in fact bound to them by bonds of service rather than economic exchange.

This flirtation with the purchasing relation (it has some of the excitement and danger of the sexual flirtation) in part explains the delicacy about the precise amount that one should give. To give a derisory amount, or what comes to the same thing, to count out exactly the 10% or 12% enjoined by local custom, risks reducing the relation to simple calculation. But to give more than is customary, or rather a great deal more, since slightly more than customary is really what is enjoined, also carries the risk of being insulting, since it may seem to destroy the fiction of the free giving of gifts beyond, or rather beneath calculation. Gratuities require the nicest possible mensuration of the nuances of the approximate.

The giving of gratuities is closely though obscurely related to the giving of bribes, which itself has a nocturnal relation to the act of begging. In its earliest use in Middle French, *briber* meant to beg, and in Middle English too a *bribe* meant a gift obtained through begging. In modern French a *bribe* still means a scrap, such as a piece of bread, and *par bribes* means piecemeal or in snatches. *The Pilgrimage of the Lyf of the Manhode*, a translation of around 1430 of Guillaume de Deguileville's *Pèlerinage de vie humaine*, refers to 'thilke that hideth brybes in his sak ... thilke that biseecheth bred for the loue of god' (Deguileville 1869, 147). Lydgate's translation of the passage evokes 'Thys hand I vse in bryberye,/In beggyng and in lasyngrye [trickery]' (1904, 477). A bribe came to mean something pilfered or extorted, or obtained through swindling; but by the middle of the sixteenth century, it had altered its orientation again, to mean to give a gift with some ulterior motive. From begging for bribes, one began to beg through bribes. When Isabella is begging for her brother's life from Angelo in *Measure for Measure*, she brings him up short with the momentarily breathtaking suggestion 'Hark how I'll bribe you', but then rescues the situation with a witty comparison of the act of prayer to bribery (even if it also lets slip the acknowledgement that all prayer may constitute a bribe-like inducement):

> Not with fond sickles of the tested gold,
> Or stones, whose rate are either rich or poor
> As fancy values them: but with true prayers,
> That shall be up at heaven and enter there
> Ere sunrise: prayers from preserved souls,
> From fasting maids. whose minds are dedicate
> To nothing temporal. (Shakespeare 2011, 811)

The giving of a gratuity is a financial inducement to behaviour that demonstrates a social relation that is not merely financial, but expressive of respect and recognition of status. Hence the various shifts to disguise the gift, as for example in the giving of gratuities in restaurants or other circumstances of service, which is always done discreetly and without ostentation or proclamation, in the acknowledged ways of making it possible not to have to acknowledge it: having the waiter come back with the change in order to be able to wave it away with a smile, or leaving a banknote coyly tucked in the folder, or under the plate. The fact that the gratuity comes after the meal has been served, or the overcoat needlessly transported to the hook, disguises the bribe relation, though with the gratuity one is not paying for an action, but recognising a prior act of recognition, or at least the performance of one.

If in one sense the gratuity symbolically reduces the one to whom it is given to the condition of a vassal or bondservant, rather than merely a contracted agent, it also exacts complex and difficult demands on the one who gives it, demands that actually amount to a kind of petition. The one who gives the gratuity must seek acknowledgement that their offering is not only acceptable but made in an acceptable manner that does not impugn the dignity of the receiver. To give gratuities ignorantly or without attention to these delicacies is in fact to reveal oneself as unworthy of the relations of service one may seek, and indeed as shamefully grovelling with mere money for what one ought to be able to expect as of right, but does not in fact deserve. In service transactions, one requisitions the temporary performance of a relation in which one would not have to ask for what would anyway be one's due. The institution of the gratuity ensures that the one temporarily contracted to such service is given the fictive warrant to decide freely on the acceptability of the gift offered to them.

This history of impostures and cross-identifications is at work in the strange, stately pavane which attends the stalking and offering of the gratuity, and the relations of service more generally that it dulcifies (since the eighteenth century a *douceur* has been a gentle euphemism for a bribe). The awkwardness and self-consciousness around the gratuity, as at once an extension of commercial and contractual relations and the engineered exception to them, is an expression of the relations of mutual dependence and reciprocal petition that arise from the generalisation of service in many modern societies.

When relations of petition and parasitical dependence become as interlocked and omnilateral as this, they can participate in a larger structural perturbation – a perturbation of a structure and a structure of perturbation – of the relations between what is inside and what is outside any system. The one who petitions must always do so from some position of relative exteriority, either seeking to insinuate themselves into their host or seeking to insinuate some part of their host, or what belongs to them, into themselves. In both cases, what is at issue, in the double sense both of being in question and of itself issuing from the process of asking the question, is the nature of the *in* – one of the most elementary and yet complex words in any language. I have wondered whether there has ever been a text entitled simply *In*, the complement perhaps to Christine Brooke-Rose's *Out* (1964). Search for texts with that title and you will find it exceedingly hard to flush any out, precisely because the word *in* is buried in so many titles. We seem to need nominalised adjectives like 'innerness' or 'interiority' to be able to come at the question of what it means to be in, which is otherwise kept so implicit, meaning that the meaning of the in is always already implied by our use of the term, and so never able to be fully explicated without finding oneself being drawn back in to the tangle from which one might seek to draw it out.

Indeed, the question of what is in and what is out is at the heart of all formal questioning whatsoever. All of biology, the greater part of linguistics and metaphysics, the categorial work of philosophy, the whole of theology and set-theory, and indeed perhaps every form of investigation, turns around the nature of the *in*. Such investigation must also always presuppose some understanding of the relations between the in and the out, since one will always be in question in the question one pursues, and so far in as to be unable to put it straightforwardly into question. Every search for principles is a *petitio principii*, a begging of the question, or assuming of the answer to the question one affects to be seeking to answer.

Perhaps this is also the parasitic inquiry that all petition institutes. Petition asks for what will not come to me otherwise, of itself, or by right. Every petition establishes an outside, from which it comes, even as it affirms an inside with which it seeks to establish a newly inclusive relation through that very petition. The parasite is petitory, as petition is parasitic. The parasite is not a relation so much as a question, a question of whether there is to be a relation, and so in fact and after all a question which is a relation. Every question is an interruption, which begs for an answer that would acquit that interruption. And petition is parasitic because it is this relation between inside and outside, rather than belonging to one side or other of it.

Michel Serres evokes this relation of asking and giving in the principle of intercession represented by the parasitically intermediate Holy Ghost-Paraclete, which is anticipated in the ordinary word παρακαλῶ used still in modern Greek both for asking or saying please and for saying 'please, don't mention it, you're welcome'. Παρακαλώ, formed from παρα, beside, alongside + καλέσω means to call, summon, exhort, demand or beseech, hence *bitte*, please, I beg or bid you. The Paraclete is from παράκλητος, one called to one's side, as witness or advocate, as in a court of law, after παρα + καλεῖν to call in, call to one's aid. The word *advocate*, the one summoned, as counsel, helper, supporter, assistant, mediator, which is used in English as an equivalent to paraclete, is formed in parallel, from *ad*, towards + *vocare*, to call, invoke. All seems to concur in the relation between the call and its answer, supplication and supplying:

> Παρακαλώ is, as we know, the closing response. Don't mention it and, yes, you're welcome. I call you, I call, I beg you. Who is invited, the one prayed to, the one called to? Say his name, say your name, say a name. *Παράκλητος*, the Paraclete, the common

name of the Holy Ghost, the third person. He intervenes,
interrupts, comes in through the walls, during meals or meetings;
he intercedes and proceeds both from the Father and the Son.
He is the wind, the being of the wind, the gust, the one the Jews
called *Ruach*. He is the gift, the being of the gift, the universal
donor. You say you're welcome because he has received, because
it is he who gives. Fire flies above exchange and above the group,
jumps from last place to first, closes the irreversible chain and
constitutes the community. The parasite Paraclete becomes the
host. (Serres 2007, 46)

But the relations between parasite and host are always intensely moralised,
and oscillate between questions of community and appropriation, property,
gift and theft. The economy of the parasite oscillates between the condition
of ecology, and the different modes and meanings of political and theological
economy. The parasite relies upon a sort of primary giving, represented by
the abundance of what we call resources. But there is in fact no such primary
giving, flying above all kinds of exchange, in the manner rather rapturously
evoked by Michel Serres. In asking for a gift, in offering the gift of being able
to become a giver, the beggar, parasite or supplicant asks in advance for the
cancellation of the debt and condoning of what would otherwise be a theft.
Condonare means to give someone the gift of their own debt. The gift of air is
only a freely-given gift for the oxygen-breathing organism that can exploit it;
atmospheric carbon is only a gift if there are plants to fix it; the gift of water is
only a gift once it has been siphoned off by the epiphyte or aqueduct. Supply
arises out of supplication, for the gift can only be supplied in relation to the
diversion proposed by the supplicant-parasite. But if, rather than being one
or other of the partners to the relation of asking and granting, the parasite is
the relation itself, then perhaps neither supply nor supplication, neither gift
nor theft, can be regarded as primary. For it is seeking – appetite, petition,
competition, impetus – that determines the sequences and relations that arise
through time, and in the process give rise to temporality itself. In the end,
then, and perhaps also at the beginning of things, the force of petition is the
disturbance that makes things, or anything at all, happen.

References

Abbot, George (1600). *An Exposition Vpon the Prophet Ionah Contained in Certaine Sermons*. London: Richard Garbrand.

A.D.B. (1619). *The Court of the Most Illustrious and Most Magnificent Iames, the first King of Great-Britaine, France, and Ireland: &c. VVith diuers rules, most pure precepts, and selected definitions liuely delineated*. London: Edward Griffin.

Agamben, Giorgio (2004). *The Open: Man and Animal*. Trans. Kevin Attell. Stanford: Stanford University Press.

Agamben, Giorgio (2010). *The Sacrament of Language: An Archaeology of the Oath (Homo Sacer II, 3)*. Trans. Adam Kotsko. Cambridge: Polity.

Andrews, Clare P. and Per T. Smiseth (2013). 'Differentiating Among Alternative Models for the Resolution of Parent-Offspring Conflict.' *Behavioral Ecology*, 24, 1185-91.

Anon (1559). *The Booke of Common Prayer, and Administracion of the Sacramentes, and Other Rites and Ceremonies in the Church of England*. London: Richard Jugge and John Cawood.

Anon (1654). *Cabala, sive, Scrinia Sacra Mysteries of State & Government: In Letters of Illustrious Persons, and Great Agents*. London: G. Bedel and T. Collins.

Anon (1666-8). *Love without Measure: Or, The Young-Mans Delight, and the Maidens Joy*. London: for William Thackery and Thomas Passinger.

Anon (1668). *A Poor Scholar's Thred-Bare Suit: Described in a Petitionary Poem to His Patron*. London: William Whotwood.

Anon (1672). *The Last, and Now Only, Compleat Collection, of the Newest and Choisest Songs and Poems*. London: William Gilbert and Thomas Sawbridge.

Anon (1708). *The Art of Tickling-Trouts; or, the Grand Secret of Philosophers: Shewing The Method How All Faculties and Professions in the World Affect the False Arts of Wheedle, Cant and Flattery, to Please Fools and Deceive Wise Men*. London: John Morphew.

Anon (1873). *The Myroure of Oure Ladye*. Ed. J. H. Blunt. London: Trübner/ Early English Text Society.

Anon (1932). 'The Three Wishes.' *Béaloideas*, 3, 434.

Aquinas, St. Thomas (1922). *Summa Theologica, Part II (Second Part)*. Trans. The Fathers of the English Dominican Province. London: Burns, Oates and Washbourne.

Atkinson, Sarah and Glen O. Gabbard (1995). 'Erotic Transference in the Male Adolescent-Female Analyst Dyad.' *Psychoanalytic Study of the Child*, 50, 171-186.

Aubrey, John (1847). *The Natural History of Wiltshire (Written Between 1656 and 1691)*. Ed. John Britton. London: J.B. Nichols and Son.

Auden, W.H. (1994). *Collected Poems*. Ed. Edward Mendelson. London: Faber and Faber.

Austin, J.L. (1962). *How to Do Things with Words*. Oxford: Clarendon.

Awdelay, John (1603). *The Fraternitie of Vacabondes as Well of Ruflyng Vacabondes, as of Beggerly, of Women as of Men, of Gyrles as of Boyes, with their Proper Names and Qualities*. London: W. White.

Baker, John (2003). *The Oxford History of the Laws of England: Volume VI 1483– 1558*. Oxford: Oxford University Press.

Baldwin, David (2009). *Royal Prayer: A Surprising History*. London and New York: Continuum.

Barbauld, Anna Letitia (1994). *The Poems of Anna Letitia Barbauld*. Ed. William McCarthy and Elizabeth Kraft. Athens and London: University of Georgia Press.

Barrett, Grant (2007). 'Whimperative.' *A Way With Words* (7th September). https://www.waywordradio.org/whimperative/

Bartholomaeus Anglicus (1398). *Liber de Proprietatibus Rerum*. Trans. John Trevisa. BL: Harley 614.

Bartholomaeus Anglicus (1505). *Liber de Proprietatibus Rerum*. s.I. Georg Husner

Bartholomaeus Anglicus (1582). *Batman vppon Bartholome His Booke De proprietatibus rerum, Newly Corrected, Enlarged and Amended*. Trans. John Trevisa. Ed. Stephen Batman. London: Thomas East.

Bateson, Gregory (2000). *Steps to an Ecology of Mind: Collected Essays in Anthropology, Psychiatry, Evolution, and Epistemology*. Chicago: University of Chicago Press.

Baudrillard, Jean (2001). *Seduction*. Trans. Brian Singer. Montreal: CultureTexts.

Beckett, Samuel (1984). *Complete Dramatic Works*. London: Faber and Faber.

Beckett, Samuel (2010a). *More Pricks than Kicks*. Ed. Cassandra Nelson. London: Faber and Faber.

Beckett, Samuel (2010b). *Texts for Nothing and Other Shorter Prose, 1950-1976*. Ed. Mark Nixon. London: Faber and Faber.

Begus, Katerina and Victoria Southgate (2012). 'Infant Pointing Serves an Interrogative Function.' *Developmental Science*, 15, 611–617.

Beier, A. L. (1985). *Masterless Men: The Vagrancy Problem in England 1560-1640*. London and New York: Methuen.

Berdoy, M., J.P. Webster and D.W. Macdonald (2000). 'Fatal Attraction in Rats Infected with *Toxoplasma gondii*.' *Proceedings of the Royal Society B: Biological Sciences*, 267, 1591–1594.

Bergen, Mary E. (1958). 'The Effect of Severe Trauma on a Four-Year-Old Child.' *Psychoanalytic Study of the Child*, 13, 407-429.

Blackie, John Stuart (1876). *Songs of Religion and Life*. Edinburgh: Edmonston and Douglas.

Blaine, Marcia Schmidt (2001). 'The Power of Petitions: Women and the New Hampshire Provincial Government, 1695-1770.' In *Petitions in Social History*, ed. Lex Heerma van Voss, *International Review of Social History*, 46 (Supplement 9), 57-77

Blake, William (1965). *The Poetry and Prose of William Blake*. Ed. David V. Erdman. Garden City: Doubleday.

Blount, Thomas (1656). *Glossographia; Or, a Dictionary Interpreting All Such Hard Words, Whether Hebrew, Greek or Latin... As Are Now Used in Our Refined English Tongue*. London: Thomas Newcomb for Humphrey Moseley.

Boyle, Kay (1932). *Year Before Last*. New York: Greenberg.

Bradshaw, John (2014). *Cat Sense: How the New Feline Science Can Make You a Better Friend to Your Pet*. New York: Basic Books.

Brecht, Bertolt (1974). *Collected Plays: Volume 7: The Visions of Simone Machard; Schweyk in the Second World War; The Caucasian Chalk Circle; The Duchess of Malfi*. Ed. Ralph Mannheim and John Willett. New York: Random House.

Brome, Richard (1652). *A Joviall Crew; or, The Merry Beggars*. London: for E.D. and N.E.

Brunschwig, Hieronymus von (1527). *The Vertuose Boke of Distyllacyon of the Waters*. Trans. Laurence Andrewe. London: Laurence Andrewe.

Bruys, François (1730). *The Art of Knowing Women: or, the Female Sex Dissected, in a Faithful Representation of Their Virtues and Vices*. Trans. John Macky. London.

Burghardt, Gordon M. (1998). 'The Evolutionary Origins of Play Revisited: Lessons from Turtles.' In *Animal Play: Evolutionary, Comparative, and Ecological Perspectives*, ed. Marc Bekoff and John A. Byers (Cambridge: Cambridge University Press), 1-26.

Burke, Kenneth (1939). 'Freud and the Analysis of Poetry.' *American Journal of Sociology*, 45, 391-417.

Burrow, John (2011). 'Chaucer as Petitioner: Three Poems.' *Chaucer Review*, 45, 349-56.

Buse, Peter (2017). 'The Dog and the Parakeet: Lacan Among the Animals.' *Angelaki: Journal of the Theoretical Humanities*, 22, 133-45.

Byrom, John (1773). *Miscellaneous Poems*. 2 Vols. Manchester: J. Harrop.

Campbell, Thomas (1907). *Complete Poetical Works*. Ed. J. Logie Robertson. London: New York and Toronto: Henry Frowde/Oxford University Press.

Capellanus, Andreas (1892). *Andreae Capellani regii Francorum De amore libri tres*. Ed. E. Trojel. Havniae: Libraria Gadiana.

Capellanus, Andreas (1969). *The Art of Courtly Love*. Ed. and trans. John Jay Parry. New York: W.W. Norton.

Caputo, John D. (1997). *The Prayers and Tears of Jacques Derrida: Religion without Religion*. Bloomington: Indiana University Press.

Caro, Shana M., Ashleigh S. Griffin, Camilla A. Hinde, and Stuart A. West (2016). 'Unpredictable Environments Lead to the Evolution of Parental Neglect in Birds.' *Nature Communications*, http://dx.doi.org/10.1038/ncomms10985

Carroll, Lewis (1970). *Alice's Adventures in Wonderland* and *Through the Looking-Glass, and What Alice Found There*. Ed. Roger Lancelyn Green. Oxford: Oxford University Press.

Carroll, William C. (1996). *Fat King, Lean Beggar: Representations of Poverty in the Age of Shakespeare*. Ithaca and London: Cornell University Press.

Chappell, Mark A. and Gwendolyn C. Bachman (2002). 'Energetic Costs of Begging Behaviour.' In *The Evolution of Begging: Competition, Cooperation and Communication*, ed. Jonathan Wright and Marty L. Leonard (Dordrecht, Boston and London: Kluwer), 143-62.

Chase, Malcolm (2019). 'What Did Chartism Petition For? Mass Petitions in the British Movement for Democracy.' *Social Science History*, 43, 531-551.

Chaucer, Geoffrey (2008). *The Riverside Chaucer*. 3rd edn. Ed. Larry D. Benson and F.N. Robinson. Oxford: Oxford University Press.

Child, Francis J., ed. (1882-98) *The English and Scottish Popular Ballads*. 5 Vols. Boston: Houghton Mifflin.

Cicero (Marcus Tullius Cicero) (2014). *On Ends*. Trans. Harris Rackham. Cambridge MA: Harvard University Press.

Clare, John (1989). *The Early Poems of John Clare: 1804-1822*. 2 Vols. Ed. Eric Robinson and David Powell. Oxford: Clarendon Press.

Clark, Stephanie (2018). *Compelling God: Theories of Prayer in Anglo-Saxon England*. Toronto, Buffalo and London: University of Toronto Press.

Clouston, W.A. (1890). 'The Story of "The Frog Prince": Breton Variant, and Some Analogues.' *Folklore*, 1, 493-506.

Coleman, Julie (2004). *A History of Cant and Slang Dictionaries: Volume 1: 1576-1784*. Oxford: Oxford University Press.

Connor, Richard C. and Rachel S. Smolker (1985). 'Habituated Dolphins (*Tursiops sp.*) in Western Australia.' *Journal of Mammalogy*, 66, 398-400.

Connor, Steven (2000). *Dumbstruck: A Cultural History of Ventriloquism*. Oxford: Oxford University Press.

Connor, Steven (2003). *The Book of Skin*. London: Reaktion.

Connor, Steven (2009). 'Witchknots, Knitwits and Knots Intrinsicate.' http://stevenconnor.com/knots.html

Connor, Steven (2011). 'The Poorest Things Superfluous: On Redundancy.' http://stevenconnor.com/redundancy.html

Connor, Steven (2012). 'Panophonia.' http://stevenconnor.com/panophonia.html

Connor, Steven (2016). *Living by Numbers: In Defence of Quantity*. London: Reaktion.

Connor, Steven (2017). *Dream Machines*. London: Open Humanities Press.

Connor, Steven (2019a). 'Abstitutions.' http://stevenconnor.com/abstitutions-prospectus.html

Connor, Steven (2019b). *Giving Way: Thoughts on Unappreciated Dispositions*. Stanford: Stanford University Press.

Connor, Steven (2019c). *The Madness of Knowledge: On Wisdom, Ignorance and Fantasies of Knowing*. London: Reaktion.

Connor, Steven (2020). 'Admiring the Nothing of It: Shakespeare and the Senseless', in *Shakespeare/Sense: Contemporary Readings in Sensory Culture*, ed. Simon Smith. London: Arden Shakespeare, 40-61.

Copland, Robert (1536). *The Hye Way to the Spyttell Hous*. London: Robert Copland.

Crashaw, Richard (1927). *The Poems English Latin and Greek*. Ed. L.C. Martin. Oxford: Clarendon.

Creemers B., J. Billen and B. Gobin (2003) 'Larval Begging Behaviour in the Ant *Myrmica rubra*.' *Ethology, Ecology and Evolution*, 15, 261-72.

Culler, Jonathan (2002). *The Pursuit of Signs: Semiotics, Literature, Deconstruction*. 2nd edn. New York and London: Routledge.

Dalton, G.F. (1971). 'The "Loathly Lady": A Suggested Interpretation.' *Folklore*, 82, 124-131.

Daniel, Michael, and Andrew Spencer (2008). 'The Vocative: An Outlier Case.' In *The Oxford Handbook of Case*, ed. Andrej L. Malchukov and Andrew Spencer (Oxford: Oxford University Press), 626-34.

de Vaan, Michiel (2008). *Etymological Dictionary of Latin and the Other Italic Languages*. Leiden: Brill.

Deguileville, Guillaume, de (1869). *The Pilgrimage of the Lyf of the Manhode*. Ed. W. A. Wright. London: J.B. Nichols and Sons for the Roxburghe Club.

Deguileville, Guillaume, de (1904). *The Pilgrimage of the Life of Man*. Trans. John Lydgate. Ed. F.J. Furnivall. London: Kegan Paul, French Trübner and Co./Early English Text Society.

Dekker, Thomas (1608). *The Belman of London: Bringing to Light the Most Notorious Villanies That Are Now Practised in the Kingdome*. London: for Nathaniell Butter.

Dekker, Thomas (1616). *O per se O. Or A New Cryer of Lanthorne and Candle-Light*. London: for John Busbie.

Denham, John (1928). *The Poetical Works of John Denham*. Ed. Theodore Howard Banks. New Haven and London: Yale University Press.

Derrida, Jacques (1997). *The Post Card: From Socrates to Freud and Beyond*. Trans. Alan Bass. Chicago and London: Chicago University Press.

Derrida, Jacques (2002). 'Declarations of Independence.' Trans. Tom Keenan and Tom Pepper. In *Negotiations: Interventions and Interviews 1971-2001*, ed. Elizabeth Rottenberg (Stanford: Stanford University Press), 46-54.

Devereux, George (1960). 'The Female Castration Complex and its Repercussions in Modesty, Appearance and Courtship Etiquette.' *American Imago*, 17, 3-19.

Devlieger, Clara (2019). 'Contractual Dependencies: Disability and the Bureaucracy of Begging in Kinshasa, Democratic Republic of Congo. ' *American Ethnologist*, 45, 455-69.

Dickey, Stephanie (2013). 'Begging for Attention: The Artful Context of Rembrandt's Etching "Beggar Seated on a Bank".' *Journal of Historians of Netherlandish Art*, 5.2. https://jhna.org/articles/begging-for-attention-artful-context-rembrandts-etching-beggar-seated-on-a-bank/

Didi-Hubermann, Georges (1982). *Invention de l'hystérie: Charcot et l'iconographie photographique de la Salpêtrière*. Paris: Macula.

Diogenes Laertius (1925). *Lives of Eminent Philosophers Vol. II, Books 6-10*. Trans. R.D. Hicks. London: Heinemann; Cambridge MA: Harvard University Press.

Dixon, Henry Lancelot (1903). *'Saying Grace' Historically Considered, and Numerous Forms of Grace Taken from Ancient and Modern Sources*. Oxford and London: James Parker and Co.

Dobson, Austin (1897). *Collected Poems*. London: Kegan Paul, Trench, Trübner and Co.

Dodd, Gwilym (2007). *Justice and Grace: Private Petitioning and the English Parliament in the Late Middle Ages*. Oxford: Oxford University Press.

Dodd, William George (1913). *Courtly Love in Gower and Chaucer*. Boston and London: Ginn and Co.

Domett, Alfred (1833). *Poems*. London: Henry Leggat.

Donaldson, E. Talbot (1970). *Speaking of Chaucer*. New York: W.W. Norton.

Dorfman, Toni (1994). 'The Fateful Crossroads: "Fork" Clusters in Shakespeare's Plays.' *Shakespeare Bulletin*, 12, 31-34.

Dudley, Donald R. (1937). *A History of Cynicism: From Diogenes to the 6th Century A.D.* London: Methuen.

Dugas, M.B., S.A. Strickler and J.L. Stynoski (2017). 'Tadpole Begging Reveals High Quality.' *Journal of Evolutionary Biology*, 30, 1024-33.

Dunbar, William (1893). *The Poems of William Dunbar*. 3 Vols. Ed. John Small. Edinburgh and London: Blackwood.

Durkheim, Emile (1964). *The Elementary Forms of the Religious Life*. Trans. Joseph Ward Swain. London: George Allen and Unwin.

Eco, Umberto (1994). *Reflections on* The Name of the Rose. Trans. William Weaver. London: Minerva.

E.H. (1864). 'Observations on the Word Amen.' *Wesleyan-Methodist Magazine*, 4, 266-7.

Elgot, Jessica (2019). 'Semi-Naked Climate Protesters Disrupt Brexit Debate.' (1st April). https://www.theguardian.com/world/2019/apr/01/semi-naked-climate-protesters-disrupt-brexit-debate

Ellis, Jesse M. S., Tom A. Langen and Elenea C. Berg (2009). 'Signaling for Food and Sex? Begging by Reproductive Female White-throated Magpie-jays.' *Animal Behaviour*, 78, 615-23.

Ellmann, Maud (2014). 'Psychoanalytic Animal.' In Laura Marcus and Ankhi Mukherjee, eds., *A Concise Companion to Psychoanalysis, Literature and Culture* (Oxford: Wiley Blackwell), 328-50.

Ernout, Alfred and Alfred Meillet (2001). *Dictionnaire étymologique de la langue latine: Histoire des mots*. 3rd edn. Paris: Klincksieck.

Escobedo, Andrew (2017). 'On Sincere Apologies: Saying "Sorry" in *Hamlet*.' *Philosophy and Literature*, 14, 155-77.

Euclid (1570). *The Elements of Geometrie*. Trans. Henry Billingsley. London: John Daye.

Feline Noguera, José C., Sin-Yeon Kim and Alberto Velando (2013). 'Maternal Testosterone Influences a Begging Component that Makes Fathers Work Harder in Chick Provisioning.' *Hormones and Behavior* 64, 19-25.

Field, Jacob F. (2013). 'Domestic Service, Gender, and Wages in Rural England c. 1700-1860.' *Economic History Review*, 66, 249-72.

Folkingham, William (1610). *Feudigraphia: The Synopsis or Epitome of Surveying Epitomized*. London: Richard Moore.

Fontaine, Jacques (1611). *Des marques des sorciers et de la réelle possession que le diable prend sur le corps des hommes*. Lyon: Claude Larjot.

Fraser, Peter (1961). 'Public Petitioning and Parliament Before 1832.' *History*, 46, 195-211.

Freud, Sigmund (1953-74). *The Standard Edition of the Complete Psychological Works of Sigmund Freud*. 24 Vols. Ed. and trans. James Strachey et. al. London: Hogarth Press.

Freud, Sigmund (1991). *Gesammelte Werke*. 18 Vols. London: Imago.

Frey, William H., Denise Desota-Johnson, Carrie Hoffman and John T. McCall (1981). 'Effect of Stimulus on the Chemical Composition of Human Tears.' *American Journal of Ophthalmology*, 92, 559–67.

Fukuyama, Francis (2011). *The Origins of Political Order: From Prehuman Times to the French Revolution*. London: Profile.

Fukuyama, Francis (2018). *Identity: Contemporary Identity Politics and the Struggle for Recognition*. London: Profile.

Fumerton, Patricia (2004). 'Making Vagrancy (In)visible: The Economics of Disguise in Early Modern Rogue Pamphlets.' In *Rogues and Early Modern English Culture*, ed. Craig Dionne and Steve Mentz (Ann Arbor: University of Michigan Press), 193-210.

Gager, John G., ed. (1992). *Curse Tablets and Binding Spells from the Ancient World*. New York and Oxford: Oxford University Press.

Garry, Jane and Hasan El-Shamy, eds. (2005). *Archetypes and Motifs in Folklore and Literature: A Handbook*. Armonk NY and London: M.E. Sharpe.

Gay, John (2013). *The Beggar's Opera* and *Polly*. Ed. Hal Gladfelder. Oxford: Oxford University Press.

Geoghegan, Joseph B (1867). *Johnny I Hardly Knew You*. London: Sinclair and Co.

Gilbert, W.S. and Arthur Sullivan (1976). *The Complete Plays of Gilbert and Sullivan*. New York and London: W.W. Norton.

Godfray, H.C.A. (1991). 'Signalling of Need by Offspring to Their Parents.' *Nature*, 352, 328-30.

Gomm, Roger (1975). 'Bargaining from Weakness: Spirit Possession on the South Kenya Coast.' *Man*, NS 10, 530-43.

Goodrich, Peter (1996). *Law in the Courts of Love: Literature and other Minor Jurisprudences*. Abingdon and New York: Routledge.

Gordon, Thomas (1741). *The Humourist: Being Essays Upon Several Subjects*. London: for T. Woodward and H. Lintot.

Gould, Robert (1698). *A Satyr against Wooing with a View of the Ill Consequences That Attend It*. London: s.n.

Grafen, A. (1990). 'Biological Signals as Handicaps.' *Journal of Theoretical Biology*, 144, 517-46.

Greenson, Ralph R. (1947). 'On Gambling.' *American Imago*, 4B, 61-77,

Greer, Germaine (2008). 'Shakespeare and the Marriage Contract.' In *Shakespeare and the Law*, ed. Paul Raffield and Gary Watt (Oxford and Portland OR, Hart Publishing), 51-64.

Greville, Fulke (1907). *Life of Sir Philip Sidney*. Ed. Nowell Smith. Oxford: Clarendon.

Groos, Karl (1898). *The Play of Animals*. Trans. Elizabeth L. Baldwin. New York: D. Appleton.

Grote, George (1861). *History of Greece: Vol.1*. New York: Harper and Brothers.

Gupta, Alok (2008). 'This Alien Legacy: The Origins of "Sodomy" Laws in British Colonialism.' Human Rights Watch (17th December). https://www.hrw.org/report/2008/12/17/alien-legacy/origins-sodomy-laws-british-colonialism#

Gurny, Evan (2016). 'Going Rogue: Spenser and the Vagrants.' *Studies in Philology*, 113, 546-576.

Halstead, Robert (1685). *Succinct Genealogies of the Noble and Ancient Houses*. London. W. Burrell.

Hapgood, Isabel, ed. and trans. (1906). *Service Book of the Holy Orthodox-Catholic Apostolic (Greco-Russian) Church*. Boston: Houghton Mifflin.

Harman, Thomas (1567). *A Caueat for Commen Cursetors Vvlgarely Called Uagabones*. London: William Griffith.

Harsnett, Samuel (1603). *A Declaration of Egregious Popish Impostures*. London: James Roberts.

Hazelkorn, Rebeccah, Bruce Schulte and Tara Cox (2016). 'Persistent Effects of Begging on Common Bottlenose Dolphin (*Tursiops truncatus*) Behavior in an Estuarine Population.' *Aquatic Mammals*, 42, 531-41.

Head, Richard (1673). *The Canting Academy, or the Devils Cabinet Opened*. London: for Mat. Drew.

Heisenberg, Werner (2012). *Der Teil und das Ganze: Gespräche im Umkreis der Atomphysik*. Munich: Piper Verlag.

Held, Gudrun (1999). 'Submission Strategies as an Expression of the Ideology of Politeness: Reflections on the Verbalisation of Social Power Relations.' *Pragmatics*, 9, 21-36.

Heller-Roazen, Daniel (2013). *Dark Tongues: The Art of Rogues and Riddlers*. New York: Zone Books.

Herbert, George (2007). *The English Poems of George Herbert*. Ed. Helen Wilcox. Cambridge: Cambridge University Press.

Herbert, W.N. (1996). *Cabaret McGonagall*. Newcastle-Upon-Tyne: Bloodaxe.

Higgs, Edward (1983). 'Domestic Servants and Households in Victorian England.' *Social History*, 8, 201-210.

Hilarie, Hugh (1554). *The Resurreccion of the Masse*. Strasburgh: for H. Singleton.

Hopkinson, Francis (1792). *The Miscellaneous Essays and Occasional Writings Of Francis Hopkinson, Esq*. 3 Vols. Philadelphia: T. Dobson.

Horn, Andrew G. and Marty L. Leonard (2005). 'Nestling Begging as a Communication Network.' In *Animal Communication Networks*, ed. Peter K. McGregor (Cambridge: Cambridge University Press), 170-90.

Houghton, Hugh A.G. (2004). 'The Discourse of Prayer in the Major Apocryphal Acts of the Apostles.' *Apocrypha* 15, 171-200

Hoyle, R.W. (2002). 'Petitioning as Popular Politics in Early Sixteenth-Century England.' *Historical Research*, 75, 365-89.

Hoyle, R.W. (2011). 'The Masters of Requests and the Small Change of Jacobean Patronage.' *English Historical Review*, 126, 544-581.

Hughes, David P., Jacques Brodeur and Frédéric Thomas, eds. (2012). *Host Manipulation by Parasites*. Oxford: Oxford University Press.

Huxley, Julian S. (1923). *Essays of a Biologist*. London: Chatto and Windus.

Ingoldsby, Thomas (1881). *The Ingoldsby Lyrics*. Ed. R.H.D. Barham. London: Richard Bentley and Son.

Irigaray, Luce (2002). *Between East and West: From Singularity to Community*. Trans. Stephen Pluhàček. New York: Columbia University Press.

Jaffe, James A. (2019). 'The Languages of Petitioning in Early Colonial India.' *Social Science History*, 43, 581-597.

James, William (1985). *The Varieties of Religious Experience*. London: Penguin.

Johnson, Samuel (1755). *A Dictionary of the English Language*. 2 Vols. London: W. Strahan, for J. and P. Knaptor; T. and T. Longman; C. Hitch and L. Hawes; A. Millar; and R. and J. Dodsley.

Jong, Mayke de (1995). 'Carolingian Monasticism: The Power of Prayer.' In *The New Cambridge Medieval History. Volume 2: c.700-c.900*, ed. Rosamond McKitterick (Cambridge: Cambridge University Press), 622-53.

Juvenal (Decimus Iunius Iuvenalis) (2004). *Juvenal and Persius*. Ed. and trans. Susanna Morton Braund. Cambridge, MA and London: Harvard University Press.

Kaptein, N., J. Billen and B. Gobin (2005). 'Larval Begging for Food Enhances Reproductive Options in the Ponerine ant *Gnamptogenys striatula.*' *Animal Behaviour* 69, 293–99.

Kapust, Daniel J. (2018). *Flattery and the History of Political Thought: That Glib and Oily Art*. Cambridge: Cambridge University Press.

Kawatsu, Kazutaka (2013). 'Effect of Nutritional Condition on Larval Food Requisition Behavior in a Subterranean Termite *Reticulitermes speratus* (Isoptera: Rhinotermitidae).' *Journal of Ethology* 31, 17-22.

Kearns, Cleo McNelly (2005). 'Irigaray's *Between East and West*: Breath, Pranayama and the Phenomenology of Prayer.' In *The Phenomenology of Prayer*, ed. Bruce Ellis Benson and Norman Wirzba (New York: Fordham University Press), 105-18.

Keats, John (1970). *Poetical Works*. Ed. H.W. Garrod. London, Oxford and New York: Oxford University Press.

Kelly, Benjamin (2011). *Petitions, Litigation, and Social Control in Roman Egypt*. Oxford: Oxford University Press.

Kierkegaard, Søren (1967-78). *Journals and Papers*. 7 Vols. Ed. and trans. Howard V. Hong and Edna H. Hong. Bloomington: Indiana University Press.

Kilpatrick, Ryan Ho (2019). '"An Eye for an Eye": Hong Kong Protests Get Figurehead in Woman Injured by Police.' *Guardian* (16th August). https://www.theguardian.com/world/2019/aug/16/an-eye-for-an-eye-hong-kong-protests-get-figurehead-in-woman-injured-by-police

Kissinger, Henry (2000). 'The Viet Nam Negotiations.' In *Leadership and Diplomacy in the Vietnam War*, ed. Walter L. Hixson (New York and London: Garland), 309-32.

Knights, Mark (2018). '"The Lowest Degree of Freedom": The Right to Petition Parliament, 1640–1800.' *Parliamentary History*, 37, 18-34.

Knox, Thomas W. (1893). 'The Begging Elephant.' *The Friend: A Religious and Literary Journal* 67, 174.

Koch, Mark (1992). 'The Desanctification of the Beggar in Rogue Pamphlets of the English Renaissance.' In *The Work of Dissimilitude: Essays from the Sixth Citadel Conference on Medieval and Renaissance Literature*, ed. David G. Allen and Robert A. White (Newark: University of Delaware Press; London and Toronto: Associated University Presses), 91-104.

Kukzaj, S., K. Tranel, M. Trone and H. Hill (2001). 'Are Animals Capable of Deception or Empathy? Implications for Animal Consciousness and Animal Welfare.' *Animal Welfare*, 10, 161-73.

Kuzma, Joseph D. (2016). *The Eroticization of Distance: Nietzsche, Blanchot, and the Legacy of Courtly Love*. Lanham, Boulder, New York and London: Lexington Books.

Lacan, Jacques (2018). *The Four Fundamental Concepts of Psychoanalysis*, ed. Jacques-Alain Miller, trans. Alan Sheridan. Abingdon and New York: Routledge.

Lakoff, Robin (1973). 'The Logic of Politeness: or, Minding Your P's and Q's.' In *Papers from the Ninth Regional Meeting of the Chicago Linguistic Society*. Ed. Claudia Corum, T. Cedric Smith-Stark, and Ann Weiser. Chicago: Chicago Linguistic Society, 292–305.

Landgraf, Edgar (2004). 'Romantic Love and the Enlightenment: From Gallantry and Seduction to Authenticity and Self-Validation.' *German Quarterly*, 77, 29-46.

Langland, William (1886). *The Vision of William Concerning Piers the Plowman: In Three Parallel Texts Together with Richard the Redeless*. Ed. Walter W. Skeat. Oxford: Clarendon Press.

Levene, Dan (2013). *Jewish Aramaic Curse Texts from Late-Antique Mesopotamia: "May These Curses Go Out and Flee"*. Leiden and Boston: Brill.

Lewis, I.M. (1971). *Ecstatic Religion: An Anthropological Study of Spirit Possession and Shamanism*. Harmondsworth: Penguin.

Locke, Jill (2016). *Democracy and the Death of Shame: Political Equality and Social Disturbance*. Cambridge: Cambridge University Press.

Loher, Brian T., John T. Hazer, Amy Tsai, Kendel Tilton, and Jessy James (1997). 'Letters of Reference: A Process Approach.' *Journal of Business and Psychology*, 11, 339-55.

Luhmann, Niklas (1986). *Love as Passion: The Codification of Intimacy*. Trans. Jeremy Gaines and Doris L. Jones. Cambridge: Polity.

Luhmann, Niklas (2010). *Love: A Sketch*. Ed. André Kieserling. Trans. Kathleen Cross. Cambridge and Malden MA: Polity.

Luther, Martin, ed. (1860). *The Book of Vagabonds and Beggars: With a Vocabulary of Their Language*. Ed. and trans. John Camden Hotton. London: John Camden Hotton.

Lyly, John (1580). *Euphues and his England*. London: T. East for Gabriell Cawood.

McCabe, Ciarán (2018). *Begging, Charity and Religion in Pre-Famine Ireland*. Liverpool: Liverpool University Press.

MacLeish, Archibald (1985). *Collected Poems: 1917–1982*. Boston: Houghton Mifflin.

MacNeice, Louis (1979). *Collected Poems*. London: Faber and Faber.

Mahler, Margaret. S., Fred Pine and Anni Bergman (1975). *The Psychological Birth of the Human Infant: Symbiosis and Individuation*. New York: Basic Books.

Mandeville, Bernard de (1924). *The Fable of the Bees: or Private Vices, Publick Benefits*. Ed. F.B. Kaye. Oxford: Oxford University Press.

Mansfield, Harvey C. (2006). *Manliness*. New Haven and London: Yale University Press.

Mansfield, Harvey C. (2007). 'How to Understand Politics: What the Humanities Can Say to Science.' Jefferson Lecture (2007). Online at http://archive.li/0F73y

Marlowe, Christopher (1999). *Complete Plays*. Ed. Mark Thornton Burnett. London: J.M. Dent.

Mastrocinque, Attilio (2007). 'Late Antique Lamps with Defixiones.' *Greek, Roman, and Byzantine Studies* 47 (2007) 87–99.

Mauss, Marcel (2002). *The Gift: The Form and Reason for Exchange in Archaic Societies*. London and New York: Routledge.

Mauss, Marcel (2003). *On Prayer*. Ed. W.S.F. Pickering. Trans. Susan Leslie. New York and Oxford: Durkheim Press/Berghahn Books.

Maynard Smith, John (1991). 'Honest Signalling: The Philip Sidney Game.' *Animal Behaviour*, 42, 1034-35.

Metaxas, Eric (2018). *Martin Luther: The Man Who Rediscovered God and Changed the World*. New York: Penguin.

Miller, Henry (2012). 'Popular Petitioning and the Corn Laws, 1833-46.' *English Historical Review*, 127, 882-919.

Miller, William Ian (2003). *Faking It*. Cambridge: Cambridge University Press.

Milton, John (2004). *Paradise Lost*. Ed. Stephen Orgel and Jonathan Goldberg. Oxford: Oxford University Press.

Mock, Douglas W. (2016). 'Some Begging is Actually Bragging.' *Nature*, 532, 180-1.

Mock, Douglas W., Matthew B. Dugas, and Stephanie A. Strickler (2011). 'Honest Begging: Expanding from Signal of Need.' *Behavioral Ecology* 22, 909-917.

Montgomery, James A. (1913). *Aramaic Incantation Texts from Nippur*. Philadelphia: Philadelphia University Museum.

More, Hannah (1830). *The Works of Hannah More. Vol. II: Poems – Tragedies*. London: T. Cadell.

Morris, Desmond (2002). *Catwatching: The Essential Guide to Cat Behaviour*. London: Ebury Press.

Murphy, Jeffrie G. (1988). 'Mercy and Legal Justice.' In Jeffrie G. Murphy and Jean Hampton, *Forgiveness and Mercy*. Cambridge: Cambridge University Press, 162–86.

Murray, Michael J. and Kurt Meyers (1994). 'Ask and It Will Be Given to You.' *Religious Studies*, 30, 311-30

Neriya-Ben Shahar, Rivka (2018). 'The Amen Meal: Jewish Women Experience Lived Religion through a New Ritual.' *Nashim: A Journal of Jewish Women's Studies and Gender Issues* 33, 158-76.

Nubola, Cecilia (2001). 'Supplications between Politics and Justice: The Northern and Central Italian States in the Early Modern Age.' In *Petitions in Social History*, ed. Lex Heerma van Voss, *International Review of Social History*, 46 (Supplement 9), 35-56

Núñez, Josué A. (1970). 'The Relationship Between Sugar Flow and Foraging and Recruiting Behaviour of Honey Bees (*Apis mellifera* L.).' *Animal Behaviour* 18, 527-38.

Nutt, Alfred (1889). 'The Legend of the Buddha's Alms Dish and the Legend of the Holy Grail.' *Archaeological Review*, 3, 257-71.

O'Donoghue, Bernard, ed. (1982). *The Courtly Love Tradition*. Manchester: Manchester University Press.

Orr, W.R. (1890). 'Flattery.' *Herald of Gospel Liberty*, 82, 243.

Orwell, George (1947). *The English People*. London: Collins.

Otter, Chris (2008). *The Victorian Eye: A Political History of Light and Vision in Britain, 1800-1910*. Chicago and London: University of Chicago Press.

Ovid (Publius Ovidius Naso) (1916). *Metamorphoses Books 1-8*. Trans. Frank Justus Miller and G.P. Goold. Cambridge MA: Harvard University Press.

Ovid (Publius Ovidius Naso) (1929). *The Art of Love and Other Poems*. Trans. J.H. Mozley, rev. G.P. Goold. Cambridge MA: Harvard University Press.

Owen, Wilfred (1983). *The Complete Poems and Fragments of Wilfred Owen*. Ed. Jon Stallworthy. London: Chatto and Windus.

Peck, Linda Levy (1993). *Court Patronage and Corruption in Early Stuart England*. London and New York: Routledge.

Peirce, C.S. (1977). *Semiotic and Significs: The Correspondence Between Charles S. Peirce and Victoria Lady Welby*. Ed. Charles S. Hardwick and James Cook. Bloomington: Indiana University Press.

Pepys, Samuel (1995). *The Diary of Samuel Pepys: A New and Complete Transcription: Volume 1: 1660*. Ed. Robert Latham and William Matthews. London: HarperCollins.

Pickering, Danby, ed. (1763). *The Statutes at Large. Vol. IV: From the First Year of King Richard III to the Thirty-First Year of King Henry VIII*. Cambridge: Joseph Bentham.

Pickering, Paul A. (2001). ' "And Your Petitioners &c": Chartist Petitioning in Popular Politics 1838-48.' *English Historical Review*, 116, 368-388.

Pollard, Graham (1937). 'The Company of Stationers before 1557.' *The Library*, 4th Series, 18, 1-38.

Propp, Vladimir (1968). *Morphology of the Folktale*. 2nd edn. Ed. Louis A. Wagner. Trans. Laurence Scott. Austin: University of Texas Press.

Pugliatti, Paola (2003). *Begging and Theatre in Early Modern England*. Aldershot and Burlington VT: Ashgate

Qu'uran, The (2015). Trans. M.A.S. Abdel Haleem. Oxford: Oxford University Press.

Rank, Otto and Sachs, Hanns (1916). *The Significance of Psychoanalysis for the Mental Sciences*. Trans. Charles R. Payne. New York: Nervous and Mental Disease Publishing Co.

Ray, John (1678). *A Collection of English Proverbs*. Cambridge: for W. Morden.

Redondo, T. and J.M. Zuñiga (2002). 'Dishonest Begging and Host Manipulation by *Clamator* Cuckoos.' In *The Evolution of Begging: Competition, Cooperation, and Communication*, ed. J. Wright and M. L. Leonard (Dordrecht: Kluwer), 389-412.

Rid, Samuel (1610). *Martin Mark-all, Beadle of Bridevvell; His Defence and Answere to the Belman of London*. London: for Iohn Budge and Richard Bonian.

Rilke, Rainer Maria (1930). *Gesammelte Werke*. 6 Vols. Leipzig: Insel-Verlag.

Roberts M.J.D. (1991). 'Reshaping the Gift Relationship: The London Mendicity Society and the Suppression of Begging in England 1818-1869.' *International Review of Social History*, 36, 201-31.

Rochester, Earl of (John Wilmot) (1984). *Poems*. Ed. Keith Walker. Oxford: Basil Blackwell.

Rodríguez, Cinthia (2009). 'The "Circumstances" of Gestures: Proto-Interrogatives and Private Gestures.' *New Ideas in Psychology* 27, 288–303.

Rougemont, Denis de (1983). *Love in the Western World*. Trans. Montgomery Belgion. Princeton: Princeton University Press.

Sabatier, Auguste (1902). *Outlines of a Philosophy of Religion Based on Psychology and History*. Trans. T.A. Seed. London: Hodder and Stoughton.

Sadock, Jerrold M. (1970). 'Whimperatives.' In *Studies Presented to R.B. Lees by his Students*. Ed. Jerrold M. Sadock and A. Vanek. Edmonton: Linguistic Research, Inc. 223-228.

Schuppe, Eric R., Meredith C. Miles and Matthew J. Fuxjager, M.J. (2019). 'Evolution of the Androgen Receptor: Perspectives from Human Health to Dancing Birds.' *Molecular and Cellular Endocrinology*. doi: https://doi.org/10.1016/j.mce.2019.110577

Schwenkel, Christina (2015). 'Reclaiming Rights to the Socialist City: Bureaucratic Artefacts and the Affective Appeal of Petitions.' *South East Asia Research*, 23, 205-25

Sebeok, Thomas A. (1965). 'Zoosemiotics: Juncture of Semiotics and the Biological Study of Behavior.' *Science*, 147, 492-493.

Sebeok, Thomas A. (1968). 'Zoosemiotics.' *American Speech*, 43, 142-144.

Serres, Michel (1982). *Hermes: Literature, Science, Philosophy*. Ed. Josué V. Harari and David F. Bell. Trans. Josué V. Harari, David F. Bell et. al. Baltimore and London: Johns Hopkins University Press.

Serres, Michel (1995). *The Natural Contract*. Trans. Elizabeth MacArthur and William Paulson. Ann Arbor: University of Michigan Press.

Serres, Michel (2007). *The Parasite*. Trans. Lawrence R. Schehr. Minneapolis and London: University of Minnesota Press.

Serres, Michel (2012). *Le mal propre: polluer pour s'approprier?* Paris: Le Pommier.

Serres, Michel (2019). *Relire le relié*. Paris: Le Pommier.

Shakespeare, William (2011). *Complete Works*. Ed. Richard Proudfoot, Ann Thompson and David Scott Kastan. London, New York, New Delhi and Sydney: Arden Shakespeare.

Sharp, William (1887). *Life of Percy Bysshe Shelley*. London: Walter Scott.

Shirley, John (1688). *The Triumph of Wit, or, Ingenuity Display'd in Its Perfection*. s.l.: Nicholas Bodington.

Simmel, Georg (1984). 'Flirtation.' In *On Women, Sexuality, and Love*, ed. and trans. Guy Oakes (New Haven and London: Yale University Press), 133-52.

Sloterdijk, Peter (2010a). 'The Grasping Hand.' Trans. Alexis Cornel. *City Journal*, 20, 5-7. https://www.city-journal.org/html/grasping-hand-13264.html

Sloterdijk, Peter (2010b). *Rage and Time: A Psychopolitical Investigation*. Trans. Mario Wenning. New York: Columbia University Press.

Sloterdijk, Peter (2013). *You Must Change Your Life*. Trans. Wieland Hoban. Cambridge and Malden MA: Polity Press.

Smiseth, Per T., Michelle Pellissier Scott and Clare Andrews (2011). 'Hormonal Regulation of Offspring Begging and Mediation of Parent-Offspring Conflict.' *Animal Behaviour* 81, 507-17.

Speck, Ross V. and Attneave, Carolyn L. (1973). *Family Networks*. New York: Pantheon.

Spenser, Edmund (1591). *Complaints Containing Sundrie Small Poemes of the Worlds Vanitie*. London: for William Ponsonbie.

Stekel, Wilhelm (1940). *Impotence in the Male: The Psychic Disorders of Sexual Function in the Male*. Trans. Oswald H. Boltz. 2 Vols. London: John Lane The Bodley Head.

Stengel, Richard (2000). *You're Too Kind: A Brief History of Flattery*. New York: Simon and Schuster.

Stevens, Wallace (2015). *Collected Poems*. New York: Knopf.

Stokes, Christopher (2009). 'Coleridge's Philosophy of Prayer: Responsibility, Parergon, and Catachresis.' *Journal of Religion*, 89, 541-63.

Stone, Christopher D. (2010). *Should Trees Have Standing? Law, Morality, and the Environment*. 3rd edn. Oxford: Oxford University Press.

Takata, Mamoru, Yuki Mitaka, Sandra Steiger, and Naoki Mori (2019). 'A Parental Volatile Pheromone Triggers Offspring Begging in a Burying Beetle.' *iScience*, 19, 1256-64.

Tertullian (Quintus Septimius Florens Tertullianus) (1885). 'On Prayer.' Trans. Sydney Thelwall. In *The Ante-Nicene Fathers: The Writings of the Fathers Down to A.D. 325. Vol. 3*. Ed. Alexander Roberts and James Donaldson (Buffalo: Christian Literature Publishing Co.), 681-91.

Thomas, Dylan (1978). *The Poems*. Ed. Daniel Jones. London, Melbourne and Sydney: J.M. Dent.

Thomson, David, ed. (2019). *An Edition of the Middle English Grammatical Texts*. Abingdon and New York: Routledge.

Tiffany, Daniel (2009). *Infidel Poetics: Riddles, Nightlife, Substance*. Chicago and London: University of Chicago Press.

Tighe, Joan (1965). 'The Mendicity Institution.' *Dublin Historical Record*, 20, 100-15.

Tobias, J. A. and N. Seddon (2002). 'Female Begging in European Robins: Do Neighbors Eavesdrop for Extrapair Copulations?' *Behavioral Ecology*,13, 637–642.

Topsell, Edward (1608). *The Historie of Serpents. Or, The Second Booke of Liuing Creatures Wherein is Contained Their Diuine, Naturall, and Morall Descriptions.* London: William Jaggard.

Tuer, Andrew W. (1897). *History of the Horn-Book.* London: Leadenhall Press.

Tyler, Royall (1968). *The Verse of Royall Tyler.* Ed. Marius B. Péladeau. Charlottesville: University of Virginia Press.

Valpy, F.E.J., Rev. (1828). *An Etymological Dictionary of the Latin Language.* London: Baldwin and Co., Longman and Co and G.B. Whittaker.

Voss, Lex Heerma van (2001). 'Introduction.' In *Petitions in Social History*, ed. Lex Heerma van Voss, *International Review of Social History*, 46 (Supplement 9), 1-10.

Waters, Thomas (2020). 'Irish Cursing and the Art of Magic: 1750-2018.' *Past & Present*. https://doi.org/10.1093/pastj/gtz051

Webster, Joanne P. (2007). 'The Effect of *Toxoplasma gondii* on Animal Behavior: Playing Cat and Mouse.' *Schizophrenia Bulletin*, 33, 752-6.

Whigham, Frank (1981). 'The Rhetoric of Elizabethan Suitors' Letters.' *PMLA*, 96, 864-882.

Whigham, Frank (1984). *Ambition and Privilege: The Social Tropes of Elizabethan Courtesy Theory.* Berkeley, Los Angeles and London: University of California Press.

White, Lynn, Jnr. (1960). 'Tibet, India, and Malaya as Sources of Western Medieval Technology.' *American Historical Review*, 65, 515-26.

Wichmann, Anne (2005). '*Please* – from Courtesy to Appeal: The Role of Intonation in the Expression of Attitudinal Meaning.' *English Language and Linguistics*, 9, 229–253.

Williams-Jones, Bryn (2012). 'Reference Letters and Conflict of Interest: A Professor's Dilemma.' *Bioéthique Online*, 1.10, 1-4

Windeatt, Barry (2012). 'Plea and Petition in Chaucer.' In *Chaucer in Context: A Golden Age of English Poetry*. Ed. Gerald Morgan. Oxford: Peter Lang, 189-215.

Winder, Marianne (1992). 'Aspects of the History of the Prayer Wheel.' *Bulletin of Tibetology*, 28, pp 25-33.

Wright, Joseph (1905). *The English Dialect Dictionary: Vol. 4 M-Q.* Oxford et. al. Henry Frowde.

Wright, Thomas, ed. (2012). *Political Poems and Songs Relating to English History, Composed during the Period from the Accession of Edward III to that of Richard III.* 2 Vols. Cambridge: Cambridge University Press.

Würgler, Andreas (2001). 'Voices From Among the "Silent Masses ": Humble Petitions and Social Conflicts in Early Modern Central Europe.' In *Petitions in Social History*, ed. Lex Heerma van Voss, *International Review of Social History*, 46 (Supplement 9), 11-34.

Yeats, W.B. (1950). *Collected Poems*. London and Basingstoke: Macmillan.

Yeats, W.B. (2007). *The Collected Works of W.B. Yeats. Volume IV: Early Essays*. Ed. Richard J. Finneran and George Bornstein. New York: Scribner.

Zahavi, Amotz (1975). 'Mate Selection: A Selection for a Handicap.' *Journal of Theoretical Biology*, 53, 205-14.

Zahavi, Amotz and Avishag Zahavi (1997). *The Handicap Principle: A Missing Piece of Darwin's Puzzle*. New York and Oxford: Oxford University Press.

Zaret, David (1996). 'Petitions and the "Invention" of Public Opinion in the English Revolution. ' *American Journal of Sociology*, 101, 1497-1555.

Zhang, Da-Yong and Xin-Hua Jiang (2000). 'Costly Solicitation, Timing of Offspring Conflict, and Resource Allocation in Plants.' *Annals of Botany*, 86, 123-31.

Zipes, Jack (2008). 'What Makes a Repulsive Frog So Appealing: Memetics and Fairy Tale.' *Journal of Folklore Research*, 45, 109-43.

Žižek, Slavoj (1994). 'Courtly Love, or Woman as Thing.' In *The Metastases of Enjoyment: Six Essays on Women and Causality* (London and New York: Verso), 89-112.

Index

.

www.ingramcontent.com/pod-product-compliance
Lightning Source LLC
Chambersburg PA
CBHW020153090426
42734CB00008B/803